MicK

(Mums !

WELLS

GH00836713

The Book of
THE BEDWYNS

A Rich History

COMPILED BY THE BEDWYN HISTORY SOCIETY

HALSGROVE

First published in Great Britain in 2003.

British Library Cataloguing-in-Publication Data.
A CIP record for this title is available from the British Library.

ISBN 1 84114 252 2

HALSGROVE

Halsgrove House
Lower Moor Way
Tiverton, Devon EX16 6SS
Tel: 01884 243242
Fax: 01884 243325
email: sales@halsgrove.com
website: www.halsgrove.com

Frontispiece photograph: *Church Street, Little Bedwyn.*

Printed and bound by CPI Bath Press, Bath.

Foreword

The project which culminated in the publication of *The Book of the Bedwyns* started quietly on a November evening in 2001 at a convivial meeting of the Bedwyn History Society in the Cross Keys. At the suggestion of our chairman, Ian Mackintosh, who recognised the importance of updating existing records and archives at the beginning of a new millennium, work was then initiated by a team coordinated by Bill Marchant Smith.

Almost immediately it became clear that the enterprise would complement the efforts of villagers concurrently compiling a Village Design Statement and a revised Conservation Area Statement for Little Bedwyn.

Two years later all three adorn our bookshelves and are widely recognised to be of exceptionally high quality. Indeed, here is proof of the vitality of a community and its spirit, for these demanding projects were the fruit of voluntary effort and commitment.

In a landscape which has survived unchanged to any great degree for aeons, we become keenly aware of the mystery of this survival. It runs through the chapters as great events approach fruition only to slide into oblivion, leaving the Bedwyns intact. With the sale of large parts of the Savernake estate in the late 1920s the Bedwyns were exposed to speculative development, but the depression and the Second World War intervened and little changed at that time.

However, substantial development did occur in Great Bedwyn in the 1970s and '80s and it was only towards the close of the last century that the Bedwyns gained the protection of more stringent planning laws as part of the North Wessex Downs Area of Outstanding Natural Beauty. A powerful combination of planning law, landscape value and the demand for sustainable development should provide the Bedwyns with a relatively tranquil passage into the era of the technological revolution.

As we look ahead, we can take heart from the belief that a community which has produced *The Book of the Bedwyns* will perpetuate its life-enhancing spirit of community enterprise and service well into the future.

It is a great privilege to welcome the publication of this book and to offer our thanks and congratulations to the authors and to all those who have contributed to the publication of this invaluable addition to the archives of Wiltshire.

Rosemary Cummins
Kennet District Councillor
Great Bedwyn, July 2003

GREAT BEDWIN.

Above: *Envelope showing postmark of December 1845.*

Left: *Bedwyn crest and coat of arms.*

Great Bedwyn Friendly Society at the north end of Brook Street in Victorian times. The photograph was taken from the first floor of the Cross Keys.

Contents

1773 map,
prepared by
John Andrews
and Andrew
Dury.

7

Acknowledgements

Over the past two years, the Bedwyn History Society has made a number of appeals to residents in the area in order to obtain information for this book. There has been an excellent response and we have received most useful information, reminiscences, items of local interest, photographs and sketches for which we are very grateful. Thanks must go particularly to the following for providing information and loaning photographs:

George Bailey, Eric Bally, Bill Bance, Roy Beckingham, Shirley Bishop, G.H. Breedon, Joan Chapman, Ruth Cooper, Jim Denning, David and Betty Gauntlett, Deborah Gibson, Jenny Harrison, Brian Hart, Judith Hiller, Pippa Hynes, Ralph Kennington, Michael and Sylvia Kington, Fred and Juma Lance, Ray Leonard, Percy Lewer, John Lidderdale, Ben Lloyd, John Lloyd, Mary May, Muriel Mann, John Mills, Val Patrick, Angela Rawson, Lily Samuel, Bill Simpkins, Norma Vines and Vic West and to the We're History Millennium Project, Crofton Society of the Kennet & Avon Canal Trust, Merchant's House (Marlborough) Trust, National Monuments Record Centre, Royal Observer Corps Museum, Wilton Windmill Society, Wiltshire County Archives and Wiltshire Archeological and Natural History Society.

We are also very grateful to the following talented artists who provided the sketches and drawings used in the book:

Tony Adcock, Ruth Cooper, Mick Goss, Anthony Gotley, Angela Rawson and Yvonne Slade.

Although the book has now been completed, we are most anxious that research into the history of the Bedwyns continues so that we can add to the archive maintained by the Society. If you are able to put a name to any of the unidentified faces in the photographs included, please let a member of the Society know so that the record can be amended.

Finally, to everyone who has helped with this venture, whether named or not, we offer our most sincere thanks and apologise to any whose names have been inadvertently omitted.

Ian Mackintosh
Chairman, Bedwyn
History Society,
Little Bedwyn,
July 2003

Castle Cottage, Great Bedwyn, birthplace of Dr Thomas Willis.

Introduction

Great Bedwyn Town Hall.

For over 4,000 years there have been settlements in the area of the Bedwyns. Traces of these still exist in the landscape and history books are full of the deeds and achievements of earlier local inhabitants. This book does not attempt to do more than cover the highlights of our past in a way that appeals both to serious historians and to those with a more general interest in days gone by.

One could perhaps summarise the Bedwyns' past as showing great potential at times but never quite developing into the commercial centre it once promised to become. As a result, we live, in 2003, in a group of lovely villages and hamlets surrounded by open farm land and forest, whose inhabitants are the envy of those who visit them. It is this general theme that we have followed in setting the chronology and contents of the chapters in the book. Each chapter has had its own author, drawn from members of the Bedwyn History Society; they were Graham Bathe, Anthony Gotley, Andrew Hutchison, Ann Lane, Ian Mackintosh, Bill Marchant Smith and Val Patrick.

Hopefully we have minimised unnecessary duplication and avoided serious errors and omissions. If the latter is not the case, then we hope we have inspired others to investigate and to publish the outcome of their research – perhaps through the Society's quarterly publication, *The Bedwyn Chonicles.*

Bill Marchant Smith
Chairman, Bedwyn History Steering Group,
Great Bedwyn, July 2003

Geology of the Bedwyn Area.

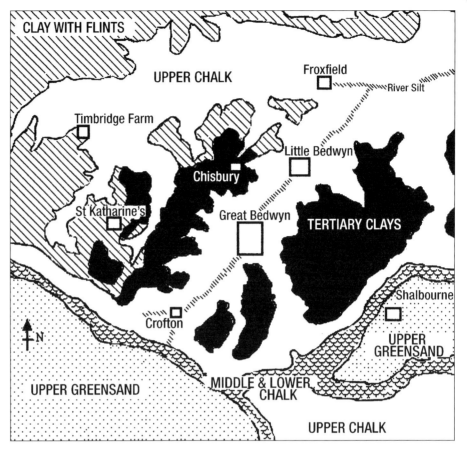

Agricultural Quality of Soil Types

Type of rock	Usefulness of soil
Upper greensand	Arable and pasture.
Lower chalk	Arable.
Middle and upper chalk	Grazing, some arable.
Tertiary clay sediments (Castle Copse and Chisbury)	Upland ground water-supply well above normal water-table (perched). Some ideal for brick making. Grassland.
Tertiary clay with flints	Poor quality, acidic soils, supports woodland and pasture.

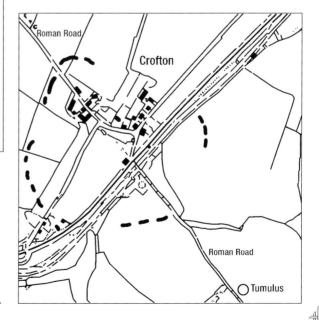

Indications of the causewayed enclosure at Crofton.

BEDWYN UP TO THE DARK AGES

EARLIEST TIMES

The Bedwyn area has probably been occupied since the climate allowed the growth of vegetation and animals, which in turn attracted hunters to the nearby forests. We do not know much about the first people to set up home on the banks of the Bedwyn Stream, but we do know that Stone-Age man did so at Crofton. To understand why we have to look at the geology of this region.

The map on the opposite page *(top)* shows the main types of rocks locally and the table below gives an indication of the agricultural usefulness of each type of soil found above these rocks.

The clay with flints, which covered large areas to the north and west of the Bedwyn Stream, would have been challenging to early cultivators even if they had been able to clear the extensive woodlands that covered large parts of eastern Wiltshire and western Berkshire. The chalk downlands, once they had been cleared, would have been far less productive than the greensands of the Shalbourne Valley and the Pewsey Vale, which extends up as far as Crofton. It is therefore no surprise that an aerial photograph in 1976 revealed the traces of a Stone-Age causewayed enclosure at Crofton. Most of the signs of this earthwork have been ploughed out but it is still possible to see some faint marks, particularly if viewed in winter from the south where the Roman road crests the hill. The diagram at the bottom of page 10 shows the area in which to look.

The enclosure is dated to around 2500BC; it would have consisted of a bank and ditch through which there would have been several gaps (causeways) which could have been temporarily blocked. Crofton's enclosure is unusual because of its size (it has a diameter of 600 metres encircling some 70 acres) and the fact that the Bedwyn Stream flows through it. Excavations have revealed that it was a wooded site with small, localised clearings. This was common practice for that time, and the enclosure would have been used to corral animals or to act as a meeting place for the nomadic people of the area.

In Neolithic (Stone Age) times the land would have been very different from that which we see today. Most of southern Britain would have been covered in forest, the downlands perhaps less densely

wooded and the valley bottoms swampy and difficult to cross, let alone cultivate. Movement would have been easier by river than over land. Thus early settlements would most likely have been close to reliable water-supplies and adjacent to natural or earlier man-made clearings. The simple wooden ploughs were only suitable for light soils. Water meadows along with other pastures and arable fields would have been important in providing fodder. There are signs of early farming in the Celtic field systems on the hillside above the Crofton pumping station, in Bedwyn Brail and at Piccadilly (the crossroads over the A338 on the way to Oxenwood). All that one can see today are the outlines of the borders of the strips of cultivated land. At an early stage permanent habitation of this area must have begun close to those fields.

As farming techniques and implements improved through the Bronze and Iron Ages, and as the population grew, so settlements would have spread and more and more land would have been brought under cultivation. Pigs would have been ideal for clearing rough scrub and creating pastures. It has been assessed that by the early Iron Age, the climatic conditions were very similar to those of today and the population of southern England would not have been that different from the rural population of the mid-1900s. To sustain these numbers, autumn planting had to take place, which led to a lot of the topsoil being washed away in the winter rains. This forced the farmers to clear more and more upland areas; spaces that became progressively less productive.

THE ANCIENT WOODLANDS OF BEDWYN

Features surviving in woodlands, including wildlife, can provide strong indicators of how the historic landscape developed. Woodlands were sources of essential building timber, fuel, hurdles, nuts and game. Occasionally they also provided timber for the nation's Navy and fuel for industry and (as at Savernake) could provide hunting entertainment fit for a king. The relative importance of these functions has changed through the centuries. Whilst some woodlands present in the countryside are recent, others are known to be centuries old, and some probably stretch back for millennia to the time when prehistoric man first settled in the area which was to

Man's Activities Through the Ages

Date	Time Period	Activity
Before 4000BC	Palaeolithic/Mesolithic	Hunter gatherers
4000–2300BC	Neolithic (Stone Age)	Farmers
2300–750BC	Bronze Age	Farmers
750–400BC	Early Iron Age	Farmers
400–100BC	Middle Iron Age	Farmers
100BC–AD50	Late Iron Age	Farmers
AD43–400	Roman	Farmers and some urban
AD400–1086	Dark Ages (early Medieval)	Farmers
AD1086–Tudors	Medieval	Farmers, urban
Tudors onwards	Post Medieval	Farmers, urban, industrial

become known as Bedwyn. Woodlands are of course dynamic, living entities. In the older examples it is the woodlands themselves, not the individual trees, that are hundreds or thousands of years old (although there are a few famous ancient oaks in Savernake).

Probably the whole of the Bedwyn area would have been wooded, or at least supported a heavily tree-covered and park-like landscape before settlement by prehistoric man. This was gradually cleared to provide pasture and arable land, but a stage was reached when woodlands had to be vigorously protected because of their importance to the local community. Evidence suggests that the basic pattern of woodland distribution in the Wiltshire landscape had been established before Domesday, and the total area of woodland has remained relatively stable ever since. The type of woodland and its local pattern changed significantly, however, as old woodlands were grubbed up and new ones planted, the latter often comprising non-native conifers. A comparison of maps depicting the different types of woodland shows that Bedwyn remains a well-wooded area. However, at least half of this woodland has been planted during the last few hundred years on areas that were formerly open fields (such as Bedwyn Common). Even in the case of those woodlands situated on ancient sites, most have been radically replanted. Only in a tiny minority of places have ancient woodlands survived, together with their complement of native British trees and shrubs.

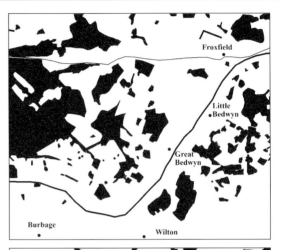

Top right: *Woodland cover in the Bedwyn area, 2000. Whilst Bedwyn remains a heavily-wooded landscape, comparison with the other maps shows that most of these woodlands have been radically altered or are of recent origin.*

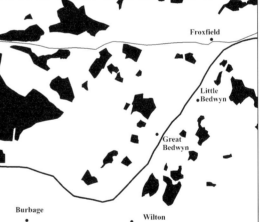

Centre: *This map shows those local woodlands standing on ancient sites, which have probably never been cleared of trees. However, most have been replanted or turned into forested plantations.*

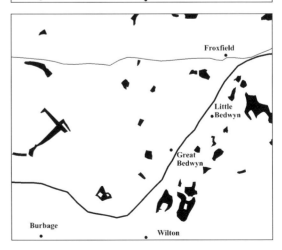

Right: *These few relics are the sole survivors of the native woodlands that once covered the whole district.*

Woodlands in Chisbury Manor, Recorded in a Court Roll of 1639

Type of Woodland	Name	Leaseholder	Area (acres)
Coppice	Parke Coppice	Edmond Hungerford	12
Coppice	Oxlease Coppice	Edmond Hungerford	40
Woody ground	Borthfield Rag	Edmond Hungerford	2
Woody ground	Burchen Hall	Edmond Hungerford	4
Coppice	Heypitt Grove	Edmond Hungerford	2
Coppice	Bennetts Grove	Chas Izard	1½
Coppice	Home Coppice	John Hayes	3
Coppice	Ballwood Coppice	John Hayes	2
Coppice	Woodfurlong	John Hayes	2
Coppice		Widow Pike	3
Coppice		Widow Kimber	8
Coppice		John Harris	6
Coppice		William Tarrant	10

Woodlands were crucial to the survival of local communities. Of particular importance was the provision of fuel and cut hazel stems from which hurdles were made to provide fencing for stock; the understory or shrub layer of hazel would be cut or 'coppiced' every few years to provide poles, and the cut stools would resprout readily. Faggots of fuel would be taken. One of the surviving relics of ancient woodlands near Bewley Farm still bears the delightful name of 'Faggotty Copse'. Most coppices were let out to local tenants and many of the older woodlands were called Copse or Coppice. A court roll of 1639 sets out meticulously how each woodland in Chisbury Manor was let.

As woodlands were so important, they were thoroughly protected. They were generally ditched and banked to mark them out (these ancient banks are still visible around the ancient woodlands of Bedwyn) and they would have been fenced to keep out deer and other animals likely to browse the regrowth. Depredations by other people, some of whom might have been desperate for firewood to survive the winter, were common. Significant rewards could be offered for informants. A broadsheet published by the Tottenham Park Association in 1826 offered rewards of three guineas for information leading to the apprehension of anyone cutting trees, and one guinea for arresting anyone stealing underwood.

The flora and fauna provide a unique insight into the history of woodlands, since there are many species of plant and animal that are almost wholly associated with ancient sites. These even include trees, such as the small-leaved lime, which (as shown through ancient preserved pollen) was probably the most common tree in southern England 6,000 years ago. Following a change in the climate in the Bronze Age, small-leaved lime became unable to set seed in England. The species can spread by suckers, and can therefore continue indefinitely in any given woodland, but it cannot spread to reach new woods which have either been planted or have established naturally on abandoned fields, even after hundreds of years. There are a surprising number of plants, some molluscs and even a few winged

Reward notice of the Tottenham Park Association. An 1826 broadsheet advertised rewards for the apprehension of offenders damaging woodlands, agricultural land and other properties, at a time of great social tension and deprivation.

invertebrates such as beetles and moths that are either confined or have a strong affinity with ancient woodlands. Ancient sites tend to be the most diverse and important for nature conservation and their identification also helps provide a picture of the landscape in historical times.

Bedwyn supports a good number of ancient-woodland indicator plants – those rarely found at ancient sites. These include toothwort (*Lathraea squamaria*), a parasitic plant with bold white flowers found on the roots of hazel, the attractive nettle-leaved bellflower (*Campanula trachelium*), the rare violet helleborine (*Helleborine violacea*) and herb paris (*Paris quadrifolia*), a plant which is almost totally confined to ancient woods. This last species has bold black berries which are apparently shunned by birds, but which (it has been conjectured) may once have been snuffled and spread by wild boar. All four of these are recorded as being present in Foxbury Wood in Little Bedwyn parish.

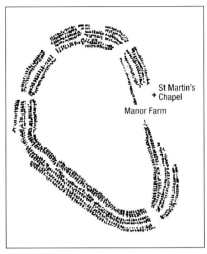

Below: *Herb paris is one of a series of plants almost wholly confined to ancient woodlands – those areas that have been continuously wooded for centuries or millennia.* ENGLISH NATURE.

Chisbury hill-fort.

CHISBURY HILL-FORT

In the fifth century BC the conditions became very wet and the growing season decreased by some five weeks compared to earlier periods. Perhaps this added to the territorial disputes which were rife in southern Britain at this time, and which led to a spate of hill-fort building. Chisbury was built possibly as early as 400BC and has at least two ditches and banks around most of its circumference; in 1819 the depth of the ditch system was reported as being 45 feet, although it is far less today. The enclosed area runs to approximately 15 acres and has an integral water-supply afforded by the underlying rock strata.

Most Iron-Age hill-forts had entry points to the east with another to the west. In Chisbury's case it has been suggested that the original entrance was from the south, but this may be based on the fact that the strongest defences appear to have been on the south-west side. There seems to be no geographical reason for the extra defences to be there as the slope of the hill varies little around the circumference of the fort. However, an entrance was always a weak point, so this might argue in favour of the southern entrance being the original one. By Saxon times there was a chapel (St Martin's) by the eastern entrance, which would indicate the importance attached to that entry point. Until some systematic archaeological investigations are done we cannot be sure when each of Chisbury's original entrances were built. The Bedwyn Dyke, in its earliest form, might have been constructed at this time, more as a boundary marker than a military obstacle, although the part nearest the fort would naturally help to reduce the vulnerability of the entrance.

At around this time, much of the low ground had become marshland, which restricted movement across country. It was only when tribal boundaries began to be firmed up that the strategic importance

The ditch at the north entrance to Chisbury fort, seen in 2003.

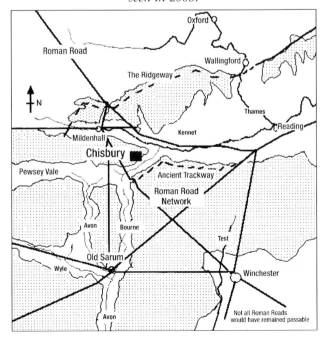

Chisbury's strategic location in the Dark Ages.

of Chisbury became apparent. It lies adjacent to some key lines of communication and in an excellent defensive position.

The valley of the Bedwyn Stream is a prime lowland communication route connecting the Thames Valley (via the Kennet) with the Pewsey Vale and the good-quality lands to the west. In those days, during the dry summer months, this would have been a good east–west route through the Chalk Downlands. Many centuries later, the Kennet & Avon Canal surveyors obviously appreciated that this route created the least engineering difficulties.

The nearest prehistoric upland route going east–west runs along the Berkshire Downs passing south of Ham and Shalbourne and through Oxenwood; and north–south goes over the Marlborough Downs after leaving the Ridgeway, and continues south towards the watershed of the Bedwyn Stream and Bourne and Avon rivers, which is near Burbage.

Chisbury itself stands on a dominating spur with extensive views overlooking the countryside to the east and south; no serious invader would have been happy to leave it unattended on his flank. Chisbury, in conjunction with the Iron-Age hill-forts at Walbury (above Inkpen) and Fosbury (to the south of Oxenwood), would have ensured the routes into eastern Wessex were well guarded.

Towards the end of the Iron Age, the Celtic people of southern England had generally established their main tribal boundaries, had their own coinage and strong trade links with the inhabitants of Gaul. Many of them would have originated from there and the term Belgic has been given to some of their artefacts. The Belgae tribe is thought to have been concentrated to the south of our area. Indeed, it can be argued that the Romans followed these traders' routes and so the tracks were instrumental in the Romans' campaign to gain control of the main settled tribal areas. Celtic coinage finds in this part of Wiltshire and Berkshire, reveal that Bedwyn lay on the borders of a number of tribal areas; a situation that continued for much of the Dark Ages. Archaeological evidence suggests that by 100BC the hill-fort at Chisbury had been abandoned in favour of a settlement just to the south-west. This settlement did not continue for long after the Roman invasion in AD43, however, and was probably completely abandoned around AD60–80. The fort might have been used for a short period some 400 years later, but it is clear that it was never a site of continuous settlement.

ROMAN BEDWYN

Roman military occupation of the fort took place for a short time between AD43 and AD100 but there would no longer have been any need for a garrison here once the main Roman base at Cunetio (Mildenhall) had been built, which was an important staging post on the network of Roman roads that passed through this area. The nearest such roads to Chisbury include the route that ran east–west just north of the present A4 (only a few traces exist near us today); and a north–south road that came from Cirencester, went through Mildenhall to Winchester and crossed the Bedwyn Stream at Crofton. Much of this route can be seen today, particularly astride Crofton. A branch from Mildenhall to Old Sarum lay to the west of Burbage, although this has all but vanished. These roads, provided they had been maintained, would have further enhanced Chisbury's strategic importance in the Dark Ages.

THE ROMAN VILLA IN BEDWYN BRAIL

Excavations carried out at the site of the Roman villa in Bedwyn Brail suggest that it was built over a Celtic settlement. The first Roman structure was probably surrounded by a ditch and might have been started soon after the Conquest. A more elaborate wooden building was built on a levelled gravel terrace around the late-second century AD. The stone (flint) building was started in the mid-third century and finally abandoned around AD450 after the collapse of the Roman administration in Britain. The villa is one of the biggest in southern England and could have grown to become the centre of a large farming complex whose economy was based on mixed farming. It is possible that the other Roman sites at Tottenham Park and Harrow Farm were satellite farms of the main villa in Bedwyn Brail. However, given that the better soils lay to the south of the Bedwyn Stream, it seems more likely that other, hitherto undiscovered sites, were part of any such estate.

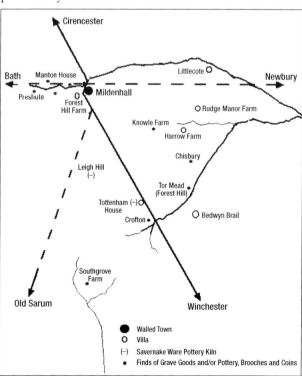

Roman sites, roads and artefacts found locally.

There are suggestions that not all of the produce was sold locally but that some grain (namely wheat and barley) contributed to British exports to Gaul along with, possibly, pork and beef. Perhaps we were not exporting British lamb in those days as sheep rearing was undergoing one of its periodic declines in Roman times. Nevertheless, given the good Roman road access, in particular to Mildenhall, it would seem more likely that the bulk of the farm produce was sold in local markets.

The late-third and early-fourth centuries AD have been described as a golden age for British farmers and manufacturers. In addition to farming there would have been local employment in forestry and possibly woollen-cloth manufacture. As well as a ready local market from those involved in defence, administration and the expansion of the economy of the province, there was a strong overseas trade, particularly to support the armies along the Rhine frontier. A buoyant money-based economy was the result, but this would soon be shattered.

In the mid- to late-fourth century AD the security situation in eastern and southern England was, at times, dire. This led to the rebuilding, between AD360 and AD380, of the walls of the Roman town at Mildenhall. There is no archaeological evidence to suggest that the inhabitants of the local villas moved into Chisbury fort to be secure and nearer their farm lands. Rather, it appears that once the Roman Army and civil administration withdrew around AD406, central control ceased and anarchy took over.

The economy collapsed, surplus food could not be reliably distributed and so production decreased, towns ceased to have a meaningful role and the bulk of the Romano-British population reverted to their agricultural Celtic past. They turned their backs on much of the Roman culture associated with central government, such as its laws and taxation and the obvious signs of urbanisation including the construction or maintenance of stone buildings and roads. In fact, the turbulence in England from the fifth century onwards was so great that, unlike France, barely a single Roman villa in southern England has passed on its name to the area it once dominated, nor did any of the previous Celtic tribal structures re-establish themselves. It seems that fragmentary local control under chieftains or warlords became the norm. The people who remained along the Bedwyn Stream and on the land overlooking it, were probably ruled by a Romano-British overlord until the area finally succumbed to Saxon control in the late-sixth and early-seventh centuries. The Dark Ages had arrived.

ARCHAEOLOGICAL FINDS

There have been numerous local discoveries to support the interpretations which have been covered so far in this chapter. Some of these can be seen in the Devizes and British Museums. The table below is not an exhaustive list but does show the variety and extent of the finds.

Some Local Archaeological Finds

Location	Period	Artefact
Crofton:		
Field above pumping station	Stone Age	Numerous worked flints
Beside Roman road to the south	Stone Age	Barrow
	Stone/Bronze Age?	Polished flint axe
Great Bedwyn:		
South-east of Stokke	Stone/Bronze Age?	Two bowl barrows
Tor Mead/Long Furlong	Early Bronze Age	Ring ditch (84 feet diameter), amber bead
?	Late Bronze Age	Bronze mace head (British Museum)
Castle Copse (Bedwyn Brail)	Roman	Mosaics, tiles, pottery, jewellery
Tor Mead	Roman	Bronze dragonesque brooch (Devizes Museum)
Little Bedwyn:		
Knowle Farm gravel pit	Stone Age	Flint axe, scrapers, knives (Devizes Museum)
Knowle Farm	Late Bronze Age	Socketed spearhead (Devizes Museum)
Chisbury hill-fort	Iron Age	Pre-Belgic pottery
	Roman	Bronze knee brooch
South-east of hill-fort	Roman	Third- and fourth-century coins
Tottenham House	Roman	Tessellated pavement

Chapter 2

THE SAXON PERIOD: A BRIGHT FUTURE

SAXON COLONISATION

It was during the Saxon period that Bedwyn achieved its greatest administrative and economic importance; its status gradually waned during the Middle Ages, the reasons for which are covered in later chapters. The Saxon take-over of parts of eastern and southern England might well have begun soon after the withdrawal of the Romans in AD406. Some of the British kings/tribal leaders are known to have used Saxon mercenaries to help them fend off raiders. This certainly happened to a great extent along the Saxon Shore (roughly from the Wash to the Isle of Wight). When the economy collapsed and the Romano-British leaders were unable to meet the economic demands of their mercenaries, the latter are believed to have taken matters into their own hands. England was seen as a rich ex-Roman province with no native defence force. As such, it is possible that these Saxon mercenaries were the catalysts for a major migration from northern Germany and the eventual colonisation of England. Perhaps the process was more akin to the settlers that moved west across the United States in the nineteenth century, than to a military invasion, such as was seen in 1066.

The initial Saxon territorial expansion was checked around AD500 by Aurelianus (a Romano-British tribal leader) at the Battle of Mons Brittanicus, which most experts agree was on the Ridgeway at Badon, south-east of where the motorway now runs near Swindon. However, within a few years the inexorable westward flow of Saxons continued to push up the Test, Bourne and Avon rivers into our area. They are known to have reached Stoke a few miles north-east of Andover by AD534, and beat a British force at Old Sarum in AD552. In conjunction with Saxons from the Thames Valley these migrants defeated the British at Barbury Castle, again on the Ridgeway, in AD556. Within a few years those Saxons who had settled in the middle and upper reaches of the Thames region themselves began to be squeezed out in a south-westerly direction by the Mercians (Angles from a different part of Germany). The Thames-Valley Saxons eventually combined peacefully and permanently with the West Saxons, who had originally colonised Hampshire and Wiltshire. As such, this union was instrumental in the establishment of the Kingdom of Wessex, which was to play a leading role in the latter stages of the Dark-Age history of this country.

SAXON BEDWYN

The earliest evidence we have of a local Saxon presence has been found at a settlement at Collingbourne Ducis. An examination of the part of the cemetery that is still accessible indicates that the initial inhabitants were pagans. Archaeologists believe that the settlement was occupied by a small farming community between the fifth and the tenth centuries. We do not know when the Saxons moved into the Bedwyn Stream valley as any traces have been destroyed, buried or built upon. The local Saxon finds at Wilton, Crofton and Grafton generally date from the sixth and seventh centuries. The features that would have attracted them to Bedwyn are: the steady flow of sufficient water to run mills; the likelihood that there were water meadows along the valley floor; and the gentle south-facing slopes above which plenty of wood could be found for building and fuel, as well as rough grazing for pigs and other livestock. Their settlements would have been instrumental in establishing a belt of arable land about 800 metres wide astride the valley floor, with a thick hedge at the edges opening on to common and heath lands.

The first documentary evidence of a possible Saxon presence here comes from the *History of Abingdon Monastery*, which records that between AD672 and AD688 Cissa, a West-Saxon overlord, ruled the Berkshire/Wiltshire-border area from his stronghold, widely believed to be Chisbury.

BATTLE OF BEDWYN, AD675

In AD675 there was another in the series of battles between Wessex and Mercia, at a place called Bedanheaford. This is reckoned to be the ford at the head of the Bedwyn Stream, thus placing the site in the area of Crofton. Some skeletons were dug up from the chalk pit above the pumping station in the nineteenth century. Unfortunately the work was not well documented but we do know that there were no grave goods. Their absence does not imply a Christian burial in this case, because the orientation of the skeletons is random; between five and seven were laid out in a pattern similar to the spokes of a wheel. The significance of this is not known. Suggested dates of the late-sixth or seventh centuries merely add to the puzzle.

Looking at this matter from a different viewpoint, we are told that previous large-scale raids from the Thames Valley into Wessex had been unsuccessful. That which took place in AD592 followed the Ridgeway and crossed over the Downs to a point overlooking Pewsey Vale above Alton Priors. The West Saxons defeated this invading force at Adam's Grave near the Wansdyke. In AD652 the Mercians kept to the low ground and tried to venture further west at Bradford on Avon in the forested and probably marshy gap between the East and West Wansdykes. This too was a failure. It is possible that in AD675 the Mercians might have tried a new route, branching off the Ridgeway and going south through Marlborough, on what remained of the Roman road system. This would have led to the gap between the East Wansdyke and Chisbury hill-fort. Savernake Forest might have been difficult going if the Roman road had not been maintained, but they would have found the watershed a relatively easier crossing. They may have hoped also to obtain an advantage through the element of surprise. In this they were unsuccessful, although the battle remained inconclusive.

WANSDYKE

It is generally reckoned that the Wansdyke had been built before, or directly as a result of, the raids southwards from the upper Thames Valley. As it is built over part of the Roman road from Mildenhall to Bath, the dyke is definitely post Roman. The deep ditch and steep banks would have made it extremely difficult for rustlers to get their stolen livestock across, except at the very few gaps in the system. These gaps were either made deliberately and probably guarded, or were in areas of very difficult going such as marshland. It had certainly been built before AD592 because reports about the Battle of Woddensbeorg (Adam's Grave), which is behind the only gap in the eastern Wansdyke, include references to the earthworks there.

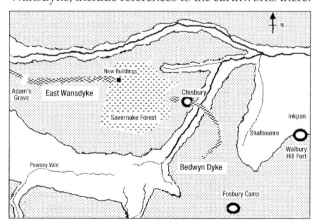

East Wansdyke and other earthworks in the Bedwyn area.

BEDWYN DYKE

The Bedwyn Dyke could well have been built at this time too or, if it had been an old Iron-Age boundary marker, then it could have been enlarged to become a serious military obstacle. The dyke was about half the size of the Wansdyke and probably 15 metres across. The bank could have been 3–4 metres high and the slope into the ditch around 40°. A possible profile is shown below as well as a comparison of the best-preserved portion by the Thames Water pumping station.

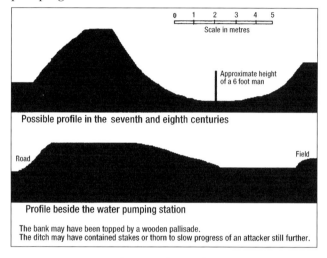

Bedwyn Dyke Profiles.

The diagram below shows the extent of the earthworks, which are believed to be part of the system designed to hinder access into north-eastern Wiltshire. To be an effective obstacle for the military, as well as for livestock, it would have been essential for the defenders to contest any attempts to cross it. From the ramparts of Chisbury hill-fort it is possible to see nearly all of the dyke as it runs west into the difficult terrain of Savernake Forest, as well as the full sweep of its main branch as it crosses the Bedwyn Stream and swings westwards behind the old Roman

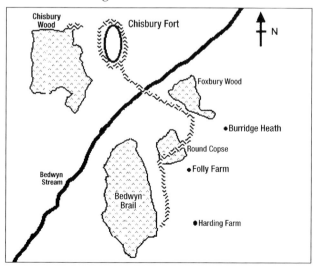

Extent of the Bedwyn Dyke.

villa. The distances involved and the difficulty of forcing a passage would mean that a defender could react effectively over those parts of the dyke.

Throughout the seventh and eighth centuries the eastern part of Wessex, which included Bedwyn, often changed its overlordship between the kings of Wessex, Mercia and sometimes Kent. We have no record of any battle being fought over the dyke but perhaps it achieved its purpose by deterring raiders into choosing a different route. For example, the Battle of Meretun (which is believed to have been at Marten) in AD871 between Mercia and Wessex is the closest to Bedwyn that we know of any major hostilities in this period. Bedwyn might have been very lucky if, as a result of the existence of such an obstacle, it did escape the attentions of the Vikings who are known to have passed through this area on a number of occasions between 1006 and 1016.

SAXON ESTATES

It is thought that by the eighth century the continual struggles between the native British and the incoming settlers had reduced the native population to a fraction of its size at the time of the Roman occupation, with the consequence that a quarter of England reverted to scrubland vegetation. The result was that most native habitation was on isolated farmsteads. It was not until there was a need for, or the prospect of, a steady return from cooperative agriculture, that villages were formed. Quite when this happened around Bedwyn is unclear, but at some stage areas of land came under some form of central control.

The first documentary evidence we have for an estate in this area comes from a tenth-century copy of England's oldest existing charter, dated AD778. The charter is written in Latin and a copy can be seen in the British Museum. It covers a grant by Cynewulf, King of the Saxons, to Earl Bica of lands around 'Bedewinde'. The descriptions of the boundaries of that land are difficult to relate to current features, particularly along the northern boundary. Nevertheless, the charter covers Chisbury and much of the present parish of Little Bedwyn. One boundary marker seems to be a reference to a very large oak called Duke's Vaunt in Savernake Forest. In 2003 an oak, which is said to be Duke's Vaunt, lies in a rather dilapidated state.

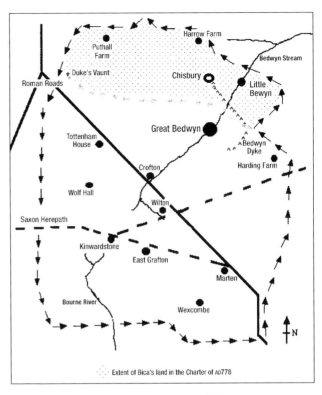

Duke's Vaunt oak tree.

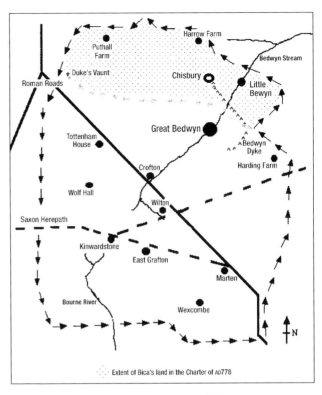

Bedwyn estate, c.AD968.

It seems that this oak was also used as a boundary marker in the Bedwyn Charter of AD968. The settlements shown in both charters exist today as villages, hamlets or farmsteads. As such, with the possible exception of St Katharine's, it appears that no new villages have been established in this area since the Saxon period.

There is a possibility that King Cynewulf only gave away part of what was a much larger royal estate in the Bedwyn area. How long Bica held on to his portion is unknown as land gifts in those days were not always hereditary and often only applied to the lifetime of the first recipient. By the middle of the eleventh century the estate was being assessed independently for taxation. In his will of the 880s King Alfred bequeathed an estate at Bedwyn to his eldest son Edward. Historians believe that Edward received the strategically crucial land, while the less important portions went to the other children. In AD968 Edgar, who was then King of England, granted to the monks of Abingdon a large tract of land at Bedwyn, which included Grafton, Tidcombe, plus parts of Burbage and South Savernake. The monks' tenure was rapidly terminated and the land again became part of a large royal estate, which flourished until soon after the Norman Conquest.

ALFRED'S FORTIFIED TOWN

As a cornerstone in his campaign to defeat the Danes, Alfred established a network of fortified

19

towns (burhs) throughout southern England in which the local inhabitants could find sanctuary. Some of these burhs, such as Worcester, required fortifications to be built, while others, such as Chisbury, used existing fortifications into which some of the local administrative functions could be easily transferred.

From information in an appendix to a mid-tenth- to eleventh-century Winchester manuscript, we learn that the number of defenders needed for each burh was based on the length of wall a man could defend. This was assessed as four men per pole or perch (5½ yards). In the case of Chisbury the circumference of the fort required around 700 men to garrison it. Landowners were required to send one man to help defend a burh for each hide of land which they owned. A hide has been calculated in a number of ways (see Glossary) but it is generally taken to be around 120 acres, depending upon the quality of the soil. Thus the manpower needed to defend Chisbury from the Danes would have to come from 700 hides or roughly 8,400 acres. We do not know from where the defenders of Chisbury came, but it would seem logical that they would have been from the land within a 15-mile radius biased towards the north-east.

BEDWYN'S DEVELOPMENT INTO A BOROUGH

Many of Alfred's burgal-hidage forts became towns, but those smaller than 15 acres tended not to, Chisbury being one such example. However, the royal estate at Bedwyn had its administrative centre moved into the fort only when the Danish threat compelled this. When the threat receded, so the old system was re-established and enhanced. Construction of a minster church was part of this process. There is a record of the Bishop of Winchester buying land for the building of a church in Bedwyn in AD905. From the size of the Saxon foundations discovered during some Victorian renovations, it is clear that this church was big enough to require more than one priest to run it. This notion is confirmed by annotations made at the back of a tenth-century copy of the Gospels (sometimes called the 'Bedwyn Bible') which is now in a museum in Berne, Switzerland (see Chapter 7). Although the church was never so big that it rivalled the bishopric in Ramsbury, it was nevertheless large enough to deal with the ecclesiastical needs of the area covered by this royal estate. Indeed, it helps to confirm that the focus of the estate was Great Bedwyn. Minster churches at that time were not necessarily in settlement centres and were often found to be a small distance from the population, in order to give the priests privacy and seclusion. A good example can be seen today with the Saxon church at Breamore, south of Salisbury. The old Saxon settlement of Great Bedwyn probably lies under the centre of the current village.

Other annotations in the Bedwyn Bible cover the freeing of two slaves and provide a clear indication of some form of guild status existing at this time. The price of freedom for each of the two women slaves was 300d. An extract from the list of commitments for the guild members includes the following:

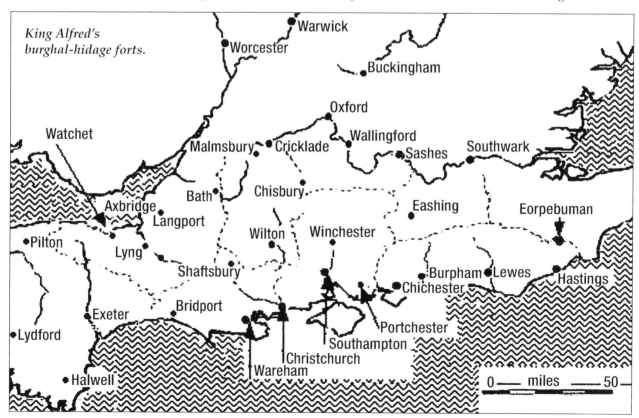

King Alfred's burghal-hidage forts.

And if a member's house is burnt (members shall contribute), by two and two, a load of timber and the work on it, or two pence.

And to the mass priest on Rogation Days, two geldsmen together shall pay a young sheep or two pence.

That sets an interesting price on the value of a slave. The Bedwyn Bible has been dated to AD975, which some believe is too early for the guild to have been a true guild of craftsmen. Instead it could have been a parish or frith guild which had administrative duties. Either way, it demonstrates that those people with a large stake in the community felt a need for mutual support in times of trouble and to formally record the responsibilities that went with this early version of an insurance policy.

For there to be a trade guild there would have to have been an economic outlet for the guild members – in other words, a market. A look at the shape of the High Street in 2003 gives a good indication of where that market might have been. However, perhaps the best clue to the existence of a flourishing market is the local communications system. A single road in and out and no radial network would be indications of a backwater. The crucial point for Bedwyn would be the existence of an all-weather crossing over the Bedwyn Stream to permit year-round movement of trade to the south and east. We know there was a Saxon herepath (army road) which ran from Pewsey to Burbage and, it is believed, on through East Grafton and Marten to where it linked up with the upland route across the Berkshire Downs. Reliance on a crossing at Crofton, if the Roman road had been maintained, would seem to involve too big a detour. Proof of the existence of a nearer crossing point comes from a report concerning work on a sewage pipe in the 1920s. A flint causeway 16 feet wide and 6 feet thick was found leading across the valley from behind the church. If this existed in Saxon times it would be strong evidence of a significant market at Bedwyn, which would then have been at the centre of a radial network of routes.

In addition, we know that Bedwyn had its own mint in the eleventh century that produced coins of Edward the Confessor and very early ones (1066–68) for William I. The British Museum holds some of these, as does a local well-known stonemason.

THE MINT

There was a multitude of mints in southern England in the tenth and eleventh centuries. Their existence is evidence for the use of coinage as payment for tithes and fines in preference to goods or labour. It also tends to confirm wider trade arrangements covering large areas – indeed, one coinage hoard found in southern England came from numerous mints, which helps to support this theory. Mints requiring a greater output of coins because they supported a large trade

had more than one moneyer. Winchester had six such men whilst Bedwyn (where coins were produced for a short time either side of the Norman Conquest) had but one. Winchester was the capital of Wessex with a sizeable population, while Bedwyn was more of a market than a population centre.

Surviving coins suggest that there were never more than six mints operating in Wiltshire concurrently in late-Saxon times. Coins were minted only within a port (a fortified location). Mints were established to meet local demands and possibly to give a good geographical spread, and Bedwyn was the only mint within a radius of 25 miles in any county. Other Wiltshire mints were at Cricklade, Malmesbury, Warminster, Wilton and Salisbury. Most of these were in places held by the Crown, where there were defences for the town either around them or close by and containing a strong building capable of use as a treasury.

Although there were more than 70 mints at the time of Edward the Confessor (1042–66), it should not be thought that this multiplicity indicated localised coinage or limited distribution. All coins were part of a national currency under sophisticated controls and standards. Coins from Bedwyn would have been widely circulated, in a society characterised by rapid interchange of money and constant travel across the country. All coinage was changed every three to six years, with the old issue being demonetised, effectively imposing a wealth tax, and keeping good coinage in circulation. Weights of new coins could be adjusted, thus affecting exchange rates and the price of imports and exports. All dies were cast in London, from where the moneyer had to collect his dies when the design changed.

After the reign of King Edgar in the mid-tenth century, coins bore the name of the sovereign and the moneyer. This is how we know that Cild or Cilda was Bedwyn's moneyer in the time of King Edward the Confessor (1042–66).

SHIRES & HUNDREDS

By the beginning of the eleventh century all of England south of the Tees was divided into shires (reflecting the expansion of the shire administrative system that had existed in Wessex since before the end of the eighth century). Wiltshire is derived from Wilton, which in turn refers to the people who lived near what is now called the River Wylie. Shires were used for local administration and their boundaries remained largely unchanged for 900 years. By the time of King Edgar (AD959–975) it was found necessary to divide shires into a number of 'equal' units. They dealt with local adjustments to taxation, law and order, and settled local pleas. These units were called hundreds as each one covered about 100 hides. Bedwyn lies in the Kinwardstone Hundred, which, like many in this part of Wiltshire, is large in area to make up for the poor agricultural quality of much of the land. It comprised just over 196 hides and was the second most highly assessed hundred in Wiltshire in 1084. It stretched from Pewsey to Hungerford and from Froxfield to Collingbourne Kingston. Savernake Forest was, at times, excluded from the hundred, the jurisdiction of which, between the twelfth and sixteenth century, went with the lordship of Wexcombe Manor, although Great Bedwyn was the administrative centre.

In every hundred there was at least one estate, a market, a minster church, a judicial place of execution and a meeting place where justice was done or where individuals could air their concerns with the reeve (the senior administrator). The meeting place for the Bedwyn royal estate was Cynewarde's Stone, which, until being shifted to the Chute Causeway, (GR303552) in the twentieth century, was on the road between West Grafton and Burbage. This move cannot have been easy as the stone weighs many tons. Places for judicial executions tended to be on boundaries. This tradition continued for many centuries and perhaps explains why there was a gibbet (gallows) on the parish boundary near the Wilton windmill in the eighteenth century.

BEDWYN ON THE EVE OF THE NORMAN CONQUEST

Everyone, apart from slaves, had to pay taxes in some form or other. The collective tax for the Bedwyn estate was to supply the king and his entourage with sustenance for 24 hours. This was referred to as food-rent. The tax was due once a year and was collected by the reeve. Of course this was not the only collective tax that was raised, but royal estates were often excused or very lightly assessed for contributing to opportunity costs, such as the Danegeld. This was part of a policy of encouraging those with wealth to either settle or make greater use of royal estates. Another advantage of trading from a king's property was the additional security and stability that the location was likely to afford.

If one assumes that there were no enormous changes in agricultural holdings or population sizes in the few years between the Norman Conquest and the production of the Domesday Book, it is possible to gain an insight into Bedwyn's local importance. The surrounding manors were at Harding, Crofton, Chisbury, Wolfhall, Marten, Grafton and Burbage. Harding was a single farmstead of around 120 acres

under cultivation. Crofton had a mill, some 600 arable acres, 10 acres of water meadow and 6 of pasture. The manorial wood was 3 furlongs in length and 1 wide. The hamlet contained seven village families and a Frenchman with a plough (who, we have to assume, came after the Battle of Hastings). Wolfhall Manor covered around 400 acres of plough land but there was no livestock raised there for reasons that are not obvious. There was a mill and, again, seven families attached to the manor. Marten, Grafton and Burbage were in multiple ownership and all contained mixed arable and livestock farms. Marten covered around 300 acres; Grafton was twice this size; and Burbage slightly larger still. Marten had four families working the land, while the other two hamlets each had three times as many.

When we compare this with Chisbury's population of 29 families and Great Bedwyn's of 154, which also included 25 free traders (burgesses), it becomes very clear that the latter was the most important place locally. Historians have suggested that one way to assess settlement sizes is to take each recorded tenement and assume that it represents a single household. The next assumption is that a household contained five people, excluding slaves. Using this calculation Bedwyn would have had a population of around 700 people engaged in farming, trade and the administration of the royal estate and the Kinwardstone Hundred.

THE COMING OF THE NORMANS

There is no record of the independence of Hungerford at the time of Domesday. Marlborough's size is a little shrouded in mystery as its landholdings in the Domesday Book are insignificant but its assessment in urban taxation was quite high at about two-thirds that of Salisbury. It has been suggested that Marlborough developed following the Norman decision to fortify the mound and use it as a base for the domination of the outlying areas. As part of this shift, the mint being run by Cild (Bedwyn's moneyer) was transferred to Marlborough in 1070 and soon after the area around Bedwyn was made a royal hunting forest through which movement was discouraged and within which agriculture was very strictly controlled. This would undoubtedly have affected the market for wool and agricultural produce. Despite this, there was still enough trade in Bedwyn to support the eight mills mentioned in the Domesday Book.

Chapter 3

UNDER THE NORMAN YOKE

In the eleventh century Bedwyn was a prestigious and regionally important centre within a rural landscape. While most of the countryside supported a population averaging 50 people per square mile, the agriculturally poorer soils of north-east Wiltshire may have only sustained half this number. Similarly, the distribution of towns would have been very different. Ramsbury was an important centre and the seat of a bishopric until 1078, but the settlements we now associate with the main Bath–London road (the A4) were either insignificant or non-existent. Neither Hungerford nor Froxfield were mentioned at all in the Domesday Book; Marlborough (also belonging to the Crown) was small in area with the survey recording just one hide with a church, worth 30s. However, the town paid the King £4 from the third penny taxation system (based on the volume of trade) which was two-thirds that paid by Salisbury and only

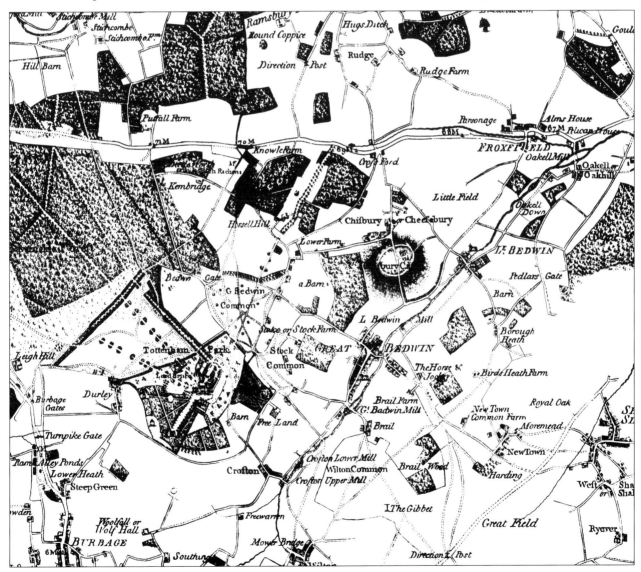

The Bedwyns in 1773. Part of the first comprehensive large-scale map of Wiltshire, prepared by John Andrews and Andrew Dury, engraved on copper sheet, 'the finest map of Wiltshire before the Ordnance Survey'.

a pound less than Cricklade. There were, in effect, few competing towns, and it is even possible that the great east–west road that later governed transport and prosperity did not exist as a realistic, passable trade route.

The Domesday entries for Bedwyn and Chisbury read as follows:

The King holds Bedvinde. King Edward [the Confessor] held it [previously]. Here is land for 79 plough-teams; 12 of which, with 18 slaves, are in demesne [untenanted land retained and farmed by the Lord]. 80 villagers, 60 cottagers and 14 colliberts [freemen] occupy the land for the other 67 plough-teams. Eight mills pay 100 shillings. Here are two woods, three miles long and a mile and a half broad; 200 acres of meadow; and the pasture is a mile and a half in length, and three quarters of a mile in breadth. Twenty-five burgesses belong to this meadow. There was a grove in this manor in the time of King Edward, three-quarters of a mile long by three furlongs wide, and it was in the King's demesne; at present Henry de Ferreres holds it. Bristoardus, a priest, holds the church; his father held it in the time of King Edward. One and a half hides belong to it. There is land for one plough-team. It is worth 60 shillings.

Gillebert of Bretevile holds Cheseberie [Chisbury]. Edricus held it in the time of King Edward, and it paid tax for five hides. There is land for nine plough-teams, four of which with seven slaves are in demesne. Twelve villagers, three smallholders and fourteen cottagers occupy land of the other five plough-teams. Two mills pay 20 shillings. Here are fifteen acres of meadow, and 40 acres of wood. The pasture is 15 furlongs in length by 3 furlongs broad. It was valued at £8, and is now worth £12.

The Anglo-Saxon kings enjoyed hunting and extensive royal estates were probably managed for deer and boar. One of Edward the Confessor's huntsmen, known as Alvic, held land at Harding. At the time of the Norman Conquest the Saxons were already developing a system of forest law for the protection of the Crown's game. It is unlikely that this was formally applied to Savernake. Although the woodland of 'Savernoc' is referred to in a Saxon charter as early as AD934, there is no mention of forest law until the pipe rolls of 1130 specify 'the Forest of Marlborough'. It was called the Forest of Savernake from the time of Henry II (1154). It is important to recognise that the term 'forest' referred specifically to an area of land where regulations concerning clearance and the killing of game were ruthlessly enforced. It did not equate with 'woodland', which is a wholly modern connotation, and it would be misleading to consider the original forest as resembling the current woodland now called Savernake, most of which would not then have carried continuous tree cover. Royal hunting forests would have

included great chases, copses, spinneys, scattered trees, scrubland and rough grazings where deer, hare and other game could prosper. The Royal Forest of Savernake would have focused on the King's estates, which may have moved in the late-eleventh century from Bedwyn to Marlborough (the site of a castle and the local centre of Norman administration).

As forests were areas to which specific laws applied, rather than lands with particular geographical characteristics, the extent of forested land could vary with political administration and royal interest. At its greatest extent, in AD1200, Savernake probably covered some 100 square miles, extending from East Kennet, along the river valley through Marlborough, Ramsbury, Hungerford and Kintbury, dropping south through Inkpen, and sweeping west to Collingbourne and Pewsey, before extending back to East Kennet. Whilst the land enclosed was not wholly unproductive, the rights of subjects were heavily constrained. Bedwyn, although exempt from forest law, was surrounded, limiting its expansion and confining the activities of its population.

Forests were a source of great resentment amongst the populace, whose ability to cultivate land and take wild food was ruthlessly controlled for the benefit of the aristocracy. Few exceptions were granted. However, Matthew de Columbarus, who held Chisbury until his death in 1269, had the privilege of retaining hounds and was thus exempt from the penalty known as expeditation [sic] for those keeping dogs within Savernake. Others were not so lucky. In 1324 the local landowner Sir Theobald Russell was found committing a trespass by hunting within the bounds of Savernake Forest. Consequently his wood at East Bedwyn was seized by Edward II 'until he should make satisfaction'.

We have no specific knowledge of the ravages of the Black Death (mid-1300s) in Bedwyn. On some Wiltshire estates one-third to a half of the population was decimated, so some impact would have been inevitable. It is just possible that the loss of certain settlements on the outskirts of Bedwyn could be related, although there is no evidence for such a link. Losses may be attributable to a widespread decline in agriculture in the fourteenth century, to famine and to epidemics in farm stock, which all predated the Black Death. Conversely, unauthorised settlements on lands to which forest laws applied may have been ruthlessly suppressed. A number of minor settlements sprang up during the medieval period, probably established on the fringes of Savernake. These included Knowle, Puthall and Henset (now integral to Little Bedwyn parish), Teteridge (now part of Froxfield), and maybe even some of Froxfield itself. The lost villages of Henset, the outline of which can still be seen north of Puthall Farm, and Teteridge were jointly given by King Henry I to St Maurice Cathedral, Angers, in 1119. The Bishop of Winchester later acquired them before they passed back to the Crown

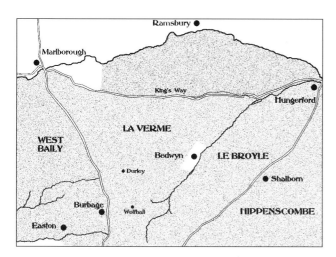

*Savernake Forest at its greatest extent in about 1200
when it stretched as far as Ramsbury. The shaded area
shows the land subject to forest laws protecting game and
its habitat for the purposes of hunting. This would have
been a wild landscape, but not necessarily wooded.*

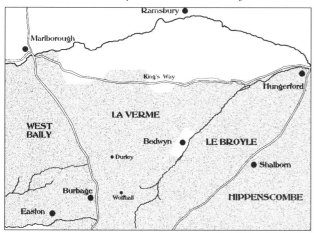

*By 1280, the land subject to protective forest law had
been withdrawn to the King's highway between
Hungerford and Marlborough.*

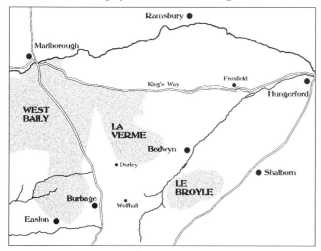

*By 1330 the forest had contracted to a fraction of
its former extent with the bailiwick of La Verme
corresponding more closely with the woodland of
Savernake seen today, and Le Broyle now partly
represented by Wilton and Bedwyn Brail.*

in 1241. Deserted for a period, the land was claimed by Knowle Farm. Subsequently the manor of Puthall was included in the gift of Froxfield to the Trinitarian Friars of Easton in the fourteenth century.

The area around Bedwyn remained a relatively wild and uncultivated area for several hundred years after the Norman Conquest. Henry VIII's cantankerous and sour antiquary and library keeper, John Leland, was on his research tour of England in 1540 and his comments concerning the landscape are revealing:

From Ramesbyri on to Great Bedwine a three miles moste parte throughe the forest of Savernake. The toune is prevelyged with a Burges at the Parliament, yet it is but a poor thinge to sight. Thens a two miles by woddy ground to Little Bedwine where I passed over Great Bedwine brooke.

It seems likely that Leland approached Great Bedwyn from the west, since there was probably no road across from Froxfield at that time and he makes no reference to Chisbury. He says acerbically:

… whereas I harde ons that there was a castelle or forteres at Great Bedwine, the ruines and plot whereof is yet seene, I could there heere nothing of it.

The area of Savernake Forest was reduced considerably through the centuries as its importance for hunting declined and increasing amounts of land came under cultivation. By 1600 the vast majority of the area had been cleared and was being managed in accordance with manorial customs, for the benefit of commoners and the lords of the manor.

THE BEDWYN MINT

Coins from Bedwyn have been identified only for the reign of Edward the Confessor (1042–46) and the first part of William the Conqueror's reign (1066 87). It is unclear whether any for Harold II were struck (1066) in the nine months that he was King. Silver pennies from Bedwyn made in 1056–59 show Edward seated on a throne holding an orb and sceptre. They bear the inscription 'EADPARRD RE' on the face, with the mint name 'BEDEPINDE' on the reverse, although this appears variously as 'BEDEP' or 'BEDE CIN'. A halfpenny dating from the same reign also survives. An early penny of William I showing the new King's head in profile also exists.

There were no major immediate changes in coinage associated with the Norman Conquest. The controls, range of mints and moneyers remained virtually the same. However, Cild's Bedwyn mint was transferred to Marlborough where he continued to strike coins of the last six types of William I and of William II. The Bedwyn mint was always insignificant in national terms. It was one of 13 that each

Above: *Minting coins. A woodcut from* Holinshed's Chronicles.

Right: *Coins of the type minted at Bedwyn in the eleventh century, showing Edward the Confessor seated on a throne holding a sceptre and orb. William I's head can be seen in profile.*

produced less than one thousandth of the realm's coins, whilst the ten largest mints produced over half of all coinage. Its demise and transfer to Marlborough, where it survived a few years more, would have been instituted in order to take advantage of increased security there as well as to ensure that it could operate under the watchful eye of the Norman overlord of this area, Henry de Ferrers. Over time, the number of mints continued to fall; 70 operated at the time of the last Anglo-Saxon kings but, by the end of the thirteenth century, all coinage was centralised in London and Canterbury.

An incident recorded in the Wiltshire Assizes some six centuries later shows that these silver pennies were not the only money ever to be minted in Bedwyn. The right to strike coins was a privilege held and ruthlessly enforced by the monarchy. With the execution of Charles I at the end of the English Civil War, it was no longer possible to infringe royal prerogative and a number of people started striking coins to make up an apparent shortfall. By 1660 at least 50 people were in the habit of issuing money, and not all of these desisted from the practice after the Restoration of the Monarchy. In 1668 orders were given to stop this 'evill practize' and to take evidence 'of those coyning or venting unlawfull coynes'. In July 1670 two Great Bedwyn men were charged with the use of unlawful coinage. John Bushell, mercer, and Thomas Greene, baker, were indicted for striking farthings not worth above 16d. per hundred. The witness was Edward Brunsden, a former churchwarden of Great Bedwyn, and it is likely that this incident was the latest episode in a long-running feud between him and Bushell.

Both the latter and Greene pleaded guilty, and they were fined, although this was later respited. Bushell was a local dignitary, probably a portreeve for the borough, and was later commemorated through the charity founded at his death in 1721. It is possible that these unauthorised farthings were simply an attempt to provide small change rather than engage in serious counterfeiting. Unlike the pennies from the time of the Norman Conquest, they were probably never circulated beyond the village.

THE BOROUGH OF BEDWYN: MARKET & FAIRS

The term 'borough' derived from the Old English term burh, which was originally applied to any defended place (notably lands belonging to the King) endowed with a royal guarantee of the enforcement of law and order. The establishment of Bedwyn as a borough conveyed on both the town and certain individuals special status, rights and responsibilities. During the wars between the Anglo-Saxons and Danes it was particularly applied to centres of population with defensive earthworks. Boroughs also enjoyed a significant element of self-government, and one of the principal tasks of local administration was to regulate commerce and industry. In 1086 the borough of Bedwyn contained 25 burgage plots, probably reflecting how the village was settled. These plots may have extended either side of the road north-east of the church. The reason for supposing this is that burgage plots often comprised long narrow strips of land extending at right angles to the street. Behind such plots was often another path, or back lane. In Hungerford the outlines of the burgage plots survive on both sides of the High Street, together with back lanes either side, while in Great Bedwyn, Back Lane could also mark the rear of original plots. Burgage plots were held by way of certain distinctive customs (known as 'burgage tenure') involving a monetary rent. This was unusual, since other properties generally involved an obligation to provide service to the lord of the manor. They could also be sold, inherited or otherwise disposed of more freely than most other rural property. Rental from these plots would have become an important source of income for the town. The burgesses or freemen were required to pay suit at the borough court and held various responsibilities. That said, they could carry out such administration to their own advantage, guarding their rights jealously and administering the affairs of the less privileged populace.

Bedwyn's 'common seal' would have been affixed to official documents to confirm authorisation. As an important instrument of borough authority, the seal would have been locked securely and its use controlled by a constitution. By the late Middle Ages the seal symbolised the power of local government. A fine solid-silver seal, formerly in the custody of the Marquess of Ailesbury, has survived and is now held by the Ashmolean Museum, Oxford. It is nearly 4 inches in height, weighs 5½ ounces and on the globular handle is written 'The Gvift of the Honorable Daniel Finch Esq'. Daniel Finch was the local MP who gave the seal in 1661. The seal bears the inscription 'The Common Seale of the Corporation of Great Bedwyn.'

BEDWYN IN COMPETITION

Bedwyn was one of 112 boroughs mentioned in the Domesday Book. Most of them had a mint, and although there were many other English towns that never achieved borough status; in many ways boroughs had the greatest chance of developing into towns. At this time the country had entered a period of considerable population growth and corresponding economic development, as more land was put under cultivation, and more intensive farming and improved techniques produced a surplus of foodstuffs for trade. In addition, markets were able to benefit from an expanding trade in luxury goods. Even though we suspect that Bedwyn, as the centre of the Kinwardstone Hundred, held a market in Saxon times, it is not until the thirteenth century that we have documentary proof. There are records that it was called Chepingbedewynde or Chippingbedewynde in the 1270s, suggesting a reference to its market status. The road now called the High Street, which held the wide market-place, was formerly called Chipping Street or Cheap Street. From later medieval times, Bedwyn's market would have been in competition with neighbouring towns, especially Marlborough and Hungerford, which were also granted borough status. Competition could even have been deliberately suppressed. The King's market at Marlborough, granted by John to the burgesses in 1204, was reportedly damaged by competition from Ramsbury, which accordingly was ordered to close immediately. Bedwyn at this time was doubtless jostling for position amongst other towns in the area, and already probably falling behind. The 1334 Lay Subsidy, a tax levied on movable wealth and collected by townships, reveals that Bedwyn was taxed at £23, whilst Ramsbury collected £37, Marlborough £80, and Aldbourne £155. These figures have to be interpreted with caution, but they do suggest that Bedwyn's primacy at the time of Domesday had already been supplanted by the mid-1300s.

King Edward IV granted a Monday market to the burgesses of Bedwyn in 1468, with a four-day fair in spring, and a six-day fair at Michaelmas, although there is no evidence that these occurred. Open butchers' stalls, known as 'shambles', were recorded

in the market-place in the fifteenth century. The Monday market was replaced by one on Tuesday in 1641 (Marlborough's remained on Wednesday and Saturday). A market or court-house stood in the market-place from at least the seventeenth century. Soon after the fire of 1716, which extensively damaged the centre of the village, the market house, together with the shambles, and the profits of fairs and tolls, were let in 1720 for only 5s. per year. In 1741 the same was let for 21 years at £1 per year. These do not suggest a very profitable market-place at this time. The market house itself was disused in the mid-nineteenth century, when a corn market was held at the Three Tuns public house. It was finally demolished in 1870, owing to its crumbling stone pillars, although it was reported that the beams could have stood for another 100 years or more.

Bedwyn seemed unable to compete with the burgeoning towns of Hungerford and Marlborough. At the time of the Norman Conquest the borough of Bedwyn had been a provincial centre of commerce in a landscape devoid of rivals. However, Marlborough thrived in the shadow of its castle and, together with Hungerford, could benefit from trade along the King's highway to London. In contrast, poor transport routes hampered Bedwyn, and it gradually dwindled from a regional centre to the rural settlement it remains today.

BEDWYN'S WOOLLEN INDUSTRY

Bedwyn's comparative prosperity during early medieval times was partly associated with the textile industry. Sheep had been kept on the chalk uplands of Wiltshire for more than 4,000 years and the discovery of spindle-whorls and tools at numerous sites across the Marlborough Downs reveals that wool has been woven into cloth since the Iron Age. The procedure remained largely unchanged for millennia. Only a few families would have owned looms, producing fabrics in small amounts for local use by tailors and other craftsmen (vertical looms could not produce large pieces of consistent quality). Weaving could have supplemented income, but never became a full profession with commercial outlets. A revolution in weaving technique followed the development of horizontal looms that allowed the production of immense cloths 2 yards wide and 20 yards long. It stimulated the development of a new industry to satisfy markets in London and overseas. Whilst other areas of Wiltshire were to become renowned for the manufacture of finely dyed and fashionable fabrics, Bedwyn and Marlborough were at the forefront of the production of 'burel', a coarse-textured speciality of southern England and Normandy, where the local sheep were markedly small in stature. Burel was extremely rough, cheaper than almost any other fabric and was suitable for clothing the poor and for military wear. Chaucer used the same term to describe the supposedly ignorant, unlearned folk of the laity.

Despite burel's suitability for the lowest ranks of society, manufacture was organised and sophisticated. 'Burellers' were entrepreneurs who employed weavers to complete piece-work. Cloth production was highly regulated. Proclamations were issued specifying that it had to be sold at a fixed standard width, although both Marlborough and Bedwyn obtained licences of exemption with respect to their burel cloth (it is likely that the 'laws of the weavers and fullers of Marlborough' would have applied equally to Bedwyn). These specified that weavers worked only under the direction of freemen; if any became sufficiently rich to want to become freemen, they had to cease their craft for two years and dispense with their tools. We can thus picture Bedwyn as possessing a highly differentiated society revolving around the town's borough status, with privileges jealously guarded, freemen not allowed to weave, and weavers allowed to work only under direct employment. Rather than benefit the town, however, such restrictions probably drove skilled artisans into the countryside.

Bedwyn never took advantage of industrial advancements in the fulling industry. Marlborough, Ramsbury and Chilton Foliat developed fulling mills, where water power drove mechanical hammers. At Bedwyn, however, fullers would have worked in the traditional way by treading the cloth underfoot in water troughs to which urine or other substances may have been added, removing natural oils, thickening and felting the fabric, pounding and rolling, pre-shrinking and pulling out the fibre using teasels and combs.

The Bedwyn textile industry was short-lived. Although it may have suffered because of its failure to embrace increasing mechanisation and adapt to changing markets, it also fell victim to a malaise affecting the whole country. Whilst the numbers of weavers, dyers and fullers declined, drapers were on the increase, which suggests that foreign imports were a root cause. By 1379 the poll-tax return for Bedwyn lists a tailor, but no weaver. In contrast Marlborough still had five weavers and one dyer. Burel had all but disappeared as a cloth by that time, and the word itself fell into obsolescence. Whilst the weavers of Salisbury thrived and became property-owners from the production of fine textiles, inhabitants of Bedwyn had to be content with the production of unworked fleeces and shepherding on the Downs. Whilst, in subsequent centuries, local craftsmen made clothes for Bedwyn parishioners, most of this would have involved imported cloth. Tailors are frequently mentioned amongst the trades listed in parish records and an account from the Quarter Sessions in Devizes of the 'terrible fire' which affected Great Bedwyn in 1716 recalls the loss of much 'drapery stuffe, silk and other merchandise', none of which would have been

of local origin. Bedwyn's prosperity was now being enjoyed by other modern towns, better situated for trade and transport; a picture that was replicated in other respects throughout the Middle Ages.

The Manorial System & Community of Bedwyn

From late Saxon times, most land in England was divided into manors that were administered by feudal tenure. Land was held on condition of providing services. The nobility occupied estates in return for military service to the Crown, and the peasantry held land from the lord of the manor on the condition that they worked on those areas which the manor farmed directly, known as the demesne land. In 1086, 12 of Bedwyn's 79 plough lands were recorded as being in demesne, suggesting that the manorial system was already in existence locally. The Normans applied the same principle everywhere; there should be no land without a master. Through succeeding centuries service was often commuted to monetary payments and these, in turn, were used to employ workers or mercenaries.

Manors were extremely variable. They could be of almost any size, sometimes relating to parishes, but also parts of parishes, or combinations of them. In Bedwyn's parish in the thirteenth century there were separate manors associated with Bedwyn itself: Chisbury, Wexcombe, Crofton Fitzwarren and Braboef, East and West Grafton, Stokke, Wolfhall and Little Bedwyn. Manors were bought and sold, and became a principal source of wealth for the nobility, some of whom owned literally dozens, or even hundreds, and few of whom actually resided within their properties. These were let out to minor aristocrats and other gentry, who became local lords of the manor. Some manors had scattered holdings and changed hands for more than just money. In 1567 the manor of Chisbury was conveyed. It included 20 holdings, six cottages, ten parcels of land, a water-mill, dovecot, 1,500 acres of pasture, 300 of wood, and 1,500 of furze and heath, in Chisbury, Great Bedwyn, Little Bedwyn, Froxfield, Rudge and Ramsbury for £200. It carried a rental charge of 4d. and 1lb of pepper. Whilst now the phrase 'peppercorn rent' has come to mean a token or nominal sum, in former times it could retain its value better than money, and was used in property rentals or even passed on through wills.

A fine effigy of a knight in armour in St Mary's Church, Great Bedwyn, probably depicts the medieval owner of the manor of Stokke. Whilst the current manor-house is brick built, and of the seventeenth century, according to Aubrey in 1675 the fine seat of Stokke formerly had a moat around it. At one time it was the residence of the Hungerford family, some of whom were MPs for Bedwyn. In 1766 Ralph, Lord Verney, sold it to Thomas Brudenell, Lord Bruce.

Sir Adam de Stokke was guardian for the Crown of

the temporalities of the see of Sarum, after the death of Bishop Nicholas de Longspee in 1297, and until the election of Simon de Gant. For at least 500 years it has generally been believed that he oversaw the renovations of the transepts and crossing of St Mary's in Great Bedwyn and that the effigy at the end of the southern transept shows Sir Adam, who died in 1312.

Throughout the Middle Ages land was farmed using the great field system. Fields were divided into strips, each to be planted ('every man's land for himself') at specified times, but grazed communally after harvest. Fields were left fallow every two or three years. There were also common grazings on which commoners could depasture a specified number of cattle, sheep, pigs or geese and there were also rights to take fuel and wood. Everything was valuable and tightly managed. In medieval times Great Bedwyn had four open fields; Tile Field and Barr Field, comprising 67 acres, were north-west of Brown's Lane, whilst Harding Field and Conygre Field, of 27 acres, were south-east of the Bedwyn Stream.

The manorial system controlled every aspect of the community, including what land could be held, the system of tenure, obligations, rights and punishments, all based on customs. However, each manor developed its own particular, and often peculiar, customs, administered and jealously guarded through local courts, with jurors sworn in from the populace. There was no national system whereby land could be acquired or leased and everything was governed by local tradition. Even the lord of the manor did not have the right to alter rentals set by custom.

Courts Leet dealt with petty law and the administration of communal agriculture, whilst Courts Baron considered management of the land, including the wastes and commons, rights and the transfer of land. Tenants came to occupy land by agreeing terms at manorial courts, the entries for which were recorded on court rolls made of parchment, sometimes several yards long, or later recorded in court books. The tenant would be given a copy of this entry, and this system of copyhold tenure was the prevailing mechanism through which land was transferred in the Bedwyn area for several centuries.

Bedwyn is fortunate in that several court rolls survive for manors in and around the parishes, revealing much about these early communities. Of particular interest are a number of rolls from the reign of Elizabeth I; these sometimes combine Latin and English script in the same roll. At this time Edward Seymour (Earl of Hertford and son of the first Duke of Somerset), who had houses at both Wolfhall and Tottenham, was lord of many local manors. From these rolls we learn that even in the sixteenth century readiness for military service was still required of tenants. One roll records that Robert Arnold, aged 20, and William Byrche, aged 18, were each fined 6d. for not having practised archery for one year. Rights on the common lands were rigidly enforced and limited.

The rolls record that Roger Walter overburdened the common with one pig and hence was 'in mercy'. Michael Stalker took thorns from the common pasture and was fined 6d. It was agreed that nobody should have geese feeding in Okehildowne (the hill southwest of Forebridge) upon penalty of 2s. and that no tenant should have sheep feeding in the Common Down between Candlemas and (the feast of) St Thomas the Apostle. The rolls also state that no tenant could keep more animals on the common than he could feed over winter from his own tenement.

The rolls record deaths and the detail of wills. For example, there is an account of the death of William Whitehorse, who held a house by copy (of an entry in the court roll) since 1556. On his death it was reported that the lord of the manor was entitled to sequester by custom the dead man's most valuable possession, namely a cow worth 20s. His wife, Agnes, was admitted to remain in the cottage, in accordance with custom, for her widowhood. The will of the late Elizabeth Arnold was proven, and her daughter was to receive a cow, whilst her son inherited all the corn he sowed, and the church received 6d.

With so many customs, some of which were applied very rarely, there was frequent debate concerning their accurate recollection. To save dispute, the customs of Chisbury Manor were tabulated in 1612 and 1639. They comprise a miscellany of revealing and archaic entries, including the following:

> ... *estranger's* [outsiders] *and felon's goods do not belong to the Lord of this Manor, but to the Earle of Pembroke; as a herriot, by custom the Lord of the Manor is due the best beast of any deceased tenant, but if he has no beast the Lord may take his best good except corne; a tenant suffering his tenement to decay may have a penalty imposed upon him, followed by a more grievous paine if not repaired, but he will not suffer forfeiture except upon wilfully pulling downe the tenement; the farmer of Knoll has a right of pasture in the sheep common to the west of Chisbury known as the Heath for three dayes in a weeke.*

The documents also list 13 different coppices at Chisbury, showing that there was still significant woodland surviving, and that this was valuable to the community.

Whilst manorial courts continued to sit until 1837, their importance gradually declined, as later records reveal. The manor of the prebend of Great Bedwyn retained a number of antiquated customs. For example, when Thomas Hurcombe took a lease on the Swan alehouse in Church Street in 1768, his yearly rental was 1s. and a couple of good fat pullets. The shilling rent was a relic of former times; one penny per month was a trivial sum even by eighteenth-century standards. The system had not changed much from the early days of the Middle

Ages and procedures were still as they were outlined in the previous chapter. However, we now know the name of the portreeve elected in 1762 for the manor of the borough of Great Bedwyn. Thomas Potter's role, like that of a mayor in the twenty-first century, was becoming increasingly ceremonial. At the same court Thomas Roby and Thomas Potter were elected bread weighers and ale tasters for the year, charged with ensuring the quality of produce sold in the borough. As late as 1837 a hayward was elected, responsible for the repair of manorial fences, looking after the commoners' animals and impounding stray cattle. Occasionally there was reference to a tragedy, as for example in 1774, when the court ordered the removal of street rubble close to the house of a Mrs Savage, lately burnt down and opposite Pyke's. In 1780 the court ordered that no person should carry fire from house to house or elsewhere within the borough either uncovered or not properly secured from danger. However, this warning was not heeded, as subsequently the court remarked that Elizabeth Barrett, a widow residing in Farm Lane, was in the habit of going about by night with a lighted candle in an improper manner.

Jurors increasingly concentrated on complaining about minor nuisances and the inadequate behaviour of their fellow citizens. Some people are listed repeatedly and we get a picture of certain poor neighbours being hounded by, but not feeling compelled to heed, the dictates of the manorial courts. One such

Above: *An account of the customs of Chisbury Manor set down in 1612. As the laws of manors were applied through custom, rather than statute, it was important that these were accurately remembered or recorded. The early-seventeenth-century script can be difficult to decipher. It reads as follows:*

A writing whereof this is a copie was brought unto me upon the eleventh day of January 1612 by John Pyke, John Newe, John Haws, William Tarrant and other tenements of Chesbury, whoe reported unto me that the same wrytinge was found in the house of John Newe after the decease of Thomas Newe his father deceased late one of the copie hould tenements of the said manor of Chesbury which writinge followeth in these words viz The Customs of the Manor of Chesbury. If a widow be convicted of incontinence *[meaning here loose morals]* she is to forfeit her estate and that a customarie tenant beinge attainted and lawfully convicted of felony is to forfeit his estate. The customarie tenant have usually taken (on this manor) cartboote, ploughboote, hedgeboote, fouldboote, and fierboote, gatboote, and stileboote *[meaning the right to take timber for these purposes]* uppon their owne tenements for their necessarie uses.

case is that of Edward Morgan, whose name is frequently raised in association with having erected a wooden house and pigsty on the waste ground of the borough, having a dangerous well without a cover, allowing his house to decay and causing an obstruction with his sarsen stones. The fact that the same misdemeanours are mentioned in a series of courts suggests that these institutions were effectively ignored as irrelevant and powerless.

In 1770 the court of the manor of Great Bedwyn borough 'presented' all the dung lying in the streets

and ordered the same to be removed by the respective owners thereof within one month, under penalty of 10s. One can imagine the effectiveness of such a decree, and disputes about the origins and ownership of all the piles of old dung. The manorial courts, which at one time would have governed life in the community, had become an anachronism and were doubtless derided. Once sources of pride and respect, the great hunting forest of Savernake, the borough status, the cheap local cloth and the fair at Bedwyn had all outgrown their usefulness.

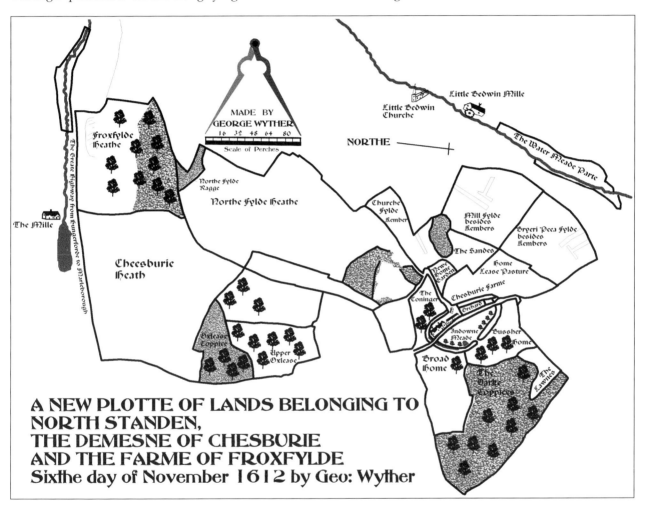

The western part of a redrawn map prepared by George Wyther in 1612, possibly the earliest detailed map showing any part of Bedwyn.

Above: *Easton Royal today. In the foreground, the uneven terrain probably indicates where the Priory (and later a Seymour house) had been sited, which was closed during the Reformation. When the Priory church decayed, the tomb of 'the worthie Sir John' was brought to Great Bedwyn.*

Right: *Painting of Sir John Seymour of Wolfhall.*

Below: *A nineteenth-century drawing by Edward Kite of the tomb of 'the worthie Sir John' in Great Bedwyn church, incorporating features described by John Aubrey in a sketch made 1672.*

Chapter 4

THE SEYMOUR LEGACY

It is now difficult to envisage the extraordinary influence once wielded by the most forceful residents that Bedwyn has ever known. The Seymours not only established a dynasty of unparalleled national supremacy, but also produced, within a single generation, some of the most powerful sons and daughters of all time. For amongst three children born in one household at the beginning of the sixteenth century, one married a king and gave birth to a king, one married a queen, and one became Protector of the Realm with all the power and authority of a king. It is a story focused on Bedwyn, embracing also the outlying settlements of Wolfhall, Tottenham, Easton Royal and the woodland of Bedwyn Brail. The story begins in the Church of St Mary the Virgin, in Great Bedwyn.

SIR JOHN SEYMOUR, 1476–1536

In the chancel of St Mary's Church, Great Bedwyn, is a fine sixteenth-century monument. It shows the recumbent figure of a knight in armour, sword at side, feet on a lion and head on a helmet. A series of eight shields around the tomb depict ancestral arms, including the Seymour wings and Esturmy half-lions. A plaque accompanying the monument reads:

Here lyeth intombed the worthie Sir John Seymour of Wolfhall, Knight... This knight departed this life at 60 years of age, 1536, and was first buried at Eston Priorie Church among divers of his ancestors, both Seymours and Sturmys. Howbeit, that church being ruined and thereby all their monuments either wholly spoiled or verry defaced during the minority of Edward Earl of Hertford... he as well for the dutiful love he beareth his grandfather as for the better continuance of his memory, did cause his body to be removed the last day of September 1590.

Sir John Seymour was a person of considerable standing. He was in favour with both Henry VII and

Above: *A seal of Henry Esturmy of Wolfhall, found attached to a document dated 1358. It shows the Esturmy half-lions and the famous Savernake hunting horn.*

Henry VIII. He fought for the Crown in 1497 against the Cornish rebels, and was knighted by Henry VII. He fought in France and Flanders for Henry VIII and was Sheriff of Dorset, Wiltshire and Somerset. In 1517 he was Constable of Bristol Castle and in 1520 and 1532 attended Henry on his visits to the King of France. His wife, Margery Wentworth, was a descendant of Edward III.

The plaque also tells us that Sir John had previously been buried at Easton Royal, near Burbage. Although the Seymours owned properties in Bedwyn itself, and would transfer their main residence there, their primary seat had traditionally been in Easton. They were patrons of Easton's Parish Church, and of a company of Trinitarian friars. The Parish Church fell into disrepair, and later local parishioners were entitled to worship at Easton Priory. However, at the Reformation, in which ironically the Seymours were principal champions, the Priory was closed down, and its church also decayed. Some 40 years later the tomb was removed from the ruins and brought to Great Bedwyn.

Sir John had an illustrious ancestry, stretching back to the Norman Conquest, under the names of both Seymour and Esturmy. The Esturmys became the hereditary wardens of Savernake Forest. The first reference to them comes from 1083, when it is recorded that Ricardus Estormid held land near Savernake. The Domesday Book records that he held Burbage, with other villages, and was a servant of the King. There are various references through the centuries, including a mention in about 1200 of Henry Esturmy marrying the daughter of Sir Adam of Eston, whose son Stephen became Archdeacon of Wiltshire, and founder of Easton Priory. This probably established the connection between the Esturmys and Easton. They gave 50 acres of woodland in Savernake to the brethren of Easton, who were to have a full common of pasture for their beasts of every kind. This area is still known as Priory Wood, and is situated near Leigh Hill. The Esturmys acquired Wolfhall between 1250 and 1277, although in 1330 Roger de Stokke held it when it was valued at £1.3s.4d. per year.

William Esturmy, warden of Savernake Forest from 1382 to 1427, had no male heir. His daughter Matilda had married Roger Seymour of Hache Beauchamp around 1400 and when William died in 1427, aged 80, he left to his grandson, John Seymour, the majority of the estate – the manor of Burbache, hamlet of Durle, pasture of Tymerygge, bailiwick of Savernake, plus 6s.8d. to Salisbury Cathedral, and 100 sheep and an oxen team plus books to Easton Priory. The Seymours therefore became wardens of Savernake. It was their descendant, the 'worthie' Sir John, now buried at Bedwyn, who was father of the three children who were to be so important in English history.

WOLFHALL

In 1491 Sir John became Lord of Wolfhall. Disappointingly, we know little about the appearance or even the location of the Tudor house, although it is likely that it was timbered or half timbered, was set in a rectangular pattern, and had a little court. It was in an advanced state of decay when demolished to provide material for

A nineteenth-century drawing of The Great Barn at Wolfhall, where King Henry VIII and his entourage were entertained.

Postcards such as this showing the remains of The Great Barn were popular in the early-twentieth-century. The photograph shows just the left-hand part of the larger barn depicted in the earlier drawing. A caption on the reverse of the postcard reads: 'In this barn Lady Jane Seymour was married to King Henry VIII.' This is pure fabrication; they were married in London.

The current Wolfhall, largely Victorian but with a mixture of different styles and periods, some of which may be Tudor. The earlier Wolfhall Manor House, home of the Esturmy and Seymour family, wardens of Savernake Forest, may have been sited slightly to the north.

The house peculiarly known as 'The Laundry' for many centuries, with fine Tudor chimneys, Tudor wing and mullioned windows, may have been associated with the earlier Wolfhall Manor House.

Tottenham House, by the Earl of Hertford, Sir John's grandson, the same man who brought his ancestor's tomb to Bedwyn.

The current Wolfhall is a mix of various styles from the sixteenth to the nineteenth century. It is almost certainly not on the site of the older Wolfhall, and with very little surviving that could have dated from the earlier period. The manor comprised 1,270 acres and included Suddene Park, Horse Park and Red Deer Park. Around 2½ acres at the manor-house were garden and orchard. There was the 'Great Paled Garden', 'My Young Lady's Garden' and 'My Old Lady's Garden'. We know that the original house had a chapel, because a salary of 2d. was paid to a priest. Hounds were kept there and the household had 44 male and seven female servants. The old manor-house may well have been situated across the road to the north, where an area of four acres shows levelling terraces. It would be a fascinating site for an archaeological excavation. Slightly downhill of this is a property that has been known as The Laundry for many centuries, on a site probably connected with the old manor. No satisfactory explanation has been provided as to why this house should be called

The Laundry when there is no evidence that it was anything other than a dwelling.

Through his association with the Seymours and his visits to Wolfhall, Henry VIII became acquainted with the children there including the young lady who became his third wife. Before describing the key players, however, an explanation should be given concerning a memorial in St Mary's Church.

JOHN SEYMOUR, DIED 1510

Near the lancet windows on the north side of the chancel is a brass showing the standing figure of John Seymour. This young man was the eldest son of Sir John, but died young. The inscription reads:

Here lyeth the body of John Seymour sone and here [heir] *of Sir John Seymour, Knight and of Margery oon of the daughters of Sir Henry Wentworth, Kt which decessed ye 10 day of July in the year of our Lord 1510 on whos soule thu have mercy and of your charitie and say a paternoster and a ave.*

It is likely that John, like his father, had initially been buried at Easton Priory. It is even possible that only the brass was transferred without the coffin. We know little about him since he died so young. His death, however, paved the way for his ruthlessly ambitious brothers to advance their own cause, taking special advantage of the King's increasing interest in their sister.

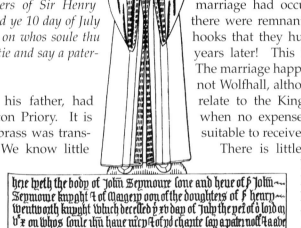

A brass memorial to John Seymour, eldest son of the worthie Sir John, in Great Bedwyn church, probably brought here from Easton Royal.

JANE SEYMOUR, QUEEN OF ENGLAND

Jane, who was probably born in about 1509, was the oldest of the Wolfhall generation. Like Anne Boleyn, she was trained in the French court as a maid-of-honour to Marie, Queen of Louis XII. She served as lady-in-waiting to Catherine of Aragon and later to Anne Boleyn when she became Queen in 1533. It is intriguing to consider the relationship between the Queen, destined for execution, and the servant who was later to occupy her throne. Anne Boleyn's fall happened very quickly. Henry had visited Wolfhall in September 1535, when Jane is likely to have been present. In January the Queen suffered a miscarriage. It was reported that Henry was making overtures to Mistress Seymour and giving her presents, although it was also said that she was of middle stature, no great beauty, and so fair as to be called pale. On 18 April 1536 Anne was being presented in Court and so was apparently still in favour. However, on 30 April a court musician admitted adultery with her,

possibly under torture. On 2 May she was arrested; on 15 May she and her brother were charged with incest, adultery and treason; on 17 May her marriage to Henry was dissolved, and two days later she was executed.

It is unclear whether Henry or other power seekers concocted the evidence, or whether it was true. What is remarkable is that within a day Henry and Jane were betrothed and 11 days later married. On the very day of Anne's execution, Cranmer issued special dispensation that allowed Henry and Jane to marry without banns. Parliament had already beseeched Henry to marry again before Anne was dead.

There is a long-standing Bedwyn tradition that Henry and Jane Seymour were married at Wolfhall, where, of course, there was a chapel. Postcards showing a dilapidated barn, drawn or photographed before it was finally demolished in the 1930s, often made claims that the marriage had occurred there, and even that there were remnants of the tapestries and the hooks that they hung by, surviving some 350 years later! This is almost certainly fantasy. The marriage happened at York Place, London, not Wolfhall, although the stories are likely to relate to the King's other visits to Wolfhall when no expense was spared in making it suitable to receive the royal entourage.

There is little doubt that Jane enjoyed being Queen, and that Henry enjoyed showing her off. He showered her with expensive gifts. He embarked on extensive developments at Hampton Court. He did, however, ensure that she should not interfere, and warned her, 'the last Queen died in consequence of meddling too much with state affairs.' Also, he was observed to pay court to other ladies at the time. He had intended her to be formally crowned in the autumn of 1536, but plague caused a postponement. Her father, Sir John, died in December 1536, after Jane had been Queen for seven months.

The Queen's pregnancy was announced on 27 May 1537, and on 11 October she gave birth to a boy, the future Edward VI. Bells rang in the city, there were bonfires, 2,000 shots were fired from the Tower, wine and beer were distributed to the poor. Typically for the time, the parents were not present at the christening, but received blessings within Jane's chamber. On 23 October, Jane fell ill and died the following day. It is thought that she had probably retained part of the placenta, leading to a catastrophic haemorrhage. On Monday 12 November her coffin, surmounted by an effigy richly apparelled and wearing a crown, with great silk banners, left Hampton Court for Windsor, where Jane was buried the next day. It is significant

In May 1537 he was sworn into the Privy Council, and three days after the christening of his nephew he was made Earl of Hertford.

During the remaining years of Henry's reign, Edward Seymour was away for much of the time. He was a military commander who served in Calais and the northern Marches, and he led the Army against Scotland. He was present at the taking of Bologna, and then again raided Scotland, burning villages and sacking monasteries. His military exploits, diplomatic skills and blood ties to the heir of the throne marked him for unrivalled prestige. Even before Henry's death, Seymour had immense Parliamentary interests in Wiltshire. In 1545, seven members were either of Seymour blood or bound by service to Seymour. By 1547 the number had increased to a dozen.

Edward Seymour had married Katherine Filliol, daughter of Sir William Filliol of Horton, Dorset. She had been repudiated by 1531. Her father's will of 1527 passed nothing to her, save for £40, which she received as long as she lived 'virtuously in a house of religion for women'. Seymour believed her to have been unfaithful and doubted the paternity of his eldest son.

Edward married, prior to 1535, Anne Stanhope, daughter of Sir Edward Stanhope and Elizabeth Bourchier, a descendant of Edward III. Anne Stanhope had a reputation of being arrogant, proud, graspingly selfish and petty, and it was possibly her driving ambition that was to lead to her husband's eventual downfall.

that, of Henry's six wives, it was with Jane that he himself would be laid to rest upon his own death. Jane of course, had retained the King's favour and died before he tired of her.

In 1880 a Mr J.E. Nightingale discovered a relic of the Seymour era at Wolfhall. In the upper part of the farmhouse, not in its original position, was some stained glass relating to Jane Seymour and Edward VI. It included the Imperial Crown, the badge of Queen Jane, a crowned bird rising from pinks and roses on a castle, the Prince of Wales' feathers and the Tudor rose. This is now mounted in a lancet window on the north side of St Mary's Church.

EDWARD SEYMOUR, LATER FIRST DUKE OF SOMERSET & PROTECTOR OF THE REALM

In many ways, Jane's brother Edward derived even greater advantage from her marriage than she did. Within days of the wedding he was made Viscount Beauchamp of Hache, and given numerous manors in Wiltshire, which added to those he had inherited.

THE RISE OF THE DUKE OF SOMERSET DURING THE REIGN OF EDWARD VI

When Henry VIII was dying, Seymour and secretary Paget reached an informal agreement on the transfer of power. The King's death was not to be announced. Young Prince Edward was to be brought to London, before anyone who might have wished to advance the cause of his sisters, Mary (the future Queen Mary) or Elizabeth (also later Queen). They agreed that a portion of Henry's will should not be divulged initially. Notwithstanding the will, Seymour was to have all the power and responsibilities of a Protector, during the King's minority, with Paget as his principal advisor. When Parliament met a few days later, Paget read some of the will, and secured the agreement that Seymour should be Protector.

Seymour was not the only person to benefit. Within two weeks of Henry's death various nobles came forward with claims that they had been promised land and titles. The Council acted rapidly to secure favourable positions, and a high proportion of all the royal wealth obtained by expropriation of the monastic lands was redistributed by sale or gift.

The Prince, son of Jane Seymour, was formally declared King Edward VI. At the ceremony in the Tower, Seymour offered his obedience to the child King in chair of state. In return Seymour was granted further privileges, including being honoured with the title Duke of Somerset.

Henry's will was actually impracticable. It required that, whilst Edward VI remained a minor, 16 executors were to be established as a Council, all with equal power. No allowance was made to remove or add names. Seymour's and Paget's position effectively violated the royal command, but made it workable. They suggested that there was a need for a man who should be preferred in name and place before other members; because of his blood connection with the boy King, and extensive experience in affairs of the realm, Seymour was to be Protector of all the realms and dominions.

Seymour also benefited in property and privileges. In May 1547 he obtained agreement for another 200 servants beyond those already employed in his considerable household, and in July his benefits were set at 8,000 marks per annum so long as he retained office. Seymour effectively had all the power needed to reign as if he were King. He could declare war, call musters and hire mercenaries, and negotiate treaties with other countries. A foreign diplomat, Van der Delft commented that Seymour had so much power vested in him that little mention was ever made of the true King.

The coronation of Edward VI, attended by his uncle the Duke of Somerset. From an engraving by Houbraken.

THE DUKE OF SOMERSET'S GRAND HOUSE

In the late 1540s, Edward Seymour started building some of the most opulent and pretentious houses England had ever seen. He had converted Syon House, Middlesex, a great monastic property granted him by the Crown, and had commenced building Somerset House in London. Seymour was also organising a huge mansion in the Brail, together with a park stretching from Bedwyn to Wilton. His properties at Wolfhall and Tottenham House were not on a scale befitting the richest noble in the land, and work commenced in 1548 to prepare for this magnificent property. A total of 280 men were engaged for the project. No designs survive, and our knowledge of the plans can be deduced only from contemporary accounts and by interpreting foundations and earthworks on the ground of the Brail itself. However, many questions remain. It is a fallacy that the current Longleat House was based on the design for the Brail. Longleat was built much later, following a fire of the former site expropriated from the monastery.

Several letters from Bryan Tesh, supervising work at the Brail, to Sir John Thynne who was charged with supervising the project, survive from this period. One, dated 25 November 1548, reads:

Concerning my Lord's house at the Broyle End... The meadow on the other side of the ponde towards Grafton is enlarged so high as the furlong goeth leaving space for a way which the Tenants of Wilton shall have from theire village to theire common where we apoynted the other pond to be made betwene both the fields in the bottom so that now my Lord shall stand at the place his house shall be and have the whole meadow in his eye, where before he should scarcely have seen it, but have looked over it.

We have taken in the felde, ryver and medowe ground from Bushell's mylne unto the very back of the mylne at Bedwyne, and so from thens to over the field towards Bushell's close... and so straight through the wood and coppice to the corner of the wood, beneath the great pit which was dygged within the wood at the upper corner of the Broyle beyond the springs, and so forth in the falling of the hill on the farther syde towards Ramphreis [sic] House.

... we have taken in a gretter compas at the corner where the chief spring is, I meane where the conduit house shall stand; and from thence straight over the felde to the close corner at Wilton's town's end viz. to the nether end of the lane which descendeth from the broke and from thence to the pond head next to Wilton where the pale standeth, and so on the other side up the close to the upper end of the medowe where we beganne, which is in compass 3 miles saving 110 lug.

Whereas I perceive that my Lord would have had the whole Broyle taken in, and so have compassed by the bottom next to Ramphries house [sic], that could not have been, for then the tenants of Wilton should have no maner of commen for their Rudder beasts [horned cattle] which would have been to their utter undoing. They kept before this tyme in their commen 180 Rudder beasts with the help of the Broyle; and if the whole wood and bottom should be taken from them then they would keep none. I pray God we may find owte [other] lands, medowe and something, to satisfy them for that which they shall now forgoe. The wild bore and the Red dere shall be sent next week.

The references give some indication as to the proposed boundaries of the park.

Dodsdown Bricks & the Construction of the Great Conduit

In March 1549, Tesh reported that the bricklayers had cast:

> ... as much earth as will make xx hundred thousand bryks [two million bricks] by estimation. I will trace and set forth my lords house according to the plan and so be ready to lay the foundation. The dich about the bounds is in a grete forwardness and will be finished these ten days saving that piece between Croughton [Crofton] and Fitzwarrens [Freewarren Farm].

Presumably at least some of the pits in Dodsdown are relics of this clay digging. Subsequent letters speak of testing various types of local stone, placing 40 men at the quarry at Wilton, 18 at Tudworth drawing chalk, and other men at quarries at Shalborne, Topnam Hill [Tottenham?], Westcombe and Martenshall Hill, as well as some further afield at Purbeck.

In May 1549 it was reported:

> ... the vault of the conduit being made well nigh a thousand feet long, would take much stuff [stone]. Touching the conduct howse, we have made ready the pavours and all things necessary for the conduct head... we shall have brycks and lead redy to begin the head and the vaute, and after that I doubte not to have running water in the base court, or at least within 3 foot where is best to make the morter heapes, because the water runneth there and the lyme below not far off.

By June 1549 the trench had been extended:

> ... the conduit is a thousand six hundred feet long and the most part thereof 15 foot depe, and tomorrow having all things prepared the rough layers shall be in to lay the vault which shall gather the water. The court next the gate be appoynted to be raysed on the lower syde and abayted on the upper syde the same wil be this night or tomorrow by noon at a point and ready finished, and the houses about my lords lodgings digged round to the depth of three foot, so that the inner court being raysed 4 foot ther remayneth 2 foot for the lights into the court to serve the 9 foot story. The gardin on the lower side of the house where the ground did fall 7 foot shall be raised to the height appoynted within these xiii dayes at most and made level in all places.

Collapse of the Plans

There is no known relevant correspondence surviving after June 1549, during which month seven letters are in existence showing considerable progress in preparations concerning the Duke's house. It is likely that works would have continued until at least October, when the Duke was arrested. Sir John Thynne, his steward, was also arrested at the time, and under cross examination by Council in November he stated that 'he disliked the great expenses of the Duke of Somersett's buildings, and often wished he would have left them' (this did not stop him building Longleat later). Unlike Seymour, Thynne was released and continued to enjoy the enormous riches he had obtained when serving his illustrious master. Many of Seymour's properties were seized by the Crown, and some redistributed amongst other members of the Council. William Herbert, Earl of Pembroke, who took part in Somerset's trial on 1 December 1551, did particularly well from the spoils. He acquired the woods at le Broyle, and 'channels, leaden pipes and brickes in a parcel of land called Doddysdowne adjacent.' These may have been taken to assist in the construction of Pembroke's new property at Ramsbury.

The Location of the House & Park

From all the written information it should be possible to trace the boundary of the park accurately. Indeed the overall ditch system must still be in existence and could be followed, especially if some of the place names given could be identified. In 1875 Canon Jackson, the great Wiltshire historian, produced his calculation of the park boundary, and this is shown below. The actual site of the proposed mansion deserves re-examination. The greatest ground feature associated with the letters is the conduit, scheduled to carry water to the house, 1,600 feet long and 15 feet

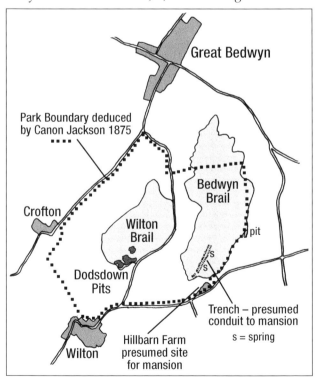

Map showing the location of the Duke of Somerset's mansion and park at Bedwyn Brail.

deep. A trench conforming to these dimensions is situated running south–west towards the southern tip of the Brail. This is shown on Ordnance Survey maps, with springs located within it; therefore this is almost certainly the true conduit. However, it has been conjectured that this trench could be associated with the Roman villa in the Brail. Certainly today it is difficult to deduce with certainty which way any water would flow, since it is all overgrown, and springs remain hidden.

So where was the house to be? Jackson believed that it may have been sited on the corner of the Brail where Hillbarn Farm is situated today. This suggestion presents some difficulties, since such a location would not have appeared to give an adequate view of the park, certainly not one befitting the likely scale of the construction, and would not accord with the description that Seymour would 'be able to stand at the place his house shall be and have the whole meadow [on the other side of the pond towards Grafton] in his eye.' The site of the house, gardens and courts, likely to be quite substantial, was terraced at the time the project was abandoned, so it should be possible to locate these terraces, even in the event that they are wooded today. Assuming that the trench through Bedwyn Brail is the original conduit, the house would have been sited close to it.

THE FALL OF THE FIRST DUKE OF SOMERSET

Towards the end of the Protectorship the countryside was unsettled as Church properties had been seized by the Crown, within a culture of traditional worship. As the date for introduction of the Book of Common Prayer drew near, there were huge uprisings in the West, and in East Anglia, where thousands of people were killed. At the same time wars with Scotland required troops to be available to the North. Inflation was rampant. Simultaneously there was a threat of invasion from France. The whole realm was beset by internal turmoil. Uprisings caused terror amongst the nobles, and Somerset stood alone as his policies of economy, war and social control were discredited. There was a claim that his power had run contrary to the will of Henry VIII. He had adopted an imperious style, using the royal 'we', addressing the French King as 'brother'; he was described as an 'Illustrious Prince'. He treated Edward VI with cold discipline, keeping him remote from others, and speaking as if he himself were the King. Somerset was also accused of enriching himself unduly during his tenure in power.

By 15 September Paget warned him of a conspiracy against him. Somerset drew up a proclamation calling on subjects to come to Hampton Court to defend the Prince and the Lord Protector. Some 4,000 peasants answered the call. Somerset realised his position was forlorn, so agreed to yield. He was taken into custody and held under strong guard, along with his eldest son and younger brother, and his steward Thynne. He was able to regain his seat for a while in Privy Council, until adequate evidence was concocted by his enemies. Somerset had alienated the nobility, shown excessive sympathy with the common peasants, and was arrogant and stubborn. That said, he was never a traitor, and retained the title of The Good Duke after his death. King Edward showed no emotion at the loss of his uncle, however, and the least emotional entry in his diary reads simply for 22 January 1552, 'The Duke of Somerset had his head cut off upon Tower Hill, between eight and nine o'clock in the morning.'

Far left: *A trench cut for carrying water to the house is all that remains of the mansion today.*

Left: *Edward Seymour Duke of Somerset, from an engraving by Houbraken.*

THOMAS SEYMOUR, BARON SUDELEY

The third member of the great Wolfhall generation was Thomas Seymour, younger brother of the Duke. Born in 1508, he too was granted considerable land after the marriage of his sister in 1536. Thomas was insanely jealous of his brother's eminence and, in an attempt to advance his own standing, secretly married the widowed Queen Catherine Parr immediately after Henry VIII's death – so soon, in fact, that if a child had been born it could have been that of either Thomas or the late King. Documents also show that he had dallied with the young Princess Elizabeth, to her embarrassment, at a time when she was immature. In due course it was revealed that he was building up military strength in the West, and he was condemned to death. His bizarre and barely concealed actions had been driven by an all-consuming and fanatical ambition which led to his inevitable demise.

THE DEATH OF EDWARD VI

The boy King suffered a lung infection in 1553, from which he did not recover; he died on 6 July, three months before his 16th birthday. His death sent England into turmoil; Lady Jane Grey (Protestant granddaughter of Henry VIII's sister) was pronounced Queen for a few days, before her arrest and trial for treason. Mary (daughter of Catherine of Aragon and Henry VIII) was declared the rightful heir to the throne, heralding a brutal return to Catholicism. The allegiances between the Seymours and the Crown were, by this time, distant and were to be tested further.

EDWARD SEYMOUR, EARL OF HERTFORD

Edward Seymour, Earl of Hertford, would have become the Second Duke, had not the Dukedom been extinguished upon the conviction of his father. Before his father's execution, Hertford had been considered as a husband for Lady Jane Grey. This would have combined royal blood on both male and female lines, and would have elevated any offspring from that marriage as a serious contender for the throne. However, his father's disgrace and execution meant that it was no longer appropriate for Hertford to be considered as a suitor for Lady Jane Grey.

Instead he adopted a risky strategy: shortly after Elizabeth I assumed the throne, he secretly courted Lady Jane's sister, Katherine Grey. They decided to marry without the Queen's consent. In December 1560, after the Queen left the palace, Katherine slipped away to a clandestine marriage arranged by Hertford's sister, Lady Jane Seymour. The priest engaged to conduct the ceremony did not appear, so Jane found another, although neither Hertford nor Katherine knew his name. This was to be important later.

The action of Katherine and Hertford put those involved at risk of execution. (Like her sister, Lady Jane Grey, Katherine was a potential contender for the Crown and as Hertford also bore royal blood any offspring could have seriously challenged the succession.) When Katherine was found to be with child she was duly arrested and ruthlessly cross-examined. Of those present at the marriage, Lady Jane Seymour, the only person who knew the priest's name, had died, and the only other witness, a servant, had fled, fearful of retribution. Hertford and Katherine were incarcerated in the Tower of London, where their son was born. He was christened Edward Seymour, Viscount Beauchamp in the Chapel of St Peter

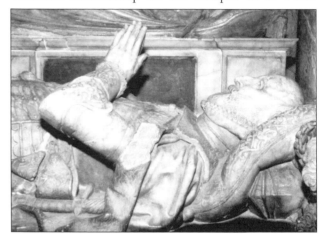

The effigy of Edward Seymour, Earl of Hertford, from his monument in Salisbury Cathedral, where he lies slightly below that of his wife Lady Katherine Grey, reputedly because of her elevated royal status.

The vast and opulent Hertford monument in Salisbury Cathedral, 30 foot high, eliminating St Lawrence's altar and eclipsing the stained-glass window.

Centre: The Earl of Hertford's coat of arms, depicting the combination of several illustrious lines, and incorporating the Esturmy half-lions.

ad-Vincula of the Tower, near the headless bodies of seven relatives, including his paternal grandfather (the Duke of Somerset), his maternal grandfather (the Duke of Suffolk, executed for pronouncing his daughter, Lady Jane Grey, as Queen), his uncle Thomas Seymour, and Lady Jane Grey herself.

The child, born at a time when there were no other obvious male contenders for the Crown, was a threat to the Queen. However, an Archbishop's commission pronounced that in the absence of witnesses, the marriage was illegal and the child illegitimate. The couple were retained in the Tower.

News reached Hertford that Wolfhall was decaying. He lamented the ruin of his beloved house, but overburdened by debts, and unable to meet his £15,000 fine, there was nothing he could do to prevent its almost total destruction. When the plague recurred in London, he and Katherine were sent under house arrest to different parts of the country. They never saw each other again. Katherine, who had remained a potential Catholic contender for the Crown, fell seriously ill and died in 1567. Her death removed her as a danger, and the Queen arranged a magnificent state funeral. Hertford was released. In due course he

arranged for Wolfhall to be pulled down, and anything salvageable to be used in constructing a new house at Tottenham. This had been a hunting lodge but was rebuilt as a grand mansion.

It was Hertford who removed his grandfather's monument from the ruined Priory at Easton to its current pride of place in St Mary's, Bedwyn. However, the church at Bedwyn was too small in size, and too modest a setting, for the scale of memorial to be erected for Hertford himself. When he died a monument of breathtaking opulence and pomposity was constructed in Salisbury Cathedral, some 30 feet high, the full height of the Lady Chapel; it blocked a stained-glass window and St Lawrence's altar, and depicted the great Tudor and Plantagenet ancestry. Here he was buried together with Katherine Grey, whose body was removed to Salisbury, some 60 years after her death. Her effigy is raised above his, in recognition of her royal status. It was only here, united in death, that these two, who had been such a threat in royal circles, had ever lain side by side for more than a few hours.

EDWARD SEYMOUR, VISCOUNT BEAUCHAMP

There is a small brass plaque in St Mary's Church that reads *'Bellocamp eram Graia gentrice Semenus Tres habui natos est quibus una Soror'*, which translates as 'I was

---

The Rotten Borough of Great Bedwyn

From 1295 until the Reform Act of 1832 the borough of Bedwyn was able to return two members of Parliament, and was represented in nearly all years between. Members of Parliament consisted of burgesses, whilst the right to vote was held by certain specified tenements. Elections were conducted by the portreeve at the market house. Whilst the right to return members was a privilege attached to borough status, the limited number of voters and the ability of the major local landowners to acquire land which brought with it the right to stand or the right to vote, made it susceptible to bribery and corruption. Bedwyn also had a small population, and the ability to return two MPs was disproportionate to the other urban centres of Britain. Hence Bedwyn became one of the renowned 'rotten boroughs'.

By the fifteenth century MPs included major landowners who had acquired burgage plots. As lords of the manor they could also wield considerable influence in ensuring the local populace supported them. Where persuasion was inadequate, monetary incentives were applied with some success. The Journal of the House of Lords in 1707 ordered Mr Pauncefoot to be taken into the custody of the serjeant-at-arms together with the arrest of his chief supporter John Bushell. Local residents with voting rights reported how they were called from their beds at two or three o'clock in the morning, and invited to go to Munday's at the King's Head, where votes were being purchased. Eight people sold their votes, and were each given two guineas and 17s. in silver, from a great sum of money on the table already divided into parcels.

In the eighteenth century Lord Bruce, later Earl of Ailesbury, managed to acquire sufficient landholdings so that he and his son Charles Brudenell-Bruce were able to take total control of elections. In fact no election was even contested after 1761.

Bedwyn returned a number of famous MPs through the years, including the antiquary and statesman John Selden, the lawyer and author Edward Hyde East, and many from the local landed gentry, especially the Seymour family. Some were clearly disreputable. Sir Giles Mompesson, MP for the borough from 1614–20, was stripped of his knighthood and sentenced for life, for having 'added impurities and sophistical drugs' to manufactured gold and silver thread 'to deceive the people'. It was reported that 'so poisonous were these deceitful components they rotted the heads and arms of work people and brought lameness and loss of eyes by the venom of the vapour.'

The Reform Act eradicated the scandal of misrepresentation and abuse which Bedwyn epitomised. In 1832 Bedwyn became one of 56 boroughs that were disenfranchised.

Beauchamp, my mother a Grey, father a Seymour, I had three sons who had one sister.' This modest memorial marks the resting place of a man once well placed to be King. At various times he was considered to be heir presumptive. In his inability to secure the Crown, and in virtually every other respect, including his inadequacy as a soldier, he was an enormous disappointment to his father, the Earl of Hertford.

Beauchamp was still in a prime position to succeed to the throne when Queen Elizabeth I lay dying. When asked who should succeed her, and Beauchamp's name was raised, she said 'I will have no rascal's son to succeed me.' Perhaps Beauchamp's supposed illegitimacy had militated against his cause. However, he also failed to advance his cause through marriage. Just like his father, Hertford, he struck up a clandestine affair without the approval of the authorities who were mindful of his potential claim to the throne. Also just like his father, he was arrested. However, it was his father who had sought to advance his son's status and it was he who was the most

furious. Beauchamp, a nobleman, had fallen in love with Honora Rogers, a simple gentlewoman. Papers preserved in Hertford's hand, many of them written from Tottenham House or from Wolfhall before it was finally razed, show his hatred of his potential daughter-in-law, and his attempts to prevent Beauchamp from 'stooping so low'. It was all to no avail. He was secretly married, and whilst Beauchamp personally is remembered for very little, his marriage was fruitful and produced several offspring who were to have some influence on the political stage.

WILLIAM SEYMOUR, LATER SECOND DUKE OF SOMERSET, & ARBELLA STUART

It is remarkable that William, a Royalist hero who distinguished himself fighting for the King in the West Country and achieved enough in his life to enable the Dukedom of Somerset to be restored to his family, has no monument of any kind in St Mary's Church, Great Bedwyn, where he was buried with

---

The English Civil War

It is difficult to assess the impact of the Civil War on Bedwyn. The town must have been torn between the different allegiances since it was so close to the strongly Parliamentary sentiments of Marlborough whilst under the influence of the overwhelmingly Royalist sympathies of the lord of the manor, William Seymour. We can be certain that townsfolk would have been aware of the food shortages caused by the wars, the removal of horses for military purposes, and the perpetual uncertainty as families and neighbours divided. They would also have been affected by a sequence of bad harvests, ongoing religious discord and uncertainty about Catholic and Protestant affiliations, as well as rural upheaval caused by the loss of common land to enclosure. The castle at Marlborough was another Seymour home, and its occupant, Sir Francis Seymour MP, was unable to swing local opinion to the King's cause. Only 12 of the county's 34 MPs were Royalist, but two of these, Walter Smyth and Richard Harding, were from Bedwyn and served at the King's Parliament in Oxford.

It was reported that in 1641 Royalist troops were quartered in Bedwyn and by 1642 the village was close to the junction of allegiances. Areas to the west, including Marlborough, Devizes, Chippenham and Swindon, were sympathetic to Parliament, whilst those to the east were more neutral or moderately Royalist.

William Seymour was a confidante of the King and had been governor to the Prince of Wales, later to become Charles II. He was appointed King's Lieutenant General of Forces in the West. In 1642 King Charles sent William Seymour to raise armies in Somerset and Wiltshire for the King's cause. Parliament had already decreed that all trained bands were under its own command, an order that these two counties had already accepted before the King had pronounced it illegal. William Seymour advanced on Bath, but finding it hostile withdrew to Wells. There he managed to raise only 900 men. In contrast some 15,000 Parliamentary sympathisers rose and met in the Mendips. Seymour withdrew to Sherborne Castle and by September had retreated to Wales. He subsequently fought the King's cause at Bristol and at the Battles of Lansdown and Roundway.

In 1642 Marlborough had been routed by Royalist forces who set fire to a good part of the town, pillaging with little enquiry about who was friend or foe. Having looted and destroyed homes, and removed 120 prisoners in chains to Oxford, they then evacuated the town. It can be imagined what brooding resentment remained. In 1643 Seymour again reoccupied Marlborough on behalf of the King and could have been singled out for retribution but at the end of the war Seymour attended the King and was a pall bearer following his execution.

There is a Bedwyn tradition that Tottenham House was attacked in retaliation for the pillage of Marlborough; this is almost certainly wrong. After being confined to Netley in Hampshire Seymour returned to Tottenham upon payment of an £8,000 fine. However, letters from William Seymour written from Tottenham after he became Second Duke of Somerset at the Restoration, indicate that by then only part of the house was habitable. It may have suffered from fire, or may simply have fallen into dereliction at a time when the family had little money available for repair. The claim of Civil-War damage may have originated from the building works undertaken there, for Aubrey reported that the great part of Wolfhall was pulled down in the decade before 1672 to build the house of Tottenham Park. Overall the war may have left Bedwyn with little alteration.

much pomp and ceremony. William was the eldest surviving son of Beauchamp. He vigorously maintained the family traditions of incurring the wrath of the authorities, being imprisoned in the Tower of London for pursuing a clandestine marriage to a woman of Royal descent. His wife was Arbella Stuart, potentially the strongest Catholic contender for the throne after the death of her aunt, Mary Queen of Scots. She had become a major threat to King James at a time when the Gunpowder Plot had spread panic in royal circles. They married secretly in 1610 and upon discovery William was incarcerated. However, he managed to escape and they tried to flee to the Continent in separate ships. Arbella was captured off Calais and brought back to the Tower, where in 1615 she died, the subject of popular ballads and laments. For a sum of £6 she was embalmed, and her remains unceremoniously interred in Westminster Abbey, in the vault of Mary Queen of Scots.

William stayed overseas until a few months after Arbella's death. He became heir to Tottenham House, Savernake, and the Seymour estates in 1621. When he returned to the Protestant fold he married Frances Devereux, the daughter of the executed Earl of Essex, and they had several sons and daughters, including a girl christened Arbella, who is buried at Bedwyn. William redeemed the family honour during the English Civil War. He fought on behalf of James' son, King Charles, and was active at engagements at Sherborne and Bristol. He was present at the execution of Charles I and carried the coffin at his funeral. He later became tutor and governor to the young Prince (later Charles II) in exile, and joined the King at York in 1642. The Dukedom of Somerset was restored to the Seymour family in 1660. William died within a few weeks of attaining the title, and the church register for Bedwyn records, somewhat peculiarly, that he was buried during the night, at the Feast of All Saints.

THE DECLINE OF THE SEYMOUR ESTATES AT SAVERNAKE & BEDWYN

Upon the death of the Second Duke, the fortunes of the Seymours underwent rapid change. The Dukedom devolved to his grandson, also called William. However, tragedy struck very quickly. As a young man William had broken away from any family control, and lived a life of liberty amongst questionable company. He soon contracted smallpox and died. A grand funeral procession, comprising a coach drawn by six horses, with ten horsemen attending the hearse, set out for St Mary's. The coffin was covered in black velvet with a silver plate bearing the titles. There was a black velvet cushion with a ducal coronet. The chancel was hung with baize, and escutcheons with the Duke's coat of arms. After the corpse had been lowered the herald spoke

all the Duke's titles and dignities. A contemporary account by Thomas Gape reads:

There was much rudeness by the common people of Bedwyn, I having above a yard of cloth of my long black coat cut and rent off in the crowd before going into church.

John Seymour, William's uncle, now became the Fourth Duke. He lived at Tottenham House, although the property was in considerable decay at this time. He was vain and haughty, appears to have been plagued by debt for much of his life, and was a gambler heavily dependent on his mother. His wife, Sarah, was critical of his wastefulness and profligacy, and within a year of his accession they separated. As part of the settlement Sarah received from him the manor of Froxfield, where she established the greatest lasting Seymour legacy, the Somerset Almshouses, still standing and fully occupied today.

Doubtless John wished for a major settlement from his mother's estate when she died in 1674, but he suffered great disappointment. She had outlived her husband William, Second Duke of Somerset, three of her sons and her grandson William the Third Duke. To carry out her will she turned not to her wasteful son John, but to Thomas Thynne, the husband of her granddaughter. Just four days before Frances died, when she was of questionable mind and reputedly unable to spell or sign her name without his guidance, she redirected an additional £20,000 to Thynne (the equivalent of millions of pounds by modern standards) with lands all over England and Ireland. Thynne became one of the richest men of his time, and when he inherited Longleat House in 1682 he brought many of the Seymour belongings there, including original family portraits which still adorn the halls and stairs. Thynne erected a memorial to his benefactor in St Mary's Church, Great Bedwyn.

John, Fourth Duke of Somerset, died the following year. He made arrangements that £1,000 should be spent on his funeral, 'according to my quality', and he was buried at the Hertford monument in

The Duchess of Somerset's monument in Westminster Abbey.

Above and below: *The Somerset Almhouses for 30 lay and 30 clergy widows, at Froxfield, also called The College and The Somerset Hospital.*

Right: *The bust of Frances Devereux, the second wife of William (Second Duke of Somerset). In the last hours of her life, when possibly not of sound mind, she changed her will, transferring a fortune to her granddaughter's husband, Thomas Thynne, who erected this memorial.*

Salisbury Cathedral. Yet more mischief was to follow, because John's will contained a gross error, something recognised by several people whilst he was alive, but which they concealed to their advantage. It listed only a fraction of his extensive properties. Hence when he died in 1675, contrary to his intentions, the bulk of his estates were transferred to his natural heir, his niece Elizabeth Seymour. John had, however, specified that certain named properties, including Great and Little Bedwyn, the manor of Wolfhall, Suddene Park, Savernake Forest, Easton, and Wootton, were left to his cousin Francis, Fifth Duke of Somerset. These properties were, in turn, to be left to the heirs of the Fifth Duke, unless he had no issue, in which case they were to revert to John's rightful heirs. Shortly afterwards, the Fifth Duke was murdered in Genoa when touring the Continent. The murderers were hanged in effigy, but never apprehended, and the Duke's body was brought back to England, where it was interred at Bedwyn on 15 October 1678.

Hence through the inadequacies of John's will, and a string of circumstances, the substantial properties of Great and Little Bedwyn, Savernake and other local estates were also transferred to John's niece, Elizabeth Seymour, alongside extensive lands in Wiltshire and Somerset already passed to her in error. Previously an ungainly girl suffering from rickets and with apparently few prospects, Elizabeth became a great heiress, whose hand was much sought after by the nobles of the land. Of various suitors suggested, she chose to marry Thomas, Lord Bruce, later Earl of

Ailesbury, whose descendants are still connected with Savernake. It is a remarkable fact that a single family has therefore been associated with Savernake for over 900 years. Initially it was in the hands of the Esturmy family who were hereditary wardens (but not owners) after the Norman Conquest, then through marriage it was transferred to the Seymours, and later again through marriage to the Bruces and Brudenell-Bruces, who retain much of the local estate.

BEDWYN ROYAL?

Bedwyn's dalliance with royalty is symptomatic of its overall history, one in which it has repeatedly approached pre-eminence, only to fall back to a sleepy backwater. Through the Seymours, Bedwyn became intimately known to royalty. The parishes were visited by Henry VIII and James I, and had been the home of Jane Seymour who in turn was the mother of Edward VI. Things could have turned out extremely differently. If Queen Jane and Edward had survived, the royal link with Bedwyn would have been sealed. If the first Duke's grand mansion in Bedwyn Brail had been finished, it would have been a palace of immense proportions, subjugating the landscape including all local villages. Lady Katherine Grey, or the pathetic Beauchamp, could easily have been crowned, instead of the indulgent King James. Subsequently the Second Duke's wife, Arbella Stuart could have been proclaimed Queen, heralding a return to Catholicism as the national religion. None of this was to be. There are three Dukes of Somerset buried in the church at Great Bedwyn , and nine other titled nobles of the Seymour family. None of the Dukes have monuments of even the simplest kind. The grand Seymour memorials are in Westminster Abbey and Salisbury Cathedral.

When St Mary's was restored in 1854, the Second Marquess of Ailesbury excavated a large part of the chancel and underpinned the walls for a family vault. In doing this some leaden coffins were found containing the bodies of the Seymours. There was William, Second Duke of Somerset; Frances his wife in a brick grave with her heart separately preserved in a lead container; Henry their son with the remains of a sprig of rosemary and other flowers laid on the coffin; and William, Third Duke, laid alongside in a coffin lined with rich crimson velvet. There was also a coffin of peculiar construction, conjectured to contain the body of Sir John Seymour of Wolfhall, with iron handles soldered onto the lead, presumably added when it was transferred from Easton Royal. For all their worldly ambitions, this is all that remains of the Seymours so long associated with Bedwyn.

However, the story does not quite end there, for no less than three of the children of William and Frances of Bedwyn are direct ancestors of twenty-first-century British royalty. One daughter, Lady Jane, gave rise to a line leading directly to Queen Elizabeth II, whilst two other children, Lord Henry and Lady Mary, are ancestors of Diana Princess of Wales. After the death of Queen Jane Seymour of Wolfhall and her son Edward VI, it was to be another 11 generations before Seymour blood again assumed supremacy. It lives on today in the monarch and heirs to the throne.

Tottenham House

Approximately two-and-a-half miles west of Great Bedwyn lies Tottenham House, surrounded by parkland enclosed in the early-sixteenth century from Savernake Forest. Most of this lies within Great Bedwyn parish.

The title of warden of Savernake Forest had passed through marriage from the original wardens, the Esturmy family, to the Seymours in the fifteenth century. In 1547 ownership of the forest was granted to Edward Seymour, Earl of Hertford, who was the uncle and regent of the young King Edward VI. This ownership was then assigned to his son, Sir Edward, in 1553 and subsequently through Seymour inheritance until 1678 when it passed to Elizabeth Seymour who married Thomas Bruce. Inheritance thereafter was through the Bruce and Brudenell-Bruce families.

The original Seymour residence in Wiltshire was Wolfhall, near Burbage, where Jane Seymour, third wife of Henry VIII, was born. Later in the sixteenth century the family moved to Tottenham Lodge in Tottenham Park and then in 1720 Charles Bruce, later to become the Third Earl of Ailesbury, commissioned his brother-in-law, Lord Burlington, to build a new mansion. Tottenham Lodge was demolished and Tottenham House built on its site. Constructed of brick with stone dressings, square in plan and moderate in size, the entrance front was set within a walled forecourt, with flanking service pavilions. In the 1730s the house was enlarged by Lord Burlington. Further alterations and rebuilding were started in the 1820s and designs by Thomas Cundy were used to convert the brick house to a stone-clad mansion. A giant Ionic portico was added to the front entrance, windows were altered and dates on rainwater heads indicate that external work to the centre and south-west parts were completed by 1825 and on the north-east by 1860.

The interior decoration was mostly nineteenth century, with French and Russian influences. The park was redesigned between the 1720s and 1740s, when a banqueting house and an octagonal temple were added, possibly to the design of Lord Burlington. From 1764 onwards Capability Brown began enlarging the park with woodland of Savernake Forest included in the overall design and with the park extending to the main fronts of the house. Trees were planted informally around the house and a column was erected in 1781 at the highest point on a ride forming the main vista from the house in the direction of Marlborough.

The house became Hawtrey's Boys' Preparatory School in 1946 until the school was moved in 1985. In 2003 the house is let to the Amber Foundation, a charity providing training and job skills to unemployed young people.

Marquess of Ailesbury's fête in Tottenham Park in honour of the Royal Wiltshire Yeomanry, 15 May 1888, taken from the Illustrated London News.

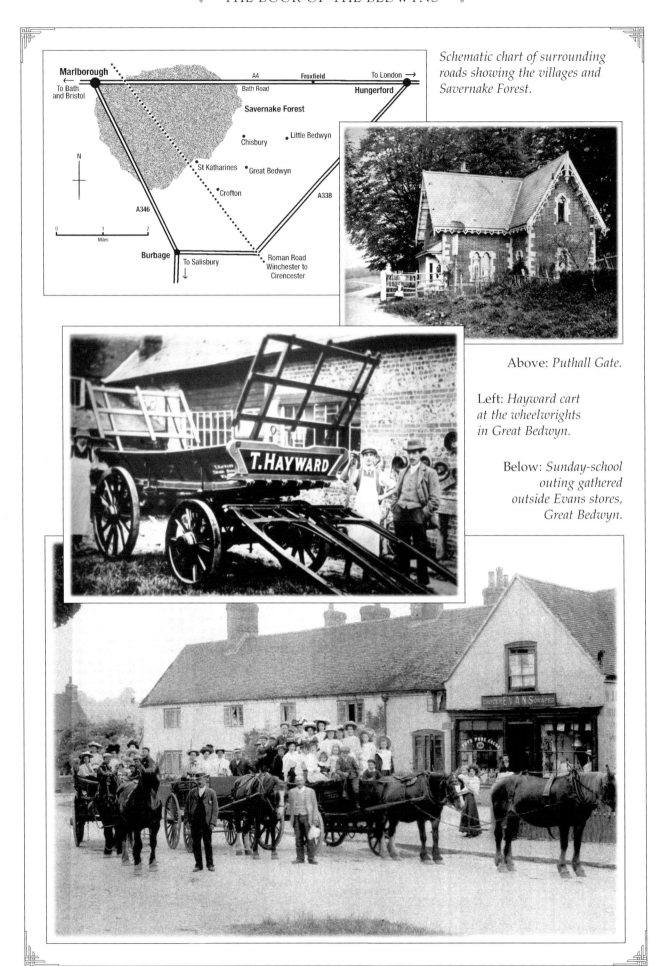

Schematic chart of surrounding roads showing the villages and Savernake Forest.

Above: *Puthall Gate.*

Left: *Hayward cart at the wheelwrights in Great Bedwyn.*

Below: *Sunday-school outing gathered outside Evans stores, Great Bedwyn.*

A Rural Retreat

Chapter 5

Travel & Communications

Many towns and large villages owe their initial establishment and subsequent development to natural communication routes, by track, road or river. Whilst Bedwyn derived its early importance from being on the best lowland route from the Thames Valley to the Pewsey Vale, the road system which developed during the Middle Ages did not follow this valley and now the Bedwyn parishes are contained within a triangle of three major and long-established roads, bounded by Marlborough, Hungerford and Burbage. To the north is the present A4 to Bath, Bristol and the West Country, one of the prime routes of the kingdom from the earliest times; to the west, the Salisbury–Marlborough road (A346); and to the south, the Hungerford–Salisbury road (A338). Not since the Roman road from Winchester–Cirencester lost its importance has a major road crossed the parishes.

A good local communication system would have been sufficient to support a local market economy but proximity to the developing trade routes would have gradually become more vital. Bedwyn was not on these developing roads and so its prosperity was always at risk.

In the seventeenth and eighteenth centuries there was a relative decline in Bedwyn's fortunes as the need for good communications became more important in a developing national economy and, at the same time, the importance of the forest declined. However, canal and railway development in the late-eighteenth and nineteenth centuries gave Bedwyn a new lease of life. Its earlier disadvantage, the lack of good road communications, has meant it has also benefited in other ways – its development in the twentieth century has, at least in part, been spared the environmental problems created elsewhere by the huge increase in road traffic.

ROADS

Prior to the late-seventeenth century, wheeled passenger traffic was rare and travel in the country-side was largely limited to horseback and on foot, with relatively few private carriages of the wealthy (Elizabeth I was the first monarch to have a coach). Farm carts and packhorses were used for larger loads. There were certain recognised King's high-ways and the Statute of Winchester as far back as

1285 affirmed the responsibility of the local manors for the upkeep of highways. The Highways Act of 1555 transferred this responsibility to the parishes and each able-bodied householder had an obligation to provide a certain number of days labour in road maintenance. By the late-seventeenth century, increased wheeled traffic led to a need for better quality maintenance of roads and turnpike trusts were developed. These, in return for maintaining specific roads, were authorised to levy a toll on users. Initially, a separate Act of Parliament was required to establish a trust and 2,000 turnpike trusts were created up to 1773 when a General Turnpike Act was passed speeding up the process. Bedwyn's relative isolation is shown by the fact that Great Bedwyn, Pewsey and Tisbury have the distinction of being the only communities in Wiltshire, approaching urban status, which were never on a turnpike road.

The turnpike provided a greater guarantee of reasonable quality roads and the economic vitality and liberalism of the eighteenth century ushered in the period of the public stagecoach. This was one of the most significant improvements in transportation, particularly for the growing middle classes in country towns. This was the first time that people who could not afford to own or hire their own carriage could easily travel much further afield. Although travel became more feasible it was relatively expensive. The regular charge on the stagecoaches in the eighteenth century was 5d. per mile for passengers inside the coach. Even for those braving the elements on the roof, the so-called 'rank outsiders', it was about half this amount. In addition, for those living in areas such as Bedwyn there was first a need to get to the main stagecoach routes at Marlborough or Hungerford, both six or seven miles away via poor-quality roads.

The A4, traversing the northern border of the Bedwyn parishes, was described in the forest bounds of 1228 and 1244 as one of the King's highways and it is shown on the fourteenth-century Gough map as one of the three main roads of the South of England. The present road is slightly south of a Roman road which linked London and Bath and which disintegrated and became impassable between the fifth and eighth centuries. A Saxon charter, dated AD778, which included much of the modern parish of Little

Bedwyn, stated that part of the charter boundary ran along 'the boundary way', as it does today, which suggests that the present line of the A4 was by then in use. The parish boundary, where it runs along the road in the east of the parish, is partly on the north side of the road and partly on the south side – undoubtedly to ensure that any parish maintenance obligations were shared between the neighbouring parishes of Little Bedwyn and Froxfield.

Another, less hilly route from Hungerford via Ramsbury to Marlborough and further west followed the valley of the River Kennet, and this was apparently preferred by many travellers as wheeled traffic increased in the seventeenth century. However, the present main road was turnpiked in 1725/6 and the resultant improved level of maintenance meant that, by the middle of that century, use of the old Ramsbury road was considered unusual. Evidence of the sites of the old turnpike gates where tolls had to be paid can be traced in the names of Voronzoff Gate, Puthall Gate and Forest Gate along this stretch of the A4.

The Bristol Road, as it was known from medieval times, came to be known as the Bath Road in the eighteenth century following the development of Bath as a desirable spa town and an important venue in the society season. By the early-nineteenth century this was the most heavily travelled route in Wiltshire. Hungerford and Marlborough were both staging posts for the coaches, where horses were changed and the passengers were able to get refreshments or lodgings for the night. Stagecoaches averaged about eight miles per hour and an 1830 timetable shows that the regular journey time between Marlborough and Hungerford was an hour.

Highwaymen were a constant threat to stagecoach passengers throughout the eighteenth century and they would probably have viewed the relatively deserted road through Savernake Forest as an excellent location for both ambush and getaway. The Cherhill Hill Gang, operating in the Devizes, Calne and Marlborough areas, gained notoriety because a gang member would strip off his clothes and leap out in front of a startled coachman and his passengers. The sudden appearance of a naked man springing from the bushes so alarmed travellers that robbing them was easy. We have no reports of their exploits being copied locally.

The major road on the west side of Bedwyn, the Salisbury–Marlborough road through Burbage, was shown on Ogilby's road atlas of 1675. This was turnpiked in 1761 and had a gate at Ram Alley, near the present Burbage Wharf. It is not certain what the normal road access between Bedwyn and Marlborough would have been before the nineteenth century but Savernake Forest would have presented a major obstruction to a direct route. The wardens would have endeavoured to limit unrestricted access to the forest and would probably have discouraged use of any route along the line of the present road,

north-west from Great Bedwyn up to the Bath Road. This road is shown on both the Andrews and Dury Wiltshire map of 1773 (see pages 6–7) and the Colonel Mudge map of 1817 as a considerably more winding route than it is today. It seems likely that the straight section, between the turning to Stokke Manor up to Sicily House at Thistleland, was constructed later in the nineteenth century, possibly when this road did become the main route to Marlborough. The principal alternative route would have been to travel to Burbage and then along the Salisbury–Marlborough road, particularly after this was turnpiked. It is unlikely that the road through Chisbury would have been practical, particularly for wheeled traffic, in view of the steep hills both up from Bedwyn and down to the A4. The Burbage route also had fairly severe gradient problems for wheeled traffic up Leigh Hill and down Postern Hill, near Marlborough, but was almost certainly better maintained. So even travel to Marlborough by Bedwyn residents was not a simple matter before the mid-nineteenth century.

It was an easier journey from Little Bedwyn to Hungerford rather than to Marlborough. The distance was shorter and it was a level route down the river valley, with roads on both sides of the river down to Froxfield, on the Bath Road. Thus, for much of the period up to the late-nineteenth century and in some respects still today, Little Bedwyn has been oriented more towards Hungerford for many of its needs and services. Until the county reorganisation in the late-nineteenth century, the western part of Hungerford, along Charnham Street, was in fact in Wiltshire.

Roads between the two villages of Great and Little Bedwyn also ran along both sides of the River Dun (Bedwyn Stream) at least until the railway was built, and these are shown clearly on the 1773 and 1817 maps. Later in the nineteenth century the road on the south-east side of the valley went only from Little Bedwyn to Parlow Bottom and then continued, as a 'green road', later a bridleway, to Great Bedwyn. There are, of course, numerous paths and bridleways throughout the parishes, many dating from Saxon and earlier times. These were used by people walking to church or to their work or, indeed, carrying coffins to the cemetery. These are now properly recorded and protected and local maps detailing the paths are available.

The road that presently passes in front of Tottenham House was not opened to the public until the nineteenth century. The western end of this road, running from near Burbage Wharf, only went as far as Durley and the link past Tottenham House, through to Thistleland, was probably opened when St Katharine's Church was built in 1861, followed by the school in 1865, both of which were designed to serve the widely dispersed population of the forest.

During the nineteenth century, as both the road system and the general economy improved, another

Little Bedwyn School outing to the seaside, 1932.

form of road transportation developed with local carriers, the precursors of modern buses, transporting people from the outlying areas to the market towns and, as the railways developed during the nineteenth century, providing links with rail services. Their routes were operated on regular schedules and used either converted farm carts or purpose-built covered wagons. In 1792 19 Wiltshire towns, including Bedwyn, held markets, but by 1888 this had declined to only nine (Bedwyn's had ceased to operate) so people had to travel greater distances to get to a market. During this period a number of carriers' businesses were developed in Great Bedwyn, some of which continued into the twentieth century.

A well-developed network of roads and tracks existed in Savernake Forest but these were generally not accessible to the public until the twentieth century and even now are still private roads. Forest roads were used for the development, management and maintenance of the forest and for leisure pursuits associated with the residents of Tottenham House and their guests. Many interesting names of these roads and tracks still exist and are evocative of the period and of their use: Grand Avenue, Eight Walks, Sawpit Drive, Postwives Walk, Marie Louise Ride, Charcoal Burners Road, Column Ride, The Gallops, Cheval Bottom and Twelve O'Clock Drive, to name but a few.

Probably the biggest change in personal transportation for the masses came with the introduction,

in the closing years of the nineteenth century, of the 'safety bicycle'. This was chain driven and had medium-sized, pneumatic-tired wheels of equal diameter, not too different from the bicycle of today. For the first time, it was possible for rural workers to travel considerable distances under their own power on a machine that was relatively cheap to own. The bicycle became one of the main means of transportation, particularly in country towns and villages, throughout the first half of the twentieth century. It was only with greater prosperity in postwar years and the relatively lower cost of motor cars that bicycles lost their position of pre-eminence. Great Bedwyn had a bicycle shop at Nash's House, the first house in Brown's Lane. Many Bedwyn residents now in their eighties and nineties have talked about the long bicycle journeys they used to make during the interwar years. Harold Painting, of Little Bedwyn, said that when he was courting he frequently used to cycle to and from Twyford, beyond Reading, on his day off.

So finally, in the 1920s, as roads were improved by the widespread use of tarmacadam, the motor car arrived. Great Bedwyn Garage opened soon after and continues in business today, although petrol sales ceased in the 1980s. In the mid-1920s omnibus services were introduced, transforming the lives of many rural people. Bus services were run to Marlborough, Hungerford, Pewsey, Devizes and further afield and charabanc tours became a regular part of village life.

CANAL

In the late-eighteenth century 'canal mania' hit England. Many canal schemes were proposed and there was usually a huge demand for investment in their shares. The Duke of Bridgewater's canal from Worsley Collieries to Manchester was opened in 1761 and presaged the development of numerous canals throughout the country. Approximately 90 major navigations had been completed or were under construction by 1820. For the first time it was possible to move large bulk loads efficiently, other than by sea; this was ideal at a time when the Industrial Revolution and the new 'steam age' were generating huge demand for the movement of raw materials to factories, particularly coal for the steam engines powering these plants, as well as transporting finished goods to customers.

Chart of Kennet & Avon Canal.

The River Kennet, which flowed through Hungerford, had been canalised between Newbury and Reading in 1723, and in the West, the River Avon had been canalised between Bristol and Bath in 1727. In 1788, some 60 years after these developments, a meeting was held in Marlborough at the Castle Inn, now part of Marlborough College, which proposed the construction of the Western Canal to connect the River Kennet at Newbury with the River Avon at Bath and so provide a through route by water between London and Bristol. This meeting was attended by many local dignitaries who became promoters of the canal and members of the initial management committee, including the Marquess of Lansdown, the Earl of Ailesbury, Lord Craven and Lord Porchester. The original proposal was for a canal to follow the line of the River Kennet to Marlborough, through a tunnel under Cherhill Down and then through Calne and Chippenham to Bath.

However, by 1793 this route and the alternatives had been thoroughly surveyed and it was recommended that the canal follow a more southerly course through Great Bedwyn, Pewsey, Devizes and Trowbridge, particularly as this avoided the need for a lengthy summit tunnel. It was proposed that there would be branches to Marlborough from Hungerford as well as to Chippenham and Calne but these were, in fact, never built. The deep cutting proposed for this route at the summit level was later changed to

the 500-yard Bruce Tunnel at the request of the Earl of Ailesbury. This new scheme was agreed by the committee in 1793 and at the same time the name was changed to the Kennet & Avon Canal. Bedwyn, therefore, got the canal almost by default.

The Kennet & Avon Canal Act was passed in 1794 and construction went ahead rapidly with John Rennie as the engineer in charge and with an expected total cost of £336,000. The course of the canal through the parishes followed the Bedwyn Stream from the Froxfield boundary in the east to its source at Crofton in the west, cutting right through the villages of Little Bedwyn and Great Bedwyn. The Act also authorised the construction of the Crofton pumping station and, as the Earl of Ailesbury did not want to see smoke from his nearby residence at Tottenham House, it was stipulated that the engines should consume their own smoke.

Construction began at both ends so that the canal could be used to transport the bricks required for the centre section. Many of these bricks were made at the brickworks at Dodsdown, between Great Bedwyn and Wilton, where brick making had taken place intermittently since the mid-sixteenth century. The building of the canal must have been a massive disruption for the local communities, with hundreds of Irish labourers ('navvies') brought in to do the laborious manual labour, almost entirely with picks, shovels and wheelbarrows and with very little in the way of any mechanical equipment. A good part of the canal through the Bedwyn area had to be built on an embankment so that it did not affect the adjacent water meadows – a major operation in itself. However, within five years a local report stated:

The navigation of the Kennet and Avon Canal was opened from Hungerford to Great Bedwyn, July 2nd 1799, when a barge of 50 tons, laden with coals and deals, arrived at the latter place. The barge, having on board a large number of the inhabitants of Hungerford, was accompanied on its passage by a vast concourse of people and received at Bedwyn with great demonstrations of joy. An entertainment was provided at the Town Hall and a quantity of beer distributed to the populace and the labourers employed on the Canal. The evening concluded with great festivity.

The canal was not finally completed until 1810 with the construction of the Caen Hill flight of locks at Devizes. The construction had taken place entirely during the period of the Napoleonic Wars and the resultant inflationary pressures had driven costs up significantly so that the budgets established 15 years earlier had been substantially exceeded.

One aspect of civil-engineering development, well evidenced on the canal near Great Bedwyn, was the construction of 'skew bridges'. Before the canal age bridges were generally built at right angles to the watercourse or other feature which they crossed. However, with already existing roads and a new man-made watercourse, the options were to alter the course of the road approaching the canal, to lengthen the bridge span and use more land to cross the canal at an angle or, the more elegant and Rennie's preferred solution, to skew the bridge so that it crossed the canal at an angle. To achieve this with arched brick bridges involved experimentation in different methods of laying the brick courses and some of this experimentation can be seen in bridges just to the west of Great Bedwyn.

One immediate effect of the construction of the canal was the loss of water to the water-mills along the course of the Bedwyn Stream and their eventual abandonment. There were six water-mills between Crofton and Froxfield and most of these ceased operations soon after the construction of the canal. The water-mill at Oakhill Down, just east of Little Bedwyn, was a survivor, at least for a period. It was owned by the Popham family of Littlecote, who clearly had influence in high places. A clause in the Kennet & Avon Canal Act required that specific measured supplies of water be made available to the Oakhill Down mill at all times and this required the construction of an unusual circular weir at the site. The loss of the water-mills also led to the construction of Wilton Windmill, just over the border in neighbouring Grafton parish, in 1821. This windmill, after a 50-year period of dereliction in the first half of the twentieth century, is now fully restored as a tourist attraction and is the only operating windmill in the Wessex region.

Above: *The derelict Wilton Windmill in the early-twentieth century.*

Wilton Windmill after restoration, 1976.

Trade on the canal brought increased business and prosperity to the towns it passed through, including Bedwyn. Half of the tonnage carried on the canal was stone and coal from the Somerset coal fields, most bound for Reading or London. It also brought much cheaper coal to Bedwyn. A Chart of the Trade for 1814 shows other cargoes crossing the wharf at Bedwyn, including gravel, chalk and whiting, timber, grain and flour.

The canal also provided improved passenger transport. Fly boats, fast passenger boats, operated from Bristol and Bath to Reading, London and intermediate towns on a regular basis. These were originally light boats which could be pulled by pairs of horses much more rapidly than barges but by the 1840s steam-propelled versions had been developed which travelled at about 8–9 miles per hour and operated through the night. These larger boats had first- and second-class passenger accommodation and some even had a string band for the entertainment of passengers. Consequently, Bedwyn residents could reach the bigger towns such as Reading and Newbury much more easily.

An additional transportation service was provided in the mid-nineteenth century by a 'market boat' running from Burbage Wharf to Devizes on market days, which must have been useful at times to Bedwyn residents. It would have been a long day, covering the 17 miles from Burbage to Devizes and then returning in the evening. A trip of this distance was only feasible because there were just four locks to be negotiated along this stretch of the canal. In the 14 miles between Wootton Rivers and Devizes the canal runs through the Pewsey Vale without any locks, the so-called Long Pound. It would not have been possible to run such a service from Great Bedwyn in view of the additional ten locks in the four miles between Great Bedwyn and Burbage.

The Kennet & Avon Canal was profitable in its early years as its tolls were less than one half of the equivalent road transport costs, but by the 1850s the new railways were providing significant competition and profitability decreased. Finally, in 1852, the canal was sold to the Great Western Railway Company and although there were certain obligations placed on GWR to maintain the canal as a waterway, which were reinforced by subsequent legislation, a steady decline in the canal's operations and its revenues proved inevitable. Navigation on the canal continued but had become severely restricted by the end of the Second World War, by which time a large backlog of maintenance requirements had built up. A proposal by GWR in 1926 to close the canal had been vehemently opposed by the local parish councils. Finally, after public petitions and appeals to save the canal, the Kennet & Avon Canal Trust was formed in the early 1960s and over the following 30 years it oversaw and raised much of the money required for restoration. In August 1990, the Queen, at a ceremony in Devizes, declared the canal reopened to navigation. Once again, the canal was contributing to Bedwyn's fortunes. With a railway station adjacent to the wharf, many narrow boats moved their moorings to Bedwyn and hire boats also began to operate from Bedwyn Wharf, bringing additional tourist income to the area. The Bruce Trust established by David and Louise Bruce, with a fleet of four narrow boats for hire to disabled groups, has its main base at the wharf.

The Kennet & Avon Canal is also justly famous as the venue of the longest canoe race in the world – from Devizes to Westminster. The race was started in 1948, with an offer of £20 to anyone who could go by boat from Pewsey to Westminster in under 100 hours; it was won by a Devizes Scout group. The Devizes to Westminster Canoe Race is held every Easter weekend and now attracts large numbers of entrants including many Armed Services teams and a substantial number of foreign crews. Bedwyn, near the middle of the canal section of the race, receives hundreds of visitors and support groups, with cars thronging the narrow roads and local viewing points over the weekend. Times have been steadily reduced from the first year's 89 hours and 50 minutes to the present 14 hours and 46 minutes for a single canoeist. This has been helped to some extent by the restoration work on the canal and the improved landing stages.

The annual Devizes to Westminster Canoe Race.

At a prize-giving ceremony in Devizes, in the 1980s, the guest of honour presenting the prizes commented that to compete successfully in this toughest of all canoe races: 'you need to have the strength of a cart-horse, the speed of a racehorse and the brains of a rocking-horse.'

One of the most remarkable features on the canal was and still is, Crofton pumping station, just one-and-a-half miles south-west of Great Bedwyn village and set in idyllic countryside. Crofton was built in 1809 to pump water from the springs feeding the River Dun (Bedwyn Stream) up to the summit level of the canal. The beam engines, restored in the 1960s, are the oldest operating steam-powered beam engines in the world, still performing the service for which they were designed.

Some 20 years after the completion of the canal the headwaters of the Bedwyn Stream were dammed to create Wilton Water, opposite the pumping station, and thereby provide a more assured supply of water.

Crofton's restored chimney, c.1997. It now stands at 82 feet.

Crofton, seen from the south side of the canal.

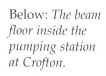

Below: *The beam floor inside the pumping station at Crofton.*

Bottom: *Stoking the boiler at the pumping station.*

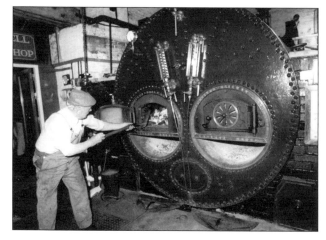

Each of the two Crofton pumps lifts approximately one ton of water 40 feet with each stroke, discharging into a feeder channel (the leat) which runs west along the contours of the valley to meet the summit level just under a mile away. The restored pumping station was opened by Sir John Betjeman in August 1970 and operates on spring and summer Bank Holiday weekends and on certain other occasions. In 1856 the original iron chimney was replaced by an 82-foot brick chimney, a landmark for miles around. This was declared unsafe in 1956, the year of its centenary, and the top 36 feet were removed. In 1996/97 the chimney was restored to its original height with funds from the Manifold Trust, the Heritage Lottery Fund and the Kennet & Avon Canal Trust's Buy-a-Brick Appeal. The pumping station now looks much as it did in its operating heyday and is a unique tourist attraction in the area. Naturally, the day-to-day operation of pumping water to the summit level has long been taken over by an unobtrusive but much less attractive modern electric pump.

To bring the canal story up to date, in the late-twentieth century a fibre-optic cable was laid under the canal towpath between Reading and Bristol, bringing additional revenue to British Waterways to fund the developing use of the canal. Once again, the canal is playing its part in improving communications links across southern England.

RAILWAYS

A railway line from Bristol to London was first mooted in 1832 and a committee was formed of various Bristol interests to examine its feasibility. Isambard Kingdom Brunel was employed to survey two possible routes, the first through the Pewsey Vale and the Kennet Valley and the second through Swindon. Brunel recommended the Swindon route and one can speculate about the different future Bedwyn might have had if this main line had taken the southern route. The GWR line opened in June 1841 and the effect was the immediate loss of virtually all the Kennet & Avon Canal's through traffic between Bristol and London. This led to its steady decline and eventual closure to traffic.

It took 20 years for the railway to finally come to Bedwyn. The Berks and Hants Railway from Reading to Newbury and Hungerford had been completed in 1847 and in 1862 this was continued to Devizes as the Berks and Hants Extension Railway. Like all GWR lines, it was broad gauge. All GWR lines were eventually converted to narrow gauge; over one weekend in 1892 the complete main line from London to Penzance, running through Bedwyn, was converted by 4,700 men working in gangs of 60 – a highly co-ordinated operation which must have delighted the small boys and railway enthusiasts of the time. The railway followed the line of the canal right through the parishes and, as with the canal 60

years earlier, its construction must have been highly disruptive to the villages. The line was operated by GWR who later purchased it in 1882. Bedwyn's fortunes were again improving. Just as the canal was in decline, the new and more flexible transportation system, which had caused the decline, came to Bedwyn. Travel to Hungerford, Newbury, Reading and London to the east and to Pewsey and Devizes to the west became remarkably easier.

Bedwyn Station and road bridge.

Two years after completion of the Berks and Hants Extension Railway, a branch to Marlborough was built. This left the main line at Savernake Junction, between the Crofton pumping station and Burbage Wharf. In 1882, the Midland and South West Junction Railway built a line from Cheltenham to Andover, which used the same track between Marlborough and Savernake. Eventually this proved impractical as, in the 1880s, it was reported that there was a train over this line every 25 minutes. Consequently, a seven-mile, north–south double track was built in 1898 between Savernake and Marlborough following a slightly shorter and more easterly course and costing £80,000. Savernake became one of the most compli-cated railway junctions in Wiltshire with high-level and low-level stations. As it was close to Tottenham House, the facilities also included the Marquess of Ailesbury's waiting room on the 'Down Platform', as stipulated in the Marlborough and Grafton Railway Act. A total of 15 staff were employed at Savernake Station and in its goods yard in 1923. This new link meant that for Bedwyn residents travel to Marlborough in the late-nineteenth and early-twentieth centuries became much simpler.

Use of the railways in the area peaked at this time, before the advent of the internal combustion engine and the move to car and bus travel. Figures given overleaf for traffic at Savernake and Bedwyn Stations (the latter of which in the 1920s had a stationmaster and three porters) show the decline in passenger traffic. This was due to the increased use of buses and cars and the growth in freight traffic as a result of heightened economic activity, and the fact that major freight movements by road had not yet developed as serious competition.

Traffic Through Savernake and Bedwyn Stations				
Savernake:	*1903*	*1913*	*1923*	*1933*
Tickets issued	18,031	19,544	16,622	8,016
Parcels handled	12,262	14,839	14,241	42,642
Bedwyn:				
Tickets issued			12,285	8,745
Parcels handled			25,485	57,715
Livestock trucks received			24	72

The north–south lines through Savernake were closed in 1964, depriving Marlborough of all rail services and Savernake Station then ceased to operate. Goods traffic also ceased at Bedwyn in 1964 but passenger services to the east have remained and their usage has increased substantially in modern times. Whilst the line continues as the main line to Exeter and express trains speed through Bedwyn, all services west from Bedwyn Station ceased in the early 1990s.

The Bedwyn area also had a closer and more personal involvement with GWR. Felix John Clewett Pole was born in Little Bedwyn on 1 February 1877, the second son of Edward Robert Pole and his wife, Emma Clewett. Edward Pole was the village schoolmaster. In October 1891, at the age of 14, Felix Pole joined the Great Western Railway at Swindon as a telegraph clerk and worked his way rapidly up the company, serving in telegraph offices, and in the office of the general manager in Paddington. There, his editing of the staff magazine attracted attention, in 1919 he became the GWR's assistant manager, and in 1921, at the age of 44, he was appointed General Manager.

In 1926 Felix helped to break the General Strike, as chairman of the Railway General Manager's conference. In 1929 he left GWR and became chairman of Associated Electrical Industries, a post he held until 1945. In this capacity he was connected with the production of radar which AEI developed and which was critical to the Battle of Britain in 1940. He was retained by GWR as a special consultant, advising on railway policy in such diverse places as the United States, Sudan and Palestine.

Poor eyesight precluded him from war service, and in later years virtual blindness obliged him to learn braille so that he could continue his many activities. He declined the honour of High Sheriff of Berkshire in 1947 because of his disability, although he was knighted in 1924. He lived in Calcot Place near Reading for the latter part of his life, although he rented Manor Cottage in Ramsbury to enjoy weekend fishing. He married Ethel Flack in 1899 and they had a son, John, and two daughters, Marjory and Ruth. Felix's younger brother, Edward Robert Pole, was an amateur historian who lived in Church Street, Great Bedwyn, and both Edward and his older brother, Randolph, also worked for the GWR, the latter in the divisional office in Bristol.

Sir Felix Pole is buried in the churchyard in Little Bedwyn. The fact that when the London Division of the GWR was established it was extended as far as Bedwyn may simply be a coincidence, but passengers from Bedwyn had good reason to thank Sir Felix for the excellent service to and from Bedwyn, particularly during his time with the GWR.

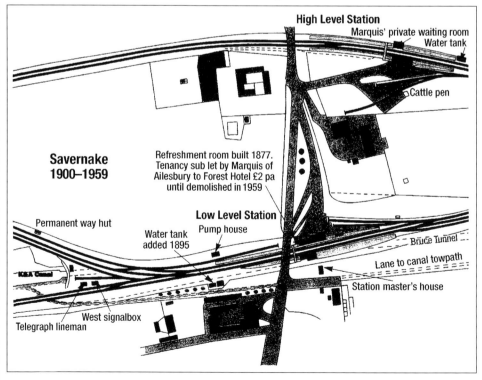

Plan of Savernake Junction.

Chapter 6
INDUSTRIES, CRAFTS & PROFESSIONS

OVERVIEW

One has only to visit the Record Office at Trowbridge to see how many traders and craftsmen Bedwyn and its surrounds had in the past and to realise how self-sufficient the settlement must have been. This has contributed in part to its continuance as a unit within the forest. Until recently, there would have been no need to leave the village to find the necessities of everyday living. To this local enterprise we must also owe the fact that Bedwyn, together with Lambourn, has the highest number of long-standing local families in the county.

Records pertaining to traders in the area are sparse prior to the eighteenth century. As we have seen in Chapters 2 and 3, the mint, which was in Farm Lane, was transferred to Marlborough as early as the eleventh century and Bedwyn owed its medieval prosperity largely to the manufacture of a coarse woollen cloth named 'burel'. We know that during the reign of Henry VIII there was a cordwainer in the village called Edmund Wynne. In 1664 there was a chapman in the village called Thomas Greene. He was a travelling seller of magazines known as 'chap books' and later the name was attached to any peddler. Iron forgers were also well established and cloth making was a cottage industry in the region in the seventeenth and eighteenth centuries, carried on by George Piper and others.

THE EIGHTEENTH CENTURY

In the early part of the century, a mercer by the name of John Bushell was selling silks and other fine cloths, and records show that there was also a more commonplace weaver working in the village in this period. Tailors were much in demand, with the Wilmotts and Newmans having a monopoly of that trade.

Carpentry was an important occupation in this period. In 1747 Thomas Robey, who followed that trade, had a house and garden in Mill Street and later moved to Portreeve Close, possibly because Joseph Gilbert, one of the village sawyers, was already there.

Horses were incredibly important in the eighteenth century and there were no less than six blacksmiths in and around Great Bedwyn. Thomas, Edward and John Walter have descendants in the area today.

An associated skill was that of the wheelwright and another ancestor of the local Pearse family, William Pearse, lived in Mill Street from 1714 to 1751. This craft was continued on the same site until relatively recent times when the Betteridges were the last wheelwrights to operate in the village.

The earliest record we have of a shopkeeper was of Thomas Greene the grocer in 1761; in the first half of the eighteenth century there were seven bakers in Bedwyn, the most notable of whom were Thomas Reeves, father of the local doctor, and Thomas Potter whose family was subsequently associated with Manor Farm. He kept a shop in Pipers Close near Brook Street and John Potter is known to have had a draper's shop in 1793. Descendants of the Potter family are still living in Collingbourne Ducis in 2003. Meanwhile, for most of the eighteenth century the Lewises of Farm Lane were the village butchers.

Lloyd's stonemason's yard, before the building to the rear was altered.

The Lloyds, still the village stonemasons at the time of writing, arrived from Wales in the late-eighteenth century to assist with the building of the canal and have carried on their business on the same site for more than 200 years. They are famed for their statue of Queen Victoria outside Buckingham Palace. Despite the large number of thatched buildings in the area, we only know of one eighteenth-century thatcher, John Fisher, who lived in Brook Street. Joseph Early secures the only mention of a glazier in 1744.

Among the less common trades and crafts recorded in the 1760s and 1770s were those of sieve maker Thomas Mason, barber and peruke maker Thomas Byrd and the collar maker, Daniel Edwards, who had a house in Church Street.

NINETEENTH & TWENTIETH CENTURIES

Many of the names associated with shops and businesses in the nineteenth century are remembered today, such as the Evans family of Bedwyn Stores. William Evans was the grocer and draper there in 1885, and the family maintained its connection with the Stores until the 1980s. In the 1920s the shop had two counters, one for provisions and one for everything else. Ted Haines, who married a member of the family, was a much-loved owner of the Stores until his retirement in the 1980s. Meanwhile, his sister and her husband, Cyril Burgess, ran the bakehouse until their

retirement, when it was sold to the Merritt family in the 1980s. John Powell was a greengrocer, and one of his descendants to this day carries on a greengrocery delivery business, which operates in and around Burbage. Thomas Shefford was the boot- and shoe-maker. Peter Shefford who, after many years of running a newsagent's business for the village from his house on the corner of Back Lane and High Street (formerly Portreeve Close), moved to Hungerford and sold his family home in 2000. It has now been extended to form two dwellings. At one time a dame school was run from this house.

At the end of the nineteenth century, the Knapp family was associated with a number of key activities in the village. Charles Knapp was the village blacksmith and his brother was the coal merchant. In the early part of the century one of the Knapps had been a village postman and The Knapp is named after another member of the family who was chairman of the Parish Council at the time it was built.

The Hart family originated in Preshute but came to Bedwyn via Froxfield. George Hart, born in 1853, came to work at the blacksmith's at No. 81 Jubilee Street (now Farm Lane) in 1890. He lived at No. 82 which was then known as Striker's Cottage, a striker being a blacksmith's helper or mate. He took over the business around 1900 when Charlie Knapp died and moved into No. 81; he made the railings at the Cross Keys as well as the rings around the chimney at Crofton, but most of his work was for the Ailesbury estate. When George died his son Frederick Albert took over and ran the business until it closed in 1946. Two of his children, Brian Hart and Anona Pounds, still live in the village.

James Martin the coal merchant was also a butcher, a somewhat improbable combination of jobs. The Wells family delivered coal from their yard at Copyhold. It is mere speculation whether Charles Tull the shopkeeper at Crofton in the nineteenth century was a descendant of the famous Jethro of Prosperous near Ham, famed for his invention of the seed drill. There are several Tulls in Hungerford today.

Of the other shops and businesses which existed within living memory in the village there was Bromley's shop in Brook Street next door to the Blue Cottage. After Mrs Bromley's death her daughter, Gladys, continued with the business selling sweets and tobacco. This shop was then taken over by the Gigg family and was a small general store. As people bought cars and went further afield to do

Evan's village shop.

Henry Killick outside Gigg's shop in Brook Street.

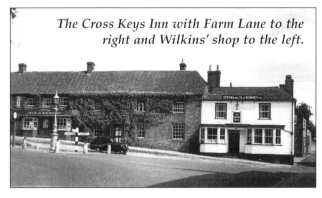

The Cross Keys Inn with Farm Lane to the right and Wilkins' shop to the left.

Today's Post Office was formerly the fire station. The original Post Office is next door.

their shopping the trade fell away. Mrs Gigg therefore closed the shop and instead opened her dining-room, where people could come and eat the fish and chips which she cooked at the back of the house.

Next door but one to the Cross Keys on the uphill side was Thomas' shop which, around 1920, sold provisions. It subsequently became Scott's shop and had one counter for provisions and the other for medicines. John Wilkins became the proprietor in about 1930 and was there for many years selling everything in the food line. As a retirement project Phil Sykes of Bedwyn House ran a general store there selling everything from 'Super Knicker' elastic to Wellington boots. After his retirement in the 1980s the shop became a private house, but the windows are still very obviously those of a shop. One of the cottages opposite Back Lane in the High Street, a hatters shop, also sold sold ice-cream.

Further along Church Street the butchers shop next door to Tudor Cottage was run (c.1920) by Cyril Bryant whose family came from Shalbourne. He kept his animals in the field behind the shop and killed them in the slaughterhouse, which was also on site. After Cyril, a firm called Riggs and Froome from Lambourn owned the business for a while. Charlie Head from Railway Terrace was their deliveryman and drove the horse and cart. The firm eventually moved back to Lambourn and Charlie went with them. For the next three or four years, Mr Kitkat was the proprietor until Jo Davis took the business over in 1930. After this it stayed within the family until the end of the 1980s. Jo was killed in an accident and it was run, latterly, by his son Les. Jo Davis was also the unofficial bookmaker for the village. Bets were placed in Mr Huntley's shop in Little Bedwyn and the money brought over to Jo. During this period, Wood's coal business was run from the yard behind Wessex House, further along the street.

The Post Office came into being after 1841 and was first run by the Lloyd family at their existing premises. They are said to have conducted much of their business on the pavement outside. By 1885 Thomas and Fanny Abery had taken over from the Lloyds and remained there until 1926 when Thomas died. While they were there, in 1886, the spelling of the Bedwyn name was changed from the earlier 'Bedwin'. During the First World War volunteer and conscript soldiers

came to the Post Office to obtain the King's shilling before enlisting. This business was taken over in 1926 by Muriel Abery, daughter of Thomas and Fanny, and an aunt by marriage of Bill Bance. She and her husband lived at Nos 11 and 12 Church Street (then all one house); the Post Office was moved across the street to their front room. She operated a telephone exchange from the premises and her first night call was to relay the message that there was a fire at the Savernake Forest Hotel. Bill and Betty Bance took over the Post Office in 1954 and Bill, who continues to live in the village, was there for nearly 32 years until his retirement. The business, then run by Don Childs, was located on the north-west side of Church Street. It has changed hands twice more since then.

Around the 1920s Mr Betteridge owned the yard at the back of the present Post Office. He traded as wheelwright, undertaker and rope maker and had a shop in the building now used by the Post Office. Another wheelwright, Mr Lovelock, was to be found on Canal Wharf for about a decade from the early 1940s until he retired. There was a shop at the house known as The Wharf from the 1920s until 1947 run by Mrs Cranstone as a sweet shop. The shop window is to the right of the front door. The Cranstones also ran their coal business from The Wharf, which they sold in 1947, moving the shop to the malt house in Farm Lane. It remained there until 1951 when the malt-house was sold to the Ryans and then to the Smiths of Axford, who were and still are coal merchants. In the 1970s it was bought by Tony Adcock. The shop window can be seen to the right of the front door on Farm Lane.

At the Crofton end of Church Street, at the far end of a row of four cottages on the left past the barn, was Mr Wootton, known as the village 'snob' (c.1920). From 1920 to 1930 Mr Saunders, who had previously been a shepherd on Salisbury Plain, lived at Cobblers Cottage in Farm Lane and was the cobbler. After his time the cottage became a private dwelling and his daughter, who later lived there, was Mrs Bennett the schoolmistress.

Chisbury Thatchers was founded by Bill Bacon in the early 1970s. A retired Army officer, he was a colourful character who kept the local thatches in good repair until his untimely death in 1996. Next to

The village school during the Edwardian era.

The Old Forge, Farm Lane.

Chisbury Thatchers at work.

Above: *Bill Bacon, of Chisbury Thatchers.*

Left: *Frank Skippence.*

the old school (which is Dr Ballard's surgery) was Neale's grocery shop. Mr Neale was related to the Neales at the Cross Keys. This became Butler's shop in the 1920s and was later taken over, firstly by Haines Edwards and then the Fitzgeralds. Monica and John Kennington lived there latterly; John ran an electrical-repair business until shortly before his death. Now a private house, it is easy to see that it was once a shop.

Powell's shop was in the Old White Hart and sold comics, fireworks, chocolate, sweets and cigarettes. A family named Birch later came from London to run the business and at the end of their occupancy it reverted to a private house. There was a bicycle shop in Brown's Lane in the early years of the twentieth century in what later became known as Nashes Farm. The Nash family had come to the village from Bristol and owned threshing machines which were used throughout the area.

The first garage in Bedwyn was started at Frogmore Farm in Frog Lane soon after the First World War by Arthur and Frank Skippence whose brother, George, had been killed on the Somme in 1916. Dissatisfied with working a smallholding, they decided to go into the motor trade and bought three landaus, which they hired out, and a 14-seater coach. Frank moved to Froxfield and started a garage there, which was eventually bought by Fawcetts of Newbury. Arthur continued at Frogmore Farm until 1925.

Today Bedwyn is well served by a Post Office, bakery, general stores and garage and has a small industrial estate at Brail Farm.

BRICKS & BRICK MAKING

The family of Merle Down made bricks at their farm until the 1930s, and the kiln where these bricks were made is still to be seen by the track leading to Burridge Heath, where an average of 900 bricks were made each day. Bricks were also made at Dodsdown and Folly Farm, and the Maltings in Farm Lane was constructed from bricks that originated from the latter. Dodsdown supplied the bricks for the almshouses in Little Bedwyn. Glazed-headed bricks were made by tipping in salt and old broken glass bottles during the process of firing; this could only be done when the firing process was performed in the traditional manner using coal or wood.

Dodsdown

Brick making at Dodsdown began in the sixteenth century. Associated with this local industry were William Dorrel from 1760, Thomas Brown in 1716 and John Piper in 1803 (all of whom were brick-layers), while John Collins was a brick burner in the early-eighteenth century.

By 1837 the Ailesbury estate had leased the property to John Bailey for an annual rent of £15 for

The Dodsdown brickworks.

which he had the use of a house and garden in the village of Wilton. In 1895 the Ailesbury estate bought 15,400 bricks from a Mark Jeans of Dodsdown. The following year a Mr Bolan is mentioned (in *The Bedwyn Chronicles, Vol. 28*) when, in December, the Ailesbury estate paid Colthurst Symons & Co. £400 in connection with buildings erected by the lessee. In 1897 Piper and Rawlings were mentioned regarding the estate seeking Counsel's advice concerning the Dodsdown brickyard. Mention was also made of four cottages and gardens. By 1901, the annual rent was £10 for the cottages and £10 for the brickyard. At this time the company came to be known as Rawlings & Co.; they paid £50 for a dead rent and wayleave (the connecting railway line from the Dodsdown brickworks to a siding at the Burbage and Grafton Stations) and compensation of £5.

The company was known by 1909 as Dodsdown Brick Company and when working to normal capacity the brickworks provided employment for between 70 and 200 men. This was dependent in part on the time of year – the bricks were made in summer and fired in winter. The yard consisted of three kilns, each with six fire holes. For many years the brick-works produced between 1.5 and 2 million dark-blue and yellow bricks annually. The bricks were transported originally by horse and cart, and later on by Sentinel steam-driven lorries.

At around 1900, the Army required large quantities of bricks for the training ground on Salisbury Plain. Tidworth Barracks was built from bricks supplied by the Wilton brickyard. In order to improve the transportation of bricks, a two-mile standard-gauge railway line was installed in 1902, and connection was made linking Dodsdown to Grafton Station. During this period the trains ran two journeys in each direction on a daily basis; the bricks were conveyed in four open wagons, and collected by MSWJR (Midlands & South West Junction Railway) goods trains every day from Grafton Station. The gradients on the line were quite severe and the railway ran by gravity from the brickyard downhill behind the chalk pit, over the lower part of Wilton Water via a small triple-arch brick-built bridge, over the level crossing at Heath Lane and uphill to Grafton Station, where it joined the Great Western Railway. We know from the Ailesbury records that in 1903 Arthur James Keeble of Peterborough was paying rent and wayleave of £50 per annum to the Ailesbury estate for the railway land.

One recorded incident with 'Progress' (an 0-4-0 outside-cylinder saddle tank, made by Peckett & Sons of Bristol) relates how the driver, having released his handbrake a little early, rushed down the 1:6 gradient with no hope of stopping at the level crossing. Luckily the local boys were there, waiting to see the train, and the gates were opened in time. The train ran on for a further half mile before it could be stopped.

The barracks at Tidworth were completed by 1910 and the line was closed and dismantled shortly afterwards. A sale was arranged by Allan Herbert, auctioneers of Andover, in May 1912, when most of the plant and machinery was sold. The engine 'Progress' was sent to Sanderson Bros & Newbold Ltd of Sheffield and in 1912 the estate received £250 for 'Compensation for Dilapidations' while paying £1.16s.8d. (approximately £1.74 in modern money) to various newspapers to advertise the brickworks as a let.

The works were eventually offered for sale in the Savernake Estate Auction, where they were withdrawn at £1,400. The brickworks finally closed in the early 1930s as a result of competition from the London Brick Company, which was selling cheaper, mass-produced, wire-cut bricks.

DODSDOWN BRICKYARD
about 2 miles from Bedwyn and Grafton Stations
Mr. Allan HERBERT will SELL by AUCTION without reserve,
on TUESDAY JUNE 11th, 1912,
the remaining portion of the
BRICKMAKING PLANT AND MACHINERY.

Including 4 Brickmaking Machines (one fitted with expression rollers), 3 lengths of Shafting, 3 Brick Presses, 2 pairs of Crushing Rollers, a Vertical Engine by Marshall, about two miles of Railway (from Dodsdown to Grafton), 200 sheets of corrugated Iron, several navvy, crowding and bearing off Barrows, about 2,000 ft. Run of Steel Wheeling Plates, quantity of useful Timber and Firewood, several second-hand Doors and Windows, about 25 cwt of Bar Iron, various sizes, quantity of second-hand Bricks and Tiles. THE CONTENTS OF THE BLACKSMITH'S SHOP, including Forge with Bellows, hand power Drilling Machine, Tools &c., Also a Brown cob Gelding. Spring Cart and several other useful and miscellaneous items.

Sale to commence at 11.30 o'clock.

Catalogue may be obtained of the Foreman at the Yard and of Mr. Allan Herbert, Auctioneers, Andover, Hants.

A sale notice for Dodsdown brickworks, as featured in the Marlborough Times, *31 May 1912.*

AGRICULTURE

In 1086 the King's estate called Bedwyn included much of what has become today's Great and Little Bedwyns and had land sufficient for 79 plough teams. Its open fields in the Middle Ages were Tile Field and Barr Field north-west of Brown's Lane, in addition to Harding or Harden Field and Conygre Field, which lay to the south-east of the River Dun. All were close to Great Bedwyn. The land to the west of Forest Hill was also arable. There were meadows beside the River Dun, and Spaines, a 20-acre pasture, lay to the north-east of the village. By 1550, the arable land to the south-west of the Marlborough Road and some of the pasture had been enclosed. Spaines, too, had been enclosed and divided.

Each village around the forest had its own designated area on which to graze sheep. This was called common land and lay open to the rest of the forest. Great Bedwyn's area was 200 acres on and around what is today known as Bedwyn Common, and included Broad Moor, to the south-west of Stokke Farm. Bedwyn residents were allowed to graze their cattle at large in the forest. Farmers of the sixteenth century included John Porter, Henry Hurcombe, James and Edward Pike, Thomas Tanner, Joseph Durril and Thomas Chidwick. Most of Great Bedwyn's land was part of the Prebendal Manor or West Bedwyn Manor, which had been built beside the church in what has been called Church Street since 1759. In the early-sixteenth century the demesne of the Prebendal Manor, later called Manor Farm, covered 100 acres, but over the next century

LOT 233
(Coloured *Yellow* on Plans Nos. 5 and 8)

THE WELL-KNOWN

Brick and Tile Works

"DODSDOWN,"

Situated within and adjoining Wilton Brail, close to Wilton Village, and about two miles from Great Bedwyn, together with Buildings and four excellent Cottages, the whole extending to an area of about 29 acres 1 rood 13 perches.

The Buildings and the Brickyard comprise :—Office built of brick with asbestos roof, brick and tiled Garage, three brick Kilns possessing 22,000 and 21,000 capacity respectively, 13 rows of Brick Hacks to shelter 8,000 bricks each, three timber and galvanised iron Storing Sheds. Brick Machine House constructed of timber and galvanised iron, fitted with Jones and Co.'s brick-making machine (capacity of 15,000 turn-out) in a nine-hour day.

The cuttings and pits contain some of the finest dark blue clay below a surface depth on an average of about 12ft. of yellow clay. The beds are extensive and capable of considerable extension for turning out large quantities.

Close by, within Enclosure Ord. No. 438a, are two well built brick and tile Cottages, Nos. 197 and 198, each containing :—Sitting Room, Kitchen, Pantry and three Bedrooms. Outside are Woodhouse and E.C., with Bakehouse for use of both Cottages. Good Gardens. Water tap in garden piped from the lake within the brickyard property. Also sunk Rain water tank.

The two similar Cottages, Nos. 195 and 196, possessing equal accommodation internally and externally. Water obtained from tap within garden of No. 197 on opposite side of road.

SCHEDULE.

Ord. No.	Description			Acreage.		
				a.	r.	p.
	Parish of Great Bedwyn.					
396	Pasture	..	..	3	2	19
399	Part Wilton Brail	..	..	3	0	30
Pt. 400	Part Wilton Brail	..	..	8	0	38
Pt. 436	Cottages Nos. 195 and 196	..	..	0	1	8
437a	Track ..	..	..	0	2	4
Pt. 438	Cottages Nos. 197 and 198	..	..	0	0	27
Pt. 438	Old Brickyard and Pasture	..	..	6	3	26
439	Part Brail	..	..	0	0	8
440	Part Old Yard and Pasture	..	..	5	3	20
442	Chalk Pit ..	..	..	0	1	33
	Total	..	A.	29	1	13

Let on lease to Mr. C. E. Maloney for 16 years from 29th September, 1925, determinable by Lessee at end of first 7 or 14 years, at a rental of £100 per annum plus Royalty Rents. Tenant pays rates.

Dodsdown brickworks sale notice, 1929.

decreased by half. From 1552 the lord of the manor of Stokke owned West Bedwyn Manor and farmed the land until by 1751 it was the largest farm in the area and was mainly arable.

Around 1770 a quarter of the farm's land was worked by Stokke and included all of Great Bedwyn's former open fields. It appears that 67 acres were in the form of closes (enclosed fields), three of which were called Bewley. John Wentworth, whose descendants farm at Aldbourne, was the farmer in 1804. Feeding rights over Bedwyn Common were extinguished in the late-eighteenth or early-nineteenth century after the lord of the Prebendal Manor had bought Stokke Manor from West Bedwyn Manor. There were at least 52 yeomen in and around Bedwyn in the eighteenth century.

Great Bedwyn's agricultural land to the north-west of its former open fields became part of Stokke's land in the early-nineteenth century and Stokke's former open-field land to the north-west of the River Dun was added to the only two farms within the village. These were Manor Farm and Jockey Green Farm. In the early-twentieth century Manor Farm and Harding Farm were worked as one. William Sheppard, a yeoman farmer from Alton in Hampshire, took the tenancy in the early years of the nineteenth century. He and his wife Catherine had three daughters, the oldest of whom married Samuel Pocock from Warminster in 1865. They succeeded to the tenancy of the farm after the death of her mother in 1867. The house was rebuilt at around this time and is the dwelling we see in 2003. Nevins Thomas Potter, whose family had been in the village since the early-eighteenth century, held Prebend Manor and Farm in 1885.

Manor Farm.

Three generations of the Kerr family were farmers at Harding and Manor Farms until moving to Marlborough Hill Farm in the 1990s when the Crown sold the Manor farmhouse and its outbuildings. The house became a private residence and the new houses beside the church were built on what had once been the pig farm.

Bewley Farm was built in the middle of the nineteenth century and, during the 1900s, worked

A traction engine at Little Bedwyn, c.1900.

nearly all of Great Bedwyn's remaining agricultural land and most of Stokke's land to the north-west of the River Dun. Since 1996 Bewley Farm has been worked in conjunction with Manor Farm, Chisbury. For more than a century the Stone family has farmed there. Years ago the villagers played cricket at Bewley as there was no pitch available in the village. Before 1773 Jockey Green Farm was known as Brail Farm and stood to the south-west of Jockey Green. In 1300 this was a detached part of Savernake Forest but by 1625 the wood had been cleared, a farmstead had been built and the land had become Brail Farm. In 2003 a pair of nineteenth-century cottages, one of which has been extended, stand on its site. The nearby farm buildings were used in the dairy part of the farm. The whole operation was later run from Merle Down Farm on the Little Bedwyn side of Jockey Green. It was sold by the Ailesbury estate in 1929 as 'a valuable and conveniently placed mixed farm together with brickyards and productive clay pits extending to more than 157 acres.' Part of the land was passed to Harding Farm and is still worked by that farm. The brickworks were at Merle Down, and for many years formed an important part of Bedwyn's economy. Messrs Charles Hawkins and son were the tenants in 1929 and paid the annual fee of £139 in rent. Charles ran the farm, while his son Len was the blacksmith. Len's brother was in charge of brick making. He was the first person in the village to own a steam wagon, a Sentinel, which he used for transporting bricks. His own son Mark (Len's nephew) continued brick making until 1932 and made 900 bricks a day.

William and Robert Hawkins had arrived at Merle Down in 1741 and started to make bricks. Robert the younger later came into the business and the family continued there in the same occupation for almost 200 years. Simon Payne was also a brick maker in the middle of the eighteenth century but we do not know at which of the several local brickworks he was employed. The old kiln (now listed) was kept alight all night to fire the bricks; there was always someone working to keep the fires going. It can still be seen covered in ivy past the fork along the Merle Down track. The village children roasted chestnuts and potatoes there. Today a tennis court has replaced the brick driers and clay pit.

A house has stood on 'Merrell Down' since the sixteenth century but the house which exists today was built in about 1770. In the sixteenth century Merrell Down was a common pasture lying along the southern boundary of the parish of Little Bedwyn. Around 1674 much of the down was enclosed but the centre part remained as common pasture. The open fields on Merrell Down were finally enclosed in 1792 and some of the land became part of Jockey Green Farm. By 1841 the farm had been added to Manor Farm and most of its buildings demolished.

Folly Farm

Folly Farm is adjacent to Merle Down Farm. In 1885 it was run by Charles Smallbones. Clay pits were also found here. It was sold in 1929 by the Ailesbury estate and at that time consisted of a thatched farmhouse, a variety of outbuildings and 97 acres. Harry Cope was the tenant. The Copes were yeoman farmers as far back as 1688 and had been around Bedwyn for more than 300 years. Ray Leonard worked at the farm in his school holidays and earned 2s.6d. a week for keeping the cows out of the clay- and sandpits. He remembers sitting on the granary steps across from the house to eat his tea. This small farm kept six cows and three horses and employed a carter and a cowman, plus Mr Cope. Rebuilt in the late 1980s, the house is in private hands.

Folly Farm.

Harding Farm

Hardene is an Old Saxon name first recorded in AD788 as Haren Dene or Hardenu, which means 'boundary valley'. It is likely that Harding Farm was built on the downland of a village that once existed within the present boundary of Shalbourne parish. Robert Harding, who is mentioned in the Domesday survey, lived in Savernake Forest, which at that time covered the area of the farm and had, in all probability, come over to England from Normandy at the

Harding Farm.

time of the Conquest with Richard Sturmid as a retainer. After the Battle of Hastings he was given land on which to farm sheep at Hardene, and adopted the name of the place as his family name.

Nearly 200 years later, in 1223, Richard de Hardene was recorded as Richard of Harding Farm, a forester of Savernake serving under the Esturmy family who served as wardens of the forest for the sovereign. The male line died out in 1330 with the death of Sir William de Hardene, who had been an important local knight, but he left two daughters, the younger of whom married Thomas de Alresford of Hampshire. They took over the farm and Thomas too became a forester covering an area named 'Broyle'. He died in 1360 leaving a son and heir called Robert, then aged 30. From then until the 1440s, the exact descent of Harding Farm cannot be proven but it is almost certain that the de Hardenes mentioned at the time were of the same family.

After the Battle of Bosworth in 1485 the farm, which was within the borough of Bedwyn and held by Sir Humphrey Stafford, Earl of Buckingham, was confiscated by the Crown for Buckingham's acts of treason committed in 1483. At around the same time, John Seymour's widow, Elizabeth, moved to Huish Manor near Pewsey, an ancient estate which had been acquired from the Byrd family who were later to be found at Stokke Manor. Descendants still live in the village. She appointed one of the Hardings to live and farm at Huish. Although the Hardings did not return to live in Bedwyn, Richard Harding, who was born into the Pewsey branch of the family in 1593, was MP for Bedwyn in 1640 in the Long Parliament of the Civil War and later became Groom of the Bedchamber to Charles II. His half-brother, Sir Giles, was MP for Bedwyn in 1614 and again in 1620–21.

Until 1767 the farm descended in the Seymour family when Hugh Percy, Duke of Northumberland, sold it to John White. During John's time a tragic accident occurred when labourer William Payne was killed by a ploughshare after the horses bolted in Den Field in 1775. John White died in 1797 and the farm was inherited by his son Thomas who in 1801 sold it to Thomas Bruce, Earl of Ailesbury. In 1929, when the Ailesbury estate sold it, the farm covered 396 acres and included land in Wilton and the former Bedwyn Brails. The house then became a private residence. In the 1980s the land was absorbed into the Stype estate in Shalbourne parish when it was bought by Mrs Vivien Duffield, daughter of Sir Charles Clore, who owned the Stype estate. The present farmhouse, which suffered serious fire damage in modern times, incorporates an early-seventeenth-century house which was timber framed. A large chimney-stack survives. The outer walls were encased in brick in the late-seventeenth century. In the eighteenth century a west wing was built providing a new entrance. Minor additions were made in the nineteenth century. A large eighteenth-century barn stands adjacent to the house.

Brail, Crofton & Stokke Farms

The other Brail Farm was at the south end of Great Bedwyn. A farmstead and seven houses and cottages stood as a group on the road from Bedwyn to Wilton in 1751. By 1773 the collection of houses was known as Brail. The farmer in 1803 was James Pike. The farmstead at the north end of the houses was called Brail Farm in 1879, when it included large farm buildings. Over the next 20 years most of these were demolished but the early-eighteenth century farmhouse survives. New farm buildings were erected in the twentieth century.

At the end of the nineteenth century and in the early years of the twentieth century Brail was farmed by Charles Smallbones, who had moved there from Folly Farm. His brother ran the Three Tuns public house. A third brother, Emerson, had a draper's shop at the front of what is now Wessex House, with an off-licence behind. During Charles' time at Brail three thatched cottages burnt down. Mr Smart was the owner and farmer who, in 1947, sold the farm to Peter and Joan Haine. Joan was a much-loved teacher at the village school. Peter died suddenly in the 1980s and the farm was sold to the Hosier family of Buttermere and Shalbourne who own it in 2003.

In the Middle Ages several small farmsteads made up the settlement of Crofton. In the seventeenth and early-eighteenth centuries, Crofton land was still worked as farms of less than 100 acres. Crofton Farm was the largest with 95 acres and was almost entirely arable. By the late-nineteenth century this farm, which stood beside the Roman road, was the only one left. The back of the farmhouse was built in the seventeenth century and was thatched. The front was built in Victorian times. The house has two staircases and is similar to two houses placed back to back. Two pairs of estate cottages were built beside the Bedwyn road in 1879 and are contemporary with the addition to the farmhouse. All survive in 2003. In 1885 Charles

Edwards farmed there, and his descendants continued there until 1954 when the Vines family, who are still present in 2003, took control of the farm. The Ailesbury estate sold the farm to the Crown in 1950.

The site of the village of Stokke is uncertain; it is thought that it probably stood beside the River Dun to the south of Bedwyn and was deserted by the Middle Ages. It had an open-field system to the south-west of Bedwyn and its common pasture lay on the higher ground at the north-west end of the parish. The open fields would have been worked by farmsteads nearby. Stokke Farm was built in the seventeenth century and was altered and enlarged in the eighteenth and nineteenth centuries, becoming Stokke Manor. Today, nothing is visible of the earlier building.

Chisbury Farms

In the fourteenth century, Chisbury hill-fort contained the chapel, which still exists today, a sizeable manor-house and farm buildings described even then as 'old'. The house was demolished in the late-eighteenth century and its building materials used to build Manor Farm in 1793.

Apart from the old farm within the fort there were five other farmsteads at Chisbury, one of which was Thorn Place, which stood in Chisbury Lane in 1552. Most of the land belonging to Thorn Place Farm was later taken over by Lower Farm Chisbury. There is no building on the site of Thorn Place today. Chisbury Lane Farm, previously known as Monk's Farm, was built in the 1800s although it carries a date stone for 1629. There has been a farmhouse on the same site since before 1719 at the west end of Chisbury Lane. The farm buildings are relatively modern. The Homer family has been there since the 1980s and before that the farm was worked by Don and Rhoda Hillier. It is a dairy farm in 2003. The Cope family worked the farm for many years, certainly from 1885 when James Cope was there. William Evans and David Needham were also farming in Chisbury at that time. In the early-twentieth century the Gazzards farmed there and with the Evans family they ran the Methodist chapel at Chisbury.

Near the parish boundary west of Chisbury Lane Farm a farmstead called Holt had been deserted by 1552. Lower Farm is a dairy farm and includes lands which were once part of Harrow Farm. Throughout the nineteenth century Chisbury Manor Farm was the largest of Chisbury's farms. From 1910, when the tenant was Sam Farmer, until the 1950s, it was worked in conjunction with Manor Farm, Little Bedwyn. At the time of writing it is mainly arable and is worked with Bewley Farm by the Whitehead family who have been there for many years.

Little Bedwyn Manor

Little Bedwyn Manor passed from the Crown to Abingdon Abbey in AD968, which owned it until AD975, after which ownership passed between the Crown and various private individuals. Two local families have reason to be proud of their ancestors, for between 1211 and 1326 the manor was owned by several generations of the Russell family and in 1458 by Emmote Mills whose descendants, both direct and indirect, owned part of the manor until 1615. William Russell, lord of the manor in the late-thirteenth century, also bought Knowle in 1291. In 1700 Thomas Streat became the owner of Manor Farm. His father, also Thomas, already owned Burridge Heath. Thomas the younger died in 1736 and both holdings passed to his son the Revd Richard Streat. When he died in 1767 his property was left to his sisters Susanna Streat and Elizabeth Kent and from them continued through three further generations of the same family until it was sold in 1809. During the nine-teenth century, Little Bedwyn estate, varying between

WILTSHIRE.

Particulars

OF THE

LITTLE BEDWIN ESTATE,

A VALUABLE

FREEHOLD PROPERTY,

SITUATE

IN THE PARISH OF LITTLE BEDWIN,

A FINE SPORTING PART OF THE

COUNTY OF WILTS.

Surrounded by the Estates of the Marquis of Ailesbury,

And about Three miles from the Hungerford Station on the Hungerford & Reading Branch of the Great-western Railway.

COMPRISING

An excellent and exceedingly comfortable Residence,

WITH STABLING AND OFFICES,

Large Pleasure & Kitchen Gardens, Orchard, Farm Cottage, Yards, & Farm Buildings,

WATER CORN MILL, BRICKFIELD,

NUMEROUS COTTAGES AND GARDENS,

TOGETHER WITH SEVERAL ENCLOSURES OF EXCELLENT

Arable, Pasture, Meadow, Water Meadow, and Wood Land,

CONTAINING IN THE WHOLE

827 Acres, 2 Roods, 34 Perches,

OR THEREABOUTS,

Which will be Sold by Auction by

MESSRS

NORTON, HOGGART, AND TRIST,

At the Mart, opposite the Bank of England,

On Friday, the 23rd of October, 1857, at 12 o'clock, in One Lot.

May be viewed, and Particulars had at the Great-Western Railway Hotel, Reading; the White Hart, Newbury; the Bear, Hungerford; of Mr. JOHN DINGWALL, Solicitor, No. 8, Tokenhouse Yard, Lothbury; at the Mart; and of Messrs. NORTON, HOGGART, & TRIST, No. 62, Old Broad Street, Exchange, London, E.C.

700 and 900 acres, was owned by Sir Robert Curtis and, later, Robert Bevan. In 1902 it was sold to Samuel Farmer who had been the tenant of Manor Farm and resident at Little Bedwyn Manor since 1875. From 1885 Sam Farmer, in partnership with his half-brother, William Gauntlett, and with Frank Stratton, acquired farms throughout Pewsey Vale (see box opposite). Following Sam's death in 1926, the estate was acquired by his nephew, Edwin Gauntlett. In 1970 it was purchased by Maria Delfina Wansbrough and in 1985 by Richard Tucker, who sold the majority of the land in 1999 to Philip Magor of the neighbouring Stype estate.

In 1719 there was a small farm at Fore Bridge but this has long gone and all the present farm buildings postdate that farm. It was one of four that existed in Little Bedwyn in the eighteenth century. Soon after Burridge Heath had been enclosed, divided and allotted, a farm named Burwood Heath was built there in 1570. In 1745 it had 72 acres. In the early years of the eighteenth century the middle of the heath was worked by other farms and the north-east part was worked by Manor Farm, Little Bedwyn. In 1929 when it was a mixed farm, it regained its heath land from Manor Farm. In 2003 the farmhouse, which has been much altered and extended, is a private home.

Inevitably some farms have had more written about them than others but this leaves the way open for those who wish to fill the gaps at a later date. Knowle, Puthall, Timbridge, Littleworth, Warren, Henset, Oakhill and Great and Little Horsehall Hill Farms have not been mentioned as they are on the fringes of the area covered by this book.

Stokke Manor

Little is known about the manor at Stokke except that it stood on the high ground and to the north and west of Great Bedwyn. At the time of writing the house probably occupies the site of the old manor, but of the latter nothing survives.

The earliest mention of the manor occurs in 1130 and fourteenth-century records show that the property was held by Thomas de St Vigeus who subsequently conveyed it to 'Adam of Stock'. From the latter half of the fourteenth century until 1630, it descended through the Hungerford family. Seventeenth-century records show it to have been moated, which suggests that the Hungerfords did indeed live there. The farm probably replaced the manor-house some time before the seventeenth century and the open fields belonging to the farm were enclosed by private agreement in 1769, at which time it was owned by Thomas Brudenell, Lord Bruce. From then until 1929 the manor descended with Tottenham House when the Marquess of Ailesbury sold land south-east of the Dun as Brail Farm. The remainder of the manor was sold to the Crown in 1950.

Sam Farmer & the Gauntlett Family

Sam Farmer was probably the most successful agriculturist in Wiltshire in the late-nineteenth and early-twentieth centuries. His forte was the commercial side of farming and he was astute and fortunate in ensuring that he had very capable partners to handle the farming side of the business.

Born at Market Lavington in 1847, Sam Farmer initially studied medicine at Aberdeen but was prevented by illness from taking his exams. His father died when he was 21 leaving him a butchering business in Market Lavington and a farming business of about 1,500 acres at Market Lavington, Easterton and Eastcott. These businesses were operated successfully for five years, but in 1874 he sold the butchering business and gave up all the land except the Eastcott Farm. At the time of his marriage that year, he took the tenancy of Little Bedwyn estate, then about 780 acres, and moved to Little Bedwyn Manor, where he lived for the next 52 years, purchasing the estate in 1902.

Completion of the railway through the Pewsey Vale enabled him to send milk to the huge market in London. During the 1880s and 1890s and extending into the early-twentieth century, he acquired tenancies of farms with easy access to the railway and negotiated supply contracts with United Dairies. This was done principally in two partnerships; one with his older half-brother William Gauntlett, and the other with Frank Stratton. At their peak, these partnerships controlled some 25,000 acres, devoted principally to dairy and sheep farming. All of this was at a time when the arable industry was in a severe depression due to cheap North American imports and many farms were going bankrupt and could be acquired at very low rentals.

While Sam Farmer had no children, William Gauntlett had seven sons and six daughters and many of these joined the family businesses and ran the farms acquired. Edwin Gauntlett, William's youngest son, worked closely with Sam Farmer from an early age and Kelston House in Little Bedwyn was built for him in 1910, when he married. The properties held by the partnerships were reduced significantly soon after the First World War when Sam Farmer correctly foresaw the advent of another agricultural depression. He died in 1926, at the age of 78, just three months before his half-brother and partner, William Gauntlett, who was then 91. Edwin Gauntlett purchased the Little Bedwyn estate which, with Chisbury Manor Farm leased from the Crown, he ran with his sons, William and David, for the next 40 years.

Sam Farmer was quick to seize the new opportunities created in agriculture by technological advances, and was one of the early converts to the new steam ploughing engines in the late-nineteenth century. These were used on the partnership's farms and on a contract basis. After establishing a number of trusts in his lifetime, he left a fortune of £400,000 on his death, a huge amount at that time. His name continues to be remembered through the trusts he set up which, amongst many other grants, have given considerable sums to the Kennet & Avon Canal, the Merchant's House in Marlborough, Savernake Hospital, Dauntseys School and Lacock Agricultural College.

MILLS

In days gone by the miller was a vital component of village life. Without him the staple diet could not be produced. In 1086 the King's estate at Bedwyn, which included several parts of what later became Great and Little Bedwyn parishes, had eight mills within its boundaries. These had dwindled to five before the coming of the Kennet & Avon Canal, which was built between 1794 and 1810.

Horsell Mill

Horsell Mill was the most easterly. A water-mill stood on Little Bedwyn Manor in the early-fourteenth century, 400 metres south-west of St Michael's Church, Little Bedwyn, and was still there in the seventeenth century. The mill was part of a holding sold by Laurence Hyde to Thomas Streat in 1665. In 1682 it was run by John Thistlethwayte. It was last mentioned in 1727 and had been demolished by 1773. Today all that remains is a grassy site near the canal, used by picnickers and fishermen. There was also a mill in Little Bedwyn village opposite the church, mentioned in the 1830s sale particulars of the estate.

Burnt Mill

Looking across to Burnt Mill Lock from The Knapp or Spaines it is hard to imagine the hive of industry which must have existed in the peaceful fields and lock area we see today. In 1086 Chisbury had two mills; one stood on the River Dun near Great Bedwyn village and was part of Chisbury Manor in the sixteenth and seventeenth centuries. In 1590 it was called Cop Mill, or Little Bedwyn Mill, and consisted of a mill and a mill house under the one roof. In the early 1700s the Revd Thomas Streat owned the mill that was then named after him and which stood close to the present lock. It was an undershot mill, which meant that the water flowed beneath the mill wheel. Crossing the small iron bridge by the canal one can look below and see the channel that once housed the wheel. For many years the mill-pond has been called the 'dog hole' and has been used as a swimming-pool by generations of Bedwyn children.

Adjacent to the mill were Little Mill Close and Great Mill Close, also owned by the Revd Streat. These are the fields which extend from the lock to the station and are between the canal and Spaines. The land on which Spaines, The Knapp and Railway

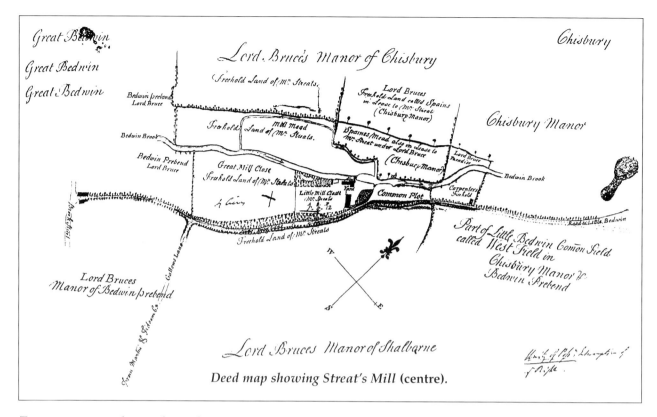

Deed map showing Streat's Mill **(centre).**

Terrace now stand was also in his possession and he leased Spaines Mead, the land to the rear of Spaines, from Lord Bruce. Thus Street had ownership of a large and contiguous area of Great Bedwyn. Spaines was described in 1792 as:

... a close of arable land and border of wood belonging, called Upper Spaines, and three pieces of water meadow adjoining all being in Little Bedwyn and all which premises had been awarded by commissioners under an Act of Parliament to the Reverend Henry Williams and the Churchwardens, Thomas Pike and William Tanner, in trust for repairing the parish church of Great Bedwyn.

With the construction of the Kennet & Avon Canal in the 1790s, the supply of water to the mill was reduced. The mill was still standing in 1802, but had been burnt down by 1812. Burnt Mill Lock is now the only reminder of the mill.

Bedwyn Mill

To the south of the village at Lower End (the Crofton end of Church Street) the name Mill Close reminds us that Bedwyn Mill (formerly known as Ford Mill) stood nearby on the road to Wilton; there was a ford here, crossing the Bedwyn Stream. The mill certainly existed in 1230. In 1751 the mill and about 20 dwellings were described as standing along the road. In 1715, this mill 'by the Broyle near a field called Stokerford' was leased by Richard Tanner, a yeoman of Great Bedwyn, from the Dean and Chapter of Sarum. In 1737 Francis Widmore became the leaseholder and passed the lease to his two nephews in 1740. Later that year John

Adams paid them £460 for absolute purchase of the lease; he died six years later. The property at the time John Adams bought it consisted of:

... a corn mill and house called Great Bedwyn Mill and the little water meadow at the east side of the watercourse belonging to the mill with the waters and water courses and fishing belonging to it and the stable and fodder house and garden usually let with the mill.

In 1758 John's widow relinquished the mill to William Reeves, the village surgeon, and Daniel Pearce, a yeoman of Chisbury. William Reeves bought the lease from the Dean and Chapter in 1763. A year before, Thomas Gale of Wexcombe had conveyed the freehold of a house and tenement adjoining the mill to William Reeves. By 1773 the Dun had been bridged on the site of the ford. On 13 September 1779 the mill, having reverted to the Dean and Chapter, was passed to the Earl of Ailesbury by John Ekins DD, Dean of Salisbury and the Chapter.

The mill was leased before 1791 to John and Thomas Potter. In that year they received £30 for their asset from Giles Sheppard who was the last miller there in 1803. The present mill house was built by the Lloyd family at the beginning of the nineteenth century after the old mill had been demolished.

Crofton

A mill stood at Crofton in 1086 and was part of Crofton Braboef Manor. In the late-fifteenth century the lord of the manor shared with the then tenant the cost of adding a malt mill to it. A century later the manor included two mills, probably under one roof. A new mill was built at Crofton in the 1590s. In 1773 Crofton still had two mills, Lower and Upper, which stood 400 metres apart and were separated by a bridge across the Dun. The former stood where the canal is now located, at the bottom of Beech Drove, and the sluice gates were visible until the 1960s. Upper Mill was near the crossing at Crofton. William Sloper was miller at the former in 1694 through to the early 1700s. In 1737 it was taken over by Richard Tanner, a local yeoman who had recently relinquished the lease on Bedwyn Mill. His son sold the lease in 1754 to William Basing of Boxford in Berkshire, almost certainly after his father's death. Between 1769 and 1783 Thomas Goodman and his son Levi were working the mill. The coroner's bills record a tragic accident in 1796 when 'George Green aged under 7 fell into the water at the mill tail and was instantly drowned.'

Lower Mill was bought by the owner of the canal and ceased to function before 1800. Upper Mill was demolished about 1773. The construction of the canal put corn grinding along the Bedwyn Stream (known today as the River Dun) into decline, so a windmill was constructed by local farmer William Edwards at nearby Wilton and completed in 1821.

THE MEDICAL HISTORY OF BEDWYN

The early medical history of Bedwyn is obscure and one can only assume that the village herbalists played a large part in the treatment of common conditions, and that treatments for the more serious illnesses would have been woefully ineffectual. Most of the sick would have remained in their homes, until help became available from religious orders.

The first mention of a hospital in the Bedwyn area occurs in 1279, when Walter Le Bret of Crofton, Great Bedwyn, by an undated deed, granted an annual rent of 4s.1d. (approximately 20p in modern money) to the brethren and sisters serving God, in the house of St John the Baptist Crofton, a messuage with croft, a meadow and wood, and six acres of land in Crofton. A Walter Le Bret of Somerset died in 1279 and another was alive in 1302/03. The family was established in Stratton St Margaret in the time of Edward I's reign (1272–1307). It seems probable that the deed was the hospital's foundation charter. Philip of Upton died in 1360, holding one-and-a-half acres of arable land in Crofton, rented at 3d. a year from the warden of the hospital. There are no further records of the hospital, but the eighteenth-century Vestry minute books witness the leases of St John's at 2s.6d. a year. In the early-twentieth century, a house called St John's was demolished to make way for The Lodge, a house that lies between the canal and Crofton Manor Farm, and adjacent to the Roman road that runs through Crofton. Pieces of ecclesiastical masonry may be seen ornamenting various gardens throughout the area,

and it is possible that they may have come from the religious establishment.

Thomas Willis

Thomas Willis MD.

In 1621, Bedwyn's most illustrious resident, Dr Thomas Willis, was born. Every medical student has heard of Willis on account of the arterial circle that bears his name; comparatively few know that he was the author of a work on the anatomy of the brain and nervous system, which was a landmark in the history of medical science; he is widely celebrated as the 'founder of the science of neurology'. Fewer still are aware of his achievement in the field of clinical medicine. He gave the first description of the disease known as myasthenia gravis. He noted that an intermittent pulse was not invariably associated with a bad prognosis. He gave the first clinical and pathological account of emphysema. After describing epileptic seizures, he concluded that they arose from explosions in the brain. This followed from his supposition that nervous energy, although derived from the blood stream, had its origins in the brain, from which it radiated through the spinal chord and peripheral nerves.

Thomas Willis was born in what is now known as Castle Cottage on 27 January 1621, the son of Thomas Willis, a lawyer who sometimes lived resided at North Hinksey near Oxford, and at other times at Great Bedwyn, where he is said to have been steward to Sir Walter Smyth, MP for Bedwyn. Thomas Willis' mother was Rachel Howell, of a family long established in North Hinksey. She was related to William of Wykeham, Bishop of Winchester and founder of New College, Oxford.

Thomas Willis received his early education under Edward Sylvester, who had a private school in the parish of All Saints, Oxford; he went there every day from his father's house in North Hinksey. As a schoolboy, he was noted for his concern for the poor, and gave them some of his own food. In 1636, at the age of 16, he became a student at Christ Church, Oxford, and intended to enter the Church, but following the death of his father and the outbreak of the Civil War, he was forced to alter his plans, and for a period served in the Royal Army, which at the time was garrisoned in Oxford. By 1645 Thomas had decided to study medicine, which had always been one of his favourite subjects. He gained his bachelor's degree in 1646 and started to practice in Oxford and the surrounding district. Steadily his fame spread so that he was in constant demand across a wide area. In 1660, on the Restoration of Charles II, he was made Sedlerian Professor of Natural Philosophy. Soon after this he took a Doctor of Medicine degree and was then appointed Physician in Ordinary to the King, who offered him a knighthood, which he modestly declined. Thomas became a Fellow of the Royal Society on its foundation. After the Great Fire of London in 1666, he was invited by Dr Sheldon, Archbishop of Canterbury, to 'go to town', and moved to a house in St Martin's Lane. By this time he was held in the highest esteem by the medical world of the time and became a Fellow of the College of Physicians.

Anthony Wood in his *Athenae Oxoniensis* describes Willis as 'a plain man, a man of no carriage, little discourse, complaisance or society', and said that for his:

... deep insight, researches in anatomy and chemistry, for his wonderful success and repute in his practice, none since has equalled, much less has outshone him, how great soever.

Willis died in his house in St Martin's Lane on 11 November 1675 and was buried in Westminster Abbey, in the north transept, near the body of Mary, his first wife (daughter of Samuel Fell DD, Dean of Christ Church, Oxford, and sister to Dr John Fell, Bishop of Oxford) who had died on All Saints Day 1670.

Before his death, Dr Willis had instigated prayers to be said in St Martin-in-the-Fields, early and late every day, for the sake of such servants and people of that parish who could not attend the ordinary daily service. His works on subjects connected with his profession, which were numerous, were published in a collective edition in two volumes, at Geneva in 1676. In 1798, a print of the doctor was in the house in Farm Lane, which was said to have been left there by his grandson, Browne Willis, the eminent antiquary, who frequently visited the house.

Local Medicine in the Eighteenth Century

Until the end of the eighteenth century, hospital training for doctors was not at all common. Surgeon apothecaries were not high on the social scale and came from a wide range of backgrounds. They learned their skills by being apprenticed to another surgeon apothecary. The title 'surgeon' is misleading, for in the days before anaesthetics they were only able to deal with minor injuries, dress wounds, drain abscesses and extract teeth. Apothecaries mixed their own prescriptions, which provided their main source of income; these mixtures were almost certainly of extremely limited use. It has been said that many a life was spared by the inability of a patient to pay for a prescription which would have cost a shilling.

By the second half of the eighteenth century, the practice of midwifery by surgeon apothecaries had become increasingly common; one guinea was the normal rate for a delivery. There were midwives working in the area, who summoned the doctor in the event of an emergency. William Reeves, the only son of Thomas Reeves, a Great Bedwyn baker, was, by the time of his father's death in 1756, an apothecary in Bedwyn, later to become a surgeon. He appeared to have taken over the lease of Bedwyn Mill from his father, and sold it to Daniel Price of Chisbury in 1758. The following year he surrendered the lease on a burgage tenement, stable and garden in Church Street, and bought the freehold of a house and tenement adjoining the mill in 1761. Two years later he purchased from the Dean and Chapter of Salisbury the freehold of the mill itself. How he received his training, or to whom he was apprenticed, is unknown, but he appears to have served his community for more than 40 years and was mentioned in the *British Universal Directory* as late as 1798.

In 1792, a young doctor named Thelwell Maurice with an MD degree from St Thomas' Hospital in London joined forces with a Dr Pinckney in his Marlborough practice. On 24 November 1794, the Kingstone family of Little Bedwyn, one of whose members was suffering from smallpox, received a visit from Dr Pinckney. Two years later, Edward Jenner, an English physician, discovered that innoculation with cowpox gave immunity to smallpox and thus pioneered vaccination. Jenner's brother, Revd Henry Jenner, was vicar of Great Bedwyn (1768–74).

Doctors covered huge distances on horseback or by carriage and had virtually no free time. The day books of the Marlborough doctors reveal that on one day in 1794, the addresses visited were in Crofton, Wootton Rivers, Ogbourne St George, Wolfhall and East Kennet, and on another day, Great and Little Bedwyn were visited, together with Wilton and Oxenwood in one direction, and Barbury, Winterbourne Basset and Swindon in the other.

Thelwell's third son David joined him in the practice in 1830 and the Bedwyns and the surrounding area continued to be served by these doctors. William Reeves was by now gone and William Bartlett was the surgeon for Great Bedwyn, being mentioned in *Pigot's Commercial Directory* of 1830. By 1842 he had joined forces with James Lidderdale, and together they provided the primary cover for Great and Little Bedwyn, Burbage, Froxfield and the neighbourhood.

The doctor's route around an area was well known, and those who required his services would stop him on his way, or ask a friend to do so. Sometimes a white garment was hung from a window to attract his attention. Three medicaments would have been of real value at that time: opium, which contained morphine (that provided pain relief), digitalis from the leaves of foxgloves (known to be useful in the treatment of cardiac failure and dropsy), and iron (used for anaemia).

In 1815 the Apothecaries Act was passed, which introduced an examination for the Society of Apothecaries. This went some way towards abolishing the right of medical practitioners to qualify by simply serving apprenticeships. In 1858 the Medical Act made it compulsory for surgeon apothecaries to pass an examination for the Royal College of Surgeons in order to practice. Thomas Brown, surgeon to Great Bedwyn in 1855, would have escaped this ruling, and would have been the last doctor there so to do.

Bartlett and Lidderdale would have seen the introduction of anaesthesia in the form of ether and chloroform in 1846, which paved the way for advances in surgery. The *Marlborough Times* of 1863 reported:

An accident occurred at Chisbury on Monday to a steady man named Henry Chandler, in the employ of Mr Cundell, whilst feeding a threshing machine (the corn was fed into the rapidly rotating drum of a steam machine). The poor fellow's days work was nearly done when he slipped and fell into the drum of the machine. He was of course removed as quickly as possible, and under Mr Lidderdale of Bedwyn, and Dr James Maurice of Marlborough, the leg was amputated at the thigh. The operation was skilfully performed under the influence of chloroform, most successfully administered by Dr James Maurice, who we understand had considerable experience in such cases at Paddington Hospital. In a quarter of an hour from inhaling the chloroform, the poor man found himself in bed, having no knowledge of the operation. We learn that he is progressing as favourably as circumstances will permit.

In 1867, the year after the opening of Savernake Hospital, James Lidderdale was joined in his practice by Henry Palmer, a surgeon and registrar of births and deaths. It had been a requirement since 1837 that births, marriages and deaths should be registered. This was the first time the job had fallen to the local doctor. As doctors earned less than £100 a year because of overcrowding in the medical profession, particularly in rural areas, there was always the need to supplement income.

After working for more than 25 years in and around Bedwyn, James Lidderdale was succeeded by his son, who bore the same name. Apart from being a surgeon, he was also medical officer to the second district of the Hungerford Union by 1875, serving the area in these roles for approximately 20 years. With the increased use of anaesthesia, his services would have been more than ever in demand, especially in the field of midwifery, where the presence of both doctor and midwife was required. In 1877, 10s. was charged for the doctor's attendance at a birth. Mothers presumably received financial assistance from the Union, but had to pay when the doctor attended the delivery. The Marlborough practice was still helping to cover the area.

The local Union had its own medical officer, and was administered by a board of guardians appointed by the ratepayers. England and Wales were divided into 21 districts, which had an assistant commissioner who supervised the boards of guardians in their area. James Lidderdale, as medical officer, would have been responsible for those registered as paupers who lived in the workhouse together with wives and children. If able-bodied, they were made to work. He would also have tended those who were disabled through illness or old age, living in the workhouse but not necessarily registered as paupers. The Union also paid for vaccinations against smallpox, which had become compulsory for children in 1853.

In about 1890, Robert Charles Garde Durdin, an Irishman who had received his medical training in Dublin, took over from Dr Lidderdale. The ledger of the Marlborough doctors for that year shows that Dr Durdin of Great Bedwyn consulted Dr Penny on numerous occasions, and sought help with carrying out surgery on patients at home. When he himself was ill, he was treated by Dr Penny.

Robert Durdin remained in the Bedwyn area until he was succeeded in 1909 by a 48-year-old Scot named Elias Fraser. Having trained in Edinburgh, Elias and his wife came to the village from Brixton with their two daughters, Renie and Katie, and son Kenneth. They lived in the Old Vicarage (now Bedwyn House) where Dr Fraser had his consulting room. Their parlour maid was Ethel Giles, later to become Cranstone. Fraser served the village, both as surgeon and medical officer for 22 years and was public vaccinator to the Great Bedwyn District of the Hungerford and Ramsbury Union until the late 1920s, when the workhouse, due to falling demand for accommodation, became a hospital. Although the Marlborough doctors were responsible for day-to-day care and dealing with all emergencies, local practitioners also gave their services. The catchment area included not only Marlborough, but Ramsbury, Hungerford, Pewsey, the Pewsey Vale, Burbage and Bedwyn. In the early days of Scouting, Dr Fraser started the first Scout troop in the village.

His life must have been a great deal easier than that of his predecessors as a result of the introduction of the motor car, and the invention of the telephone. During the time he worked in Bedwyn, Lloyd George implemented the National Insurance Act, whereby weekly wage earners were compulsorily insured and had sickness and maternity benefits for their wives. Visits to patients cost between 3s.6d. (approximately 17.5p in modern money) and 7s.6d. The hospital contributory scheme was started at Savernake Hospital in 1928, and within 18 months had 10,000 members. Artisans, tradespeople, farmers and others in like circumstances paid 6s. per annum, while labourers paid 4s. The latter were entitled to the services of the nurse for themselves and their families in cases of illness or accident, exclusive of children over the age of 16. F.S. Shefford's collector's book for 1941 is still extant and it is interesting to note how many of the names mentioned are still to be found in or around the village today: Rolfe, Wells, Lawrence, Hollister, Davis, Nash, Gigg, Kempster, Mills and Alderman, to name but a few.

On his retirement in 1931, Dr Elias Fraser and his wife moved across the road to Wayside Cottage (now Tudor Cottage) in Church Street, which had been converted by their son-in-law, Frank Wray (husband of Katie) from three dwellings into one house with three staircases! Elias died there in 1945 aged 84; his wife eventually moved to Finchley, London, where she died aged 87 in 1953.

It is interesting to note that in 1926 Dr Fraser brought the Challoner Ellis Hall from London and had it erected on the site where the Village Hall now stands. It was positioned west–east. It was initially used as a summer camp for children from London and was not used exclusively as the Village Hall until after 1949. Latterly, it was painted black outside and had a witches' hat chimney on top. Inside was a small stage, and a serving hatch on the north wall. In 1982, it was replaced by the new Village Hall.

During the working life of Dr Fraser, Emily Webster was the District Nurse, travelling everywhere by bike in an eight-mile radius of the village. Midwifery formed the principal part of her work; indeed many people living in Great Bedwyn in 2003 were brought into the world by Nurse Webster. Born in 1865 in Warwickshire, she later trained at the Queen Elizabeth Hospital, Birmingham; she and her second husband Joseph, whom she had married in Warwickshire, came to Crofton in 1903 with two children and subsequently had three more. Joseph was the crossing keeper for the GWR at Crofton and lived in the railway cottage. In 1905 they came to live in Jockey Green and after a year moved to No. 183 Brook Street. Joseph died before the end of the First World War, and Nurse Webster and her family continued to live there. During that time she adopted a young orphan named Ray Leonard, who eventually married her daughter Pat. In 1930 Nurse Webster and the family moved to a cottage in Forest Hill and in 1936, at the time of her retirement, to Sweet Briars, the thatched house in Brook Street, which is still inhabited by Ray. He said of his mother, 'she was very bright and kind, and the complete nurse'. Nurse Webster died at Sweet Briars in 1954 in her ninetieth year.

On 29 May 1936 the Bedwyn, Shalbourne and District Nursing Association was founded with the aim of providing and paying for a nurse for Bedwyn and its surrounding area. The qualifications required were CMB (Central Midwives Board) and three years' training. The salary was as much as £150 a year, with lodgings or a house to be paid for by the nurse. Nurse Currie was duly appointed. The Shalbourne representatives found her a room that she could use as a base, office or clinic. Mrs Lloyd rented her a house at Great Bedwyn at 7s. (about 35p) a week, inclusive of rates. The following items were provided by the Nursing Association: midwifery bag, £1.15s.6d., general nursing bag, £3.2s.3d. (which was presumably for use after a patient had delivered), a cupboard and necessary surgical dressings, an electric hot plate (18s.6d.) and fish-kettle steriliser, at £1. There was no uniform allowance or help with removal expenses, but £1 a month was paid for mileage. The nurse paid for her own electricity. Later in the year, Oxenwood, Fosbury, Tidcombe and Froxfield joined the Association. Among the rules was a request for the nurse's services to be made available before 9a.m. and for three month's notice to be given in midwifery cases. During the first three months she was at Bedwyn, Nurse Currie averaged 65 visits a week.

Clearly overworked and dissatisfied with her terms and conditions, she threatened to leave in 1938, and take up a County Council appointment, but at the last minute withdrew her resignation and agreed to an increased salary. By 1939, she was also fulfiling the role of school nurse and health visitor. As the threat of war loomed, the committee, consisting of Mesdames Tandy, Gage, Weight, Champion, Lawrence, Beckingham, Ayling, Lee and Bolland decided that it was more important to keep the district nursing and midwifery service going, and that a district nurse 'must not undertake any obligation that might interfere with her work.' The secretary accountant of Savernake Hospital wrote to the association asking that the number of civilian admissions be restricted to acute cases only. More patients would have to be treated in their own homes and those in hospital might be discharged earlier than would normally be the case.

The nurse's statement of extra work shows that Great Bedwyn had received 108 evacuees during the Second World War, Little Bedwyn 49, and St Katharine's 8. It also reveals that there had been nine cases of impetigo in Great Bedwyn, together with 1,000 treatments for head lice in the first nine months of 1939. To add to all this, Ham joined the Association in 1940, and a request for uniform allowance was again refused. The following year, however, Nurse Currie received £24 'War Bonus' for the year. In 1942 she resigned and was replaced by Nurse Gulley, who was immediately supplied with a car by Lord Rootes, a local resident. She was housed in a cottage in Church Street, and proved to be 'most efficient and very much liked by the patients.' She was a midwife only, and not a general nurse; she had trained at Plaistow Maternity Hospital in London. In 1946 she returned there for a brief period to learn how to use the new gas-and-air apparatus for the relief of pain, which had recently come into existence, but shortly after she moved on to another post.

On 1 June 1946, Nurse McLeod Craik, State Registered Nurse and State Certified Midwife, whose name was on the Queen's Institute Roll of Nurses, began work in Bedwyn. She is still remembered by many village residents in 2003.

With the introduction of the National Heath Service on 5 July 1948, the Nursing Association ceased to be responsible for the nursing service in the area, but continued to advise the Health Committee on health matters affecting the locality. It was also involved in all day-to-day matters connected with the conduct of the district nursing service in the area, on behalf of both the nurse and her patients until the Association was finally wound up in 1959.

Herbert Hancock

Herbert Arthur Hancock succeeded Elias Fraser as Bedwyn's doctor. Born in Cambridge in 1881, the youngest of three children, he was educated at the Perse School, Cambridge, and Emmanuel College, Cambridge, where he gained his BA. The London Hospital provided his clinical training. A cricket Blue, and half Blue at golf, he was also talented musically. After qualifying he worked as an assistant to a doctor in Harleston, Norfolk, and travelled on his rounds in a horse-drawn trap. With the outbreak of the First World War he joined the RAMC and was sent to Flanders. He became medical officer on the hospital ship *Gallipoli*, receiving an OBE for his work. He was a modest man and his family only became aware of his achievements much later. In 1916 he married May Harland, a fellow musician, and they lived in quarters at Tidworth Military Hospital and then at Fort Pitt, Chatham. Following demobilisation, he bought a small practice in Gravesend, but his wife contracted TB and the foggy climate of the Thames Estuary was unsuitable for an invalid. They came to Great Bedwyn by chance, having stopped off in Marlborough on their way to Devon. Falling in love with the area, Herbert discovered that there was a practice up for sale in Great Bedwyn, and brought his wife and two children to live in the Old Vicarage where the rest of his working life was spent. (It was during this period that Protonsil, the first of the sulphonamides, was introduced in 1937.) He started the practice in Vernham Dean and in his spare time was president of the Bedwyn Bowls Club. He died suddenly in 1940 and, in recognition of his war service, his coffin was carried to the church by members of the Royal British Legion. His widow moved away from Bedwyn, and eventually died in Devon at the age of 84. However, the family retains close links with Bedwyn as their daughter, Betty, married David Gauntlett who joined his father and brother in running Little Bedwyn estate and Chisbury Manor Farm after the war.

After Dr Hancock's death, his son-in-law, Bill Empey, who was in the Indian medical service and home on leave, did locums in the practice until it could be handed over in 1941 to Dr (Colonel) Powell, a retired medical officer for Indian Army prisons. He was of Irish extraction and came to Bedwyn with his wife and three daughters, the youngest of whom was named Patience; rumour had it that he had wanted a son! He was short in stature, but had an unmistakable military presence. He was also something of an eccentric, who would drive to Marlborough by car, forget the car, and return by bus! The family lived in the house adjacent to the Old White Hart public house until the 1950s, when it was sold to a Major Wyndham Wright. After six or seven years in the practice, Dr Powell found he could no longer cope and retired, leaving the way open for Dr Bill Kingston. Bill bought the practice soon after the Second World War and came to Bedwyn when in his early 30s, with his wife Bel. Sadly he died of a brain haemorrhage after only a short time, leaving two small daughters. They moved with their mother to Ogbourne St Andrew and Dr Fenn took over the practice. He is remembered by many people in the village in 2003. It was during this period that the maternity ward at Savernake Hospital opened, and the Princess Margaret Hospital in Swindon was built.

Death in Bedwyn

An interesting source for local historians is that provided by coroners' financial accounts. Although coroners had been established in England since the twelfth century they were not paid for this service. It was not until 1752 that they were entitled to claim £1 for each inquest held and 9d. for each mile they had to travel. Their expense accounts were kept in good order for this purpose, and retained details of each death investigated. A typical entry reads: '24 Feb 1762, West Grafton in Great Bedwyn. Thomas Mackarell: found dead in a field; sudden natural death. 18 miles. £1.13.6d.' The final figures represent the fee and travel expenses claimed by the coroner.

These bills provide information on the names of local residents at the time, places and occupations, as well as frequent causes of death. Invariably they provide only a snapshot of something that happened, and read like the headlines of a newspaper to which no further article is attached, leaving us wanting more. Amongst the causes of deaths are very many instances of suicide (typically called 'lunacy' at that time), a variety of accidents (many of which involved drowning and injury from horses), the demon alcohol and a surprising number of murders, including many which involved the killing of illegitimate babies. A selection of these follows, using Bedwyn and local examples where available, taken from R.F. Hunniset's Coroners Bills, 1752–1796, published by the Wiltshire Records Society.

Tragedies and Drownings

27 July 1755: Wexcombe, Great Bedwyn. Robert Reynolds, aged 2: drowned in a tub.

22 May 1767: Oakhill, Froxfield. John Page: fell into lock hole of mill and was drowned.

25 Apr 1772: Crofton in Great Bedwyn. Mary Cope aged 3, fell into brook and drowned.

9 Sept 1772: Westcourt near Burbage. Robert Webb, drowned in a tub of water.

20 Oct 1776: Crofton in Great Bedwyn, Thomas Pizzey, a fisherman to the Earl of Ailesbury: letting down the fishpond hatch, fell over it into the hatch-hole and was killed.

Natural Death

22 Aug 1774: Great Bedwyn. Richard Batholomew, an old man: returning from Tottenham, was found dead in an inclosure called Town Field.

1 Jan 1788: Man unknown: found dead in the snow Savernake Park.

26 Oct 1791: Little Bedwyn. Mary Cox, subject to fits: found dead in Fore Bridge Lane.

Suicides

11 May 1759: Graham Farm in Savernake Park. Stephen Peke: on 9 May shot himself; lunacy.

4 Sept 1765: Crofton in Great Bedwyn. Samuel Warde on 3 Sept hanged himself; lunacy.

11 Apr 1771: East Grafton John Sheffard. On 9 April, hanged himself in Pyke's coppice; lunacy.

6 Apr 1776: Wilton in Great Bedwyn. Joseph Vincent, hanged himself; lunacy.

13 Jan 1786: Brail in Great Bedwyn, Robert Cope: hanged himself from a tree in his garden.

6 July 1789: Savernake Park Great Lodge near Marlborough Forest, William Tuck, threw himself into a deep well and was instantly killed, lunacy from frenzy and fever.

Death from horses

6 Feb 1762: Savernake Park. Francis Wiltshire: killed by wagon going over him.

22 Feb 1767: West Grafton in Great Bedwyn, Edward Townsend: killed by a kick of a horse belonging to Mr W. Pinkney of Wolf Hall.

1 Apr 1767: West Grafton in Great Bedwyn, Thomas Pierce was riding along a lane between West Grafton Farm and Cow Leaze by the side of a ditch and the horse fell into the ditch upon Thomas by which he was drowned.

25 Aug 1775: Little Bedwyn, William Temple: received a violent blow from a horse on his abdomen or lower belly and was killed.

20 May 1775: Harding Farm in Great Bedwyn, William Payne: killed by a ploughshare, the horses taking fright in Den Field.

6 Feb 1775: Marten in Great Bedwyn, Mary Cook: thrown to the ground by the overturning of a one-horse chaise and instantly killed.

16 July 1777: Savernake Park, Mary Gale, was riding in a wagon and the driver being careless, the wheel gathered up a bank, turned over and killed her on the spot.

4 July 1778: Crofton in Great Bedwyn, Joseph Vivash, returning from plough, riding on and playing with a horse, was thrown off, entangled in and dragged by the trace of the harness, and killed.

9 July 1780: Froxfield, Little Bedwyn, John Tow, had been selling cherries and riding on a gelding, fell to the ground and was instantly killed.

3 Aug 1780: Great Bedwyn, Thomas Martin, riding on a horse very fast was thrown and killed.

25 Feb 1789: Great Bedwyn, George Tucker: returning on horseback from thence to his home in Froxfield was drowned in a stream near Great Bedwyn.

Accidents

14 Dec 1767: Savernake Lodge in Savernake Forest. Jacob Pierce: being at work in a marl-pit in the forest, part of its edge fell in upon him and killed him on the spot.

9 Jan 1774: Crofton, William King found dead in Langfield Copse; severe weather.

27 June 1775: Great Bedwyn, Alexander Meaden: had been violently exerting himself playing fives and, as imagined, thereby ruptured a blood vessel, as soon after suddenly died.

27 June 1789: Thomas Smith: was digging chalk-stone in a quarry at Wolf Hall in Great Bedwyn, the upper part of which fell in and instantly killed him.

21 May 1790: Burbage, James Savage: having got up a high tree for dry wood, fell and was killed.

2 Jan 1791: Great Bedwyn, Benjamin Grobetti, a native of Switzerland who had resided as a schoolmaster there for many years much respected: repairing to his chambers for his wonted rest, fell down the stairs and was killed.

18 Jan 1796: Burbage, Robert Skitrell: employed in cutting and forming the Kennet & Avon Canal, was killed by falling from a narrow plank while driving a wheelbarrow of earth.

Alcohol

7 Nov 1782: Westcourt in Burbage, John Hooper: returning from Appleshaw fair full of liquor, laid and slept on the ground, from which and the hard rains that fell that night he died.

1 May 1794: East Grafton in Great Bedwyn, Zabulon Carter: found dead in a coppice near there; no other violence than his having drunk too freely of hot spiritous liquors, part whereof was in the bottle by him.

Murder

6 Feb 1777: Wilton, a newborn infant found drowned in an earthen jar; murder.

21 June 1783: Buttermere. Several parts of the body of a newborn infant, only the head of which was found first by a dog, afterwards a hand in a wood at a considerable distance. The places where the parts were found were examined, and the residences of the supposed mother, who had absconded, and of the supposed father. In the night the woman Sarah Cram got from a very high window and fled a second time and escaped the most diligent search. When retaken she charged the father Scammel with taking the child from her after delivery in a wood. Murder. [At Salisbury Assizes on 2 Aug 1783, she was acquitted of murdering a male bastard child, and the case against John Scammel was not prosecuted. Sarah was convicted of entering a house and stealing a cotton gown worth 7s. and was sentenced to be whipped round Marlborough market-place between noon and 2p.m. and committed to Marlborough's house of correction on 12 months' hard labour.]

INNS & ALEHOUSES

'There is nothing which has yet been contrived by man by which so much happiness is produced as by a good tavern or Inn.' So said Dr Samuel Johnson in the 1760s. Throughout the centuries Bedwyn had its fair share of inns and alehouses. All but two have now gone.

The word 'ale' came into the English language with the Scandinavian invaders through the Danish word 'ol'. Ale booths and ale stonds were first mentioned in the laws of Ina, King of Wessex, before AD728. Among the Anglo-Saxons, there were three kinds of establishment open to the public – the alehouse, the wine house, and the inn. The first two were just for drinking, but an inn or hostel was a house used as a lodging as well. Alehouses were always the lesser establishments, and were often placed at the crossing of roads. The sign of an alehouse was traditionally a bush of greenery, hung out over the entrance on a pole. Chaucer makes allusion to this 'ale-stake' and, indeed, the bush as a symbol of the alehouse had been used as far back as Roman times.

Sellers of food and drink were called victuallers. They were already an ancient trade corporation when the Vintners Company of London was founded in 1437. Over the course of time common alehouse keepers came to be known as victuallers.

In an unlettered age, a pictorial sign was a mark of identity, which could be recognised by the illiterate. At the end of the fourteenth century, publicans were compelled by law to display signs. The earliest inn signs were those connected with brewing and agriculture, such as the sign of the harrow – the present inn at Little Bedwyn takes its name from an older inn of that name on the Bath Road.

Inn signs have been classified under 15 different headings, the last of which is the biblical and religious group of which there were a great number in pre-Reformation times. Signs having inferential reference to the old religion are still common, such as the Cross Keys, which are the arms of the Papacy. From the association of ale-brewing with monastic life comes the name the Three Tuns. Brewing beer was an accomplishment cultivated in most English monasteries and this particular sign is common in Wiltshire. (Three Tuns also appear on the coat of arms of the Brewers Company.) Beer barrels were marked with 'x' or 'xx' or 'xxx'. The mark was a guarantee of good quality, as in shape the crosses were akin to a crucifix and indicated that by the oath of the monks sworn on the cross the beer was of sound quality and fit to drink. We may assume therefore that Bedwyn beer was amongst the best! Of the monastic offices, that of cellarer was one of the most important. The Saxons regarded drunkenness as honourable, for the man who could withstand the effects of strong drink the longest was the most admired.

The first mention of drinking habits associated with 'Bedwynde' was recorded in the Dean of Salisbury's register of visitations for 10 May 1409, when Thomas Stokke, Hawkin Page, Thomas Smyth, Thomas Hurlebat, William Plomere, Hugh Luyde and Richard Waryne, parishioners, disclosed that Robert Shaket, Parish Clerk, 'frequents taverns and customarily sits with his ale when he ought to go with the vicar to go visit the sick' and 'that the vicar habitually frequents taverns'. The vicar denied this accusation on 9 July but was 'purged with the Court's indulgence'.

The Church also had an influence on beer drinking and a number of festivals were held with ecclesiastical sanction. John Aubrey, writing on Wiltshire in the mid-1600s, revealed that:

... in every parish was a church house to which belonged spits, crocks, etc., utensils for dressing provisions. Here the housekeepers met and gave there charity. The young

people were there too, and had dancing, bowling, shooting at butts... the ancients sitting gravely by and looking on. All things were civil and without scandal.

All these Church-organised festivities fell out of favour with the advent of Puritanism.

Another old custom in which copious drinking often occurred was known as 'beating the bounds' held in Rogation week. Some claim that the main attraction was the ale, which was freely distributed at inns and stopping places along the line of the parish boundaries. Drinking was interspersed with the reading of the Gospel at the various Gospel trees along the route; the latter provided a cover of respectability for the activity.

From 1552 it became necessary for any person keeping an alehouse to be licensed in Sessions or by two Justices. There was no restraint on the practice of selling malt liquors at fairs. The economic regulation on the part of the central government by statute proclamation and administrative order reached its peak between 1604 and 1627. No less than seven Acts of Parliament were directed against drunkenness and the drink trade. Tradesmen had to adhere to specific laws, such as not selling beer during Lent. On 8 March 1620, William Davis and John Keele, both alehouse keepers of Great Bedwyn, appeared before Anthony Hungerford, Justice of the Peace at Marlborough, for just such a reason. The rise of the public informer was a product of Tudor economic policy which culminated in an Act of 1623 charging every town or village official on their oaths to act as common informers against any 'tipsy man'.

In 1621 when the population of England and Wales was probably under five million there were thought to be at least 13,000 licensed premises in the country. It was common for working men to drink three or four quarts of strong, heavy ale each day of their lives. In 1648 the alehouses of Great Bedwyn were regarded as a nuisance and thought to be too numerous by inhabitants of the neighbouring parishes.

The Beer Act

The Beer Act of 1830 enabled any householder whose name was on the rate book to sell beer but no other intoxicating liquor by retail without obtaining a licence; they merely paid the sum of two guineas to the Excise. Within the first three months of the Act's coming into force 25,000 people had paid their fee. From 1830 to 1869 any person of good character could obtain a beer-house licence for a tenement of a certain rateable value.

During the middle decades of the nineteenth century ale was retailed by large numbers of small householders. Customers were accommodated in cottage kitchens, parlours and halls. Thus in 1837 Edward Champion was a maltster in his own home in Brook Street, as was William Wise in his. The

names Choules and Miles were also associated with brewing. Such men often had several occupations. Of all the inns which once existed only the Cross Keys and the Three Tuns remain in 2003.

Ancient Watering Holes

The earliest Bedwyn pub to be mentioned is the 'King's Head'. In 1675 the Visitation Court was held there. The 'Blow Lyon', was bought in 1745 by Edward Wilmott from Edward Nowmans for the princely sum of £60, having been in the tenure of John Webb, victualler. The only description is of 'a tenement or dwelling-house situate in Great Bedwyn.' The name Blow Lyon would have had heraldic origins. The exact location of these pubs remains a mystery.

In 1741 Thomas Hill of Great Bedwyn, innkeeper, took over a lease from labourer Richard Gilbert, yeoman, John Satt of Aldbourne and Elizabeth his wife. This was almost certainly the lease on the market house, for by September of that year he held a 21-year lease to run his business there and receive the profits from the tolls and market. The lessor reserved the right to use the house to hold courts and to use it at election times. It appears that Thomas Hill owned a considerable amount of property in Great Bedwyn in the mid-eighteenth century. In 1747 there is also mention of a dwelling-house, malt-house and garden lying at the west end of a ground 'abutting on Cheap Street' (later High Street). This was thought to have been on the site of Stock Tree Cottage.

The name of Thomas Hill appeared again in connection with an inn which is now barely a memory: the Fighting Cocks. This stood on glebe land between the present Vicarage Drive and Garden Cottage, opposite the church and adjacent to Back Lane. It was owned by the Church and was certainly in existence by 1745. Its name recalls the gruesome sport which would once have taken place there. The churchwardens' accounts for that year mention money received annually for the rent of the property.

In the mid-1700s inns and malt-houses proliferated in Great Bedwyn. We know for certain that there were at least 14 open at various dates; there were half a dozen in Church Street alone, although there is little documentation about them. We have some records of John Savage who appears to have been in business as a maltster for almost 20 years in the area of Back Lane. He was also involved in a land transfer when in 1742 he assigned lands called 'the Mill Bargain' in Great Bedwyn to John Adams, yeoman of the same.

John Wylde rented the adjacent Church Close, which was where Glebe House stands in 2003. In 1758 Thomas Hill paid £30 for the lease and then let the inn to Sir Harry Verney, Lord of Stokke. By 1763 it was in a poor state of repair and in 1765 was bought by Thomas, Lord Bruce, for £30 and ceased to exist as an inn. By the late 1700s, the Fighting Cocks and several adjacent cottages had been demolished.

Thomas Gaines and William Reeves had a house and garden with brew house and stable opposite, near the crossing at Crofton in 1753. This was adjacent to Crofton's Upper Mill. At the same time Joseph Bailey ran a malt-house and garden where Great Bedwyn Garage is now located. Another such establishment was leased by Thomas Goodman, the Crofton miller, and Levy his son in 1769 and was called Baccats. It consisted of house, malt-house, stable, barn, garden and part of Portreeves Close. It stood at the High Street end of Back Lane. John Savage, Thomas Kidd, Charles Elkins and William Hawkins were also maltsters in the 1700s on unspecified sites. Another maltster member of the Hawkins family was Thomas who owned land to the west of the common fields of Bedwyn in 1792 and was mentioned in the *Universal British Directory* from 1793 to 1798.

Cobham's Inn, another ancient Bedwyn watering hole, had ceased to exist by 1762, when John Chidwick, a yeoman of Bulstrode in Buckinghamshire, bought the building and surrounding land. Its exact whereabouts is unknown.

From 1759 to 1765 William Darrell, a bricklayer of Great Bedwyn, had a half share in the Greyhound Inn, which stood in Church Street on glebe lands. He leased it from the Church. After 1765 there is no further mention of the inn.

Brewing was originally a domestic industry, entirely in the hands of women, but by the nineteenth century men had become more involved than women. To prevent fraudulent sales, there was a standard measurement known as the 'sealed quarts' which were pewter measures bearing the ale-tasters' mark, which in Bedwyn would have carried the arms of the borough. The ale-taster was an officer of considerable importance, appointed and sworn to look to the assize and goodness of all the beer brewed within the jurisdiction of the lordship. (The latter half of the eighteenth century produced ale-testers instead of ale-tasters, who were employed to test purely for sugar content.)

The Horse and Jockey

Jockey Green takes its name from the public house that once stood there. The hospitality offered at the Horse and Jockey appears to have been relatively short-lived. It is shown on the Andrews and Dury map of 1773, but was a farmhouse by 1802. Giles Sheppard, who was the tenant in 1800, had a named pew in St Michael's Church in Little Bedwyn; Jockey Green was within the parish boundary of Little Bedwyn at that time. In 1804 the Horse and Jockey was converted to the three cottages which still exist in 2003. Originally thatched, they were later tiled. The middle cottage still houses the

bread oven and the right one the beer cellar. The yard was to the front of the buildings in what are now gardens and there was a stable block to the left side running at right angles to the cottages down towards the green.

The Old White Hart

Another inn is remembered in the name of a private house in Church Street – the Old White Hart. The name derives from the white hart which formed the arms of Richard II and harks back to the white hart with the golden collar of ancient Greece. Until 1720 it was known as Rosiers. Thomas Rosier of Great Bedwyn, previously a husbandman (small farmer) and by then a maltster, and Robert Coxhead of Hungerford, were the landlords. In that year they leased for 1,000 years their property described as 'house brewhouse and garden' to 'Edward Cummyns of Bedwin innholder and Joseph Balley of Bedwin innholder.'

The inn was owned from about 1725 to 1757 by the Balley family who had come to Bedwyn possibly from Newbury. John Balley, who died in 1737, and his son Joseph (1686–1755) were the town carpenters. Joseph had previously used the market or court-house with the butcher's shambles, and reaped the profits of fairs and tolls, etc. Later, both became brewers, maltsters and publicans.

A detailed description of the property at the time of the sale exists:

A house called the White Hart Inn with the shop adjoining, with a plot of garden, also a room or lower kitchen adjoining to the west end, and the chamber over the kitchen, and the stable brewhouse and other outhouses, and the upper part of Portreeve Close.

Above: *The Horse and Jockey public house was converted into three cottages in 1804. It is seen here in 2003.*

Left: *The Old White Hart, as seen at the start of the twenty-first century. It is now a private dwelling.*

Also, a house, outhouse, malt houses and garden, and the lower part of Portreeve Close with the stable. All in Great Bedwyn.

Portreeve Close was between the rear of the White Hart and Back Lane, with the High Street forming the eastern boundary.

Joseph appears to have been a great success for when he died in 1755, he had provided for his second wife Elizabeth. His middle son, Joseph, who had been the landlord of the Cross Keys was already dead, while his youngest son, William, was the village tailor. The White Hart, which had been the family home as well as a pub, passed to Joseph's eldest son John on the death of his stepmother Elizabeth in 1757. Almost immediately, John sold it to William Harrison, Doctor of Divinity of Corpus Christi College, Oxford, for £119. He and his family were to be allowed to continue in the house for 20 years if they lived as long as that. John, however, agreed to accept a leasehold estate at Collingbourne instead. In 1763 he was renting a cottage garden and an acre of land near Bedwyn Mill. William Harrison had no interest in being a brewer or publican and in 1761 left Bedwyn with his wife and family. At the time of his death in 1765 Joseph's family owned the White Hart, the Cross Keys, several houses and land called Portreeve Close.

In the closing years of the eighteenth century Thomas Vernon was landlord of the White Hart and was succeeded by Francis (Frank) Willmott in the early 1800s. After Frank's death his wife Elizabeth carried on the business until around 1855. They had no children so left their money and two grandfather clocks to Savernake Hospital. Elizabeth was succeeded by John Smallbones and his wife Hannah. He was the last landlord. In 1867 the inn closed its doors for ever and the Smallbones moved to the Three Tuns, which at that stage was divided into two houses occupied by James and Elisabeth Drew from 18 Cheap Street (High Street) and John and Ann Powell from 4 Forest Lane. At a later date the building reverted to the single dwelling which can be seen in 2003.

The Cross Keys

The Cross Keys is one of the two remaining old inns of Great Bedwyn and was built after the 1716 fire which destroyed 28 houses in the centre of the village. For a while it co-existed with the old Cross Keys in Brook Street, which was described as 'standing on a piece of ground on the south side of Brook Street, adjoining a shop with stable and outbuildings which had been recently erected.' Thomas Hill was landlord there in 1735. The old Cross Keys eventually fell into disrepair and was demolished in 1763. By 1753 he was leasing the inn from James Field, a village wheelwright, and his business partner, John Long, was landlord. The date

when he ceased to be connected with the business is not known.

Joseph Balley and his wife Joanna (née Dunning) from Little Bedwyn ran the new Cross Keys from 1736 to 1742, when Joseph died at the age of 25. Joanna continued to manage it until her old age, when she exchanged it for an annuity. On 19 June 1783, having been the landlord for 47 years, she announced:

Premises to Let. Mrs Balley wishes to retire from business at the Cross Keys and proposes to let the premises on condition that there is a lease for life of another house in Bedwyn, and an annuity of £10 for life.

She then enjoyed eleven years of retirement for she did not die until 1794.

The Cross Keys had remarkably few new names associated with it until recent times. For almost 60 years until the 1850s various members of the Thatcher family ran it as innkeepers, maltsters and publicans. They were followed by Charles Wooldridge, whose licence was issued in 1854. Two years earlier he had married Eliza, daughter of Henry Neale and Ann (née Cope) of the Three Tuns. Charles was also a land surveyor and secretary to the Great Bedwyn Friendly Society which had been formed in 1821. Their marriage was short-lived, for Charles died in 1856. Eliza carried on alone for 11 years until her death in 1867 when she was succeeded by her brother Richard Neale of the Three Tuns.

Richard and his wife Eliza had seven children and were at the Cross Keys for about 40 years. The Neales had come from Marlborough in the seventeenth century and owned land in Great Bedwyn. John Lloyd, writing at the time of Richard's death noted:

... he was the last of the old style village landlords and was also the people's Churchwarden, overseer of the parish, school manager and charity trustee, a grand old gentleman and his lady to match.

A good landlord had as strong an influence in the village as the parson. He recorded his wife's death by putting on her tombstone her favourite hymn, 'Alleluia alleluia alleluia the strife is oer, the battle won.' Brown stone jars with the Neale name imprinted on them can often be seen in local antique shops.

After the Neales came the Ayling and Calloway families whose descendants are to be found in the area in 2003. The latter arrived from London in the early 1920s. Mosden Calloway, who was landlord for about a decade, had been a police superintendent in the East End of London and arrived in Bedwyn with his sons Matt, Ruben, Albert, Frank and Charlie. The motor industry was developing and they bought two Ford taxis which Albert and Ruben drove. Tom Cummins from Andover had the pub from the 1930s until the Second World War. He is buried in the churchyard. After the war the pub changed hands frequently.

ⓞ all to whom these Presents shall come, Greeting: KNOW YE, That We, whose Hands are hereunto set, and Seals affixed, being three of the Commissioners of Inland Revenue, reposing especial Trust and Confidence in the Knowledge, Skill, Industry, Fidelity, and Circumspection of

Charles Wooldridge

HAVE, pursuant to the several and respective Powers vested in us as such Commissioners as aforesaid in this behalf, nominated, constituted, and appointed, and for Her Majesty's Service DO hereby nominate, constitute, and appoint the said

Charles Wooldridge

to be the Agent of the said Commissioners, for holding and keeping open the Office of Excise, at *the Cross Keys* in the *Borough of Bedwin* within the County of *Wilts* at all such times as shall be required for the convenience of the Collector of Excise of *Sarum* Collection, or such Person or Persons as shall be duly appointed to receive the Duties of Excise for such Collection, holding his Sittings therein, and at all times required for receiving, depositing, and securing therein any seizure of any Goods or Commodities made by any Officer or Officers of Excise under or by virtue of any Laws relating to the Revenue of Excise or Customs, and for keeping all such seizures in his safe custody at such Office as aforesaid, until the same shall be removed therefrom by the proper Officer of Excise, and for the due performance of all such matters and things touching or relating to such Office and Appointment. This our Commission to continue and be in Force during the Pleasure of the Commissioners of Inland Revenue for the Time being. *In Witness whereof, We have hereunto set our Hands and Seals, the* **Ninth** *Day of* **January** *in the* **Seventeenth** *Year of the Reign of our Sovereign Lady* VICTORIA *by the Grace of God, of the United Kingdom of Great Britain and Ireland, Queen, Defender of the Faith, and in the Year of our Lord One Thousand Eight Hundred and* **fifty four**

Entered.

Charles Wooldridge was the licensed landlord at the Cross Keys between 1854 and 1856.

Fire!

There are three clear markers to Great Bedwyn's disastrous fire in 1716. First, an absence of much thatch in the centre of the village; second, darker and possibly smoke-stained lower brick courses in some of the central village houses; and finally, an obvious spurt of 'new' brick buildings dating from the early- to mid-eighteenth century.

The records of the Quarter Sessions held at Devizes in April 1716 give clear evidence of an event which must have had an enormous impact on village life at the time. The report sent to the Lord Chancellor, the Rt Hon. William Lord Cowper, Baron of Wingham, on 1 April 1716 stated that between 11a.m. and 12 noon on 2 April a 'sudden and terrible' fire broke out 'in or near the house of Hurcombe' and that in a few hours it had burnt down the adjoining houses, barns and malt-houses 'together with most parte of the household goods, grocery, drapery stuffe, silk and other merchandises, wheat barley, malt, hay, grass seed and several other valuable commodities there.'

The schedule listed 28 names with losses ranging from £318.17s.0d. to £16.9s.0d. for houses and from £397.16s.6d. to £1.6s.0d. for goods. Roberto Hall was the biggest claimant with a total of £716.13s.6d., a very substantial amount at that time. He had the highest losses in each category and Edward Webb had the lowest, a total of £2.0s.0d. worth of goods. Sarah and Mary Hurcombe, in whose house the fire presumably started, had relatively low losses of £17 and £31 respectively.

The fire seems to have been concentrated in the centre of the village with many houses affected in Farm Lane, the High Street up to the Three Tuns and Church Street. It is not known whether these losses were refunded in any way, either from government, public subscription or village funds.

From the 1753 Tithe Map it is possible to make a guess about where the fire raged. The houses of some of the tenants on the east side of the High Street, just below the Three Tuns, are in the same sequence as reported in the list given to the Quarter Session of 10 April 1716. It could be that they moved back into their old homes once these had been repaired.

The Three Tuns

The Three Tuns in the upper part of the village is also an eighteenth-century building which opened its doors in 1784. Its landlord through the 1790s was John Scammell, a victualler. The Scammells were not in the area long and were succeeded in the 1830s by Henry Neale and his wife Anne who ran the inn with the help of their son James for more than 30 years. Every Tuesday in the 1850s a corn market was held there as the market house was no longer in use. Eventually their son Richard took over, but he moved to the Cross Keys in 1867.

The High Street and the Three Tuns.

John Smallbones and his wife Hannah (née Willmott) were the next innkeepers. A small number of families therefore had a monopoly of all the inns in the village and were a close-knit community in themselves. In 1871 Hannah died and John continued at the Three Tuns until he was succeeded by their son George, who was both publican and baker. He held the licence until the early years of the twentieth century when William Alfred Lloyd, a member of the local stonemason's family, took over. In 1925 he moved to the Bricklayers Arms in Bartholomew Street in Newbury. From then on the pub changed hands with increasing frequency. Tommy Jordan, a blacksmith from Marlborough, arrived to try his hand in the trade. He kept pigs in the field where No. 2 Forest Hill now stands and owned a hire car. His son Fred later drove the Wiltshire and Dorset buses which ran through the village. Tommy was only at the pub for five or six years until Tommy Hearst, also a taxi driver, took over until the Second World War. Ray Leonard, who still lives in the village, drove the taxi for him. After the war many different landlords came and went.

The Harrow Inn, Little Bedwyn

It seems likely that the Harrow Inn at Little Bedwyn (built around 1830) took its name from the Harrow Inn on the Bath Road, near Chisbury, which had ceased trading.

During the 1870s it was operated by John and Martha Dixon. In the late-nineteenth and early-twentieth centuries there was a Methodist hall in the narrow space between the inn and Myrtle Cottage

and for this reason the Harrow was unable to obtain a seven-day licence until 1981.

In 1932 Edward and Bertha Lance acquired the tenancy and operated the business with their family for almost 50 years, having purchased the freehold from Simmonds Brewery in 1959. At this time the Harrow also included a smallholding, provided by the estate on condition that the establishment supply the village with milk. The Lance family sold the inn in 1981 and, after initial success, the business declined in the late 1980s. The then owners tried to get permission to convert the building into a private house.

The village decided to take action and a company was formed selling shares to 85 residents of Little Bedwyn and the surrounding villages. This raised £100,000, which together with a commercial mortgage was sufficient to purchase and improve the property. The refurbishment of the premises subsequently became a village venture and the managers, Sean and Louise Juniper, had local connections, all of which created intense interest in the national media. There were countless newspaper stories and television and radio interviews on the theme of 'village buys pub'.

After successfully operating the business for five years and acquiring an excellent reputation, particularly for their food, Sean and Louise moved to larger premises closer to Marlborough. Problems with four separate unsuccessful tenancies over the following three years persuaded the shareholders to sell the business in 1998, after which it was run as a quality restaurant under the management of Roger and Sue Jones. The Harrow features in many of the national food guides and has received awards for the finest seafood restaurant in the South West.

Landlady Bertha Lance in the Harrow Inn, 1960s.

The Windsor Castle

Little Bedwyn had another pub: the Windsor Castle at Fore Bridge on the road to Hungerford. This was apparently fairly short-lived during the middle years of the nineteenth century. In 1868 it was sold to Robert Bevan, who then owned Little Bedwyn estate, for £150. The sale particulars described it as: 'Windsor Castle public house, arranged with brick kitchen, bay-windowed parlour and four bedrooms, small garden with brick and slate brewhouse…'. The building was finally condemned and demolished in 1951.

Right: Copy of 1991 newspaper article: 'village buys pub'.

Below: The locals pull together to ensure the Harrow Inn reopens.

Bottom left: Reopening of the Harrow by Johnny Morris of 'Animal Magic' fame.

Bottom right: Copy of Windsor Castle sale particulars, 1868.

MARLBOROUGH TIMES NEW

PUB REGULARS GET TOGETHER TO BUY

Doors open at a true village local

THE HARROW Inn in Little Bedwyn has been given a new lease of life, thanks to the dedicated efforts of the villagers who could not bear to live without it.

The pub had been a vital feature of community life — the only other public facility in the village besides the church — until last September, when it was closed by its owner.

But the villagers were not prepared to let it go and a group of locals got together and bought their favourite watering hole. Little Bedwyn resident Ian Mackintosh said this week, 'The negotiations to acquire the property from the previous owners have now been completed and we plan to open the pub's doors again for business on August 24.'

But before they could do that, the place had to cleaned up and a manager appointed. So at the weekend, a team of about 30 villagers turned up at the pub armed with everything from rubber gloves and scouring pads to paint brushes and ladders.

Great Bedwyn Parish Councillor Jenny Scott was one of the cleaners. 'It was tremendous,' she said on Wednesday, 'Everyone got their teeth stuck into the work — the suds were really flying.'

She added, 'And we've appointed a very experienced couple to manage the place. Louize Juniper, the daughter of the local master thatcher Bill Bacon, and her husband Sean.'

The Juniper's are both fully trained chefs, and as soon as the kitchens are refitted they will be serving food. 'What we want to do with the pub,' said Mrs Scott, 'is first get it open, and once that is done we intend to renovate and restore it back to its former reputation of being a wonderful place to eat and drink.'

TO BREWERS AND OTHERS.

FORE BRIDGE, LITTLE BEDWYN,
Wilts, One Mile from Froxfield.

VOTE FOR THE COUNTY.

FREEHOLD BRICK AND SLATE

DWELLING HOUSE

WITH BRICK AND SLATE

BREWHOUSE, STABLE AND COACHHOUSE,

KNOWN AS THE

"WINDSOR CASTLE" PUBLIC HOUSE.

MESSRS.

ALEX. DAVIS AND THOS. PALMER

Are favoured with instructions from Mr. Thos. Wise, to Sell by Auction, at the

Three Swans Hotel, Hungerford, on Friday, May 15, 1868, at 3 o'clock in the Afternoon,

A MODERN-BUILT

BRICK & SLATE FREEHOLD DWELLING HOUSE,

Known as the "Windsor Castle" public house, arranged with brick kitchen, bay-windowed parlour, and four bedrooms, small garden, with brick and slate brewhouse, with well of good water, brick and slate stable and coachhouse, facing the road leading to Little Bedwyn, and close to Fore Bridge on the Canal.

May be viewed prior to the Sale, by applying to Mr. Wise, on the Premises, and particulars with Conditions of Sale may be had of G. H. Long, Esq., Solicitor, Windsor, or of the Auctioneers, Valuers, and Estate Agents, Market Place, Newbury, Berks.

BLACKET AND SON, PRINTERS, NEWBURY.

Three Notable Priests

One of the most interesting vicars of Great Bedwyn was Revd John Ward (b.1795) who was an historian, genealogist and amateur archaeologist. He was the second son of John Ward, agent to the Ailesbury family and grandson of Revd Francis Ward of Stramshall, Staffordshire. He became vicar of Great Bedwyn in 1826, following James Hall, and married Ann Merriman at St George's, Westminster, in 1823. He resigned from Great Bedwyn in 1850. One of his five daughters, Elizabeth, married John Fall who farmed at Warren Farm (or Home Farm) in Savernake. Their descendants, the Tosh family, were living in Great Bedwyn until the late 1980s. The Falls later moved to Wharf Farm, Burbage, in 1874, and were renowned for their agricultural steam engines.

John Ward in a drawing by H. Smith.

When his first wife died in 1844, John Ward married Helen Stuart in Wath near Ripon, Yorkshire, where he was rector and rural dean. A book written by him, together with a transcript of every monumental inscription in the churchyard and church, plus notes on the history of the church is still in the parish, and he also wrote a short history of the parish and church of Great Bedwyn.

During his time in Bedwyn, Ward was responsible for the construction of the church's turret (spiral) staircase leading to the ringing chamber, the foundation-stone for which was laid by the vicar's eldest son, Samuel Hawkes Foster Ward, on 1 May 1840. The work was completed on 1 September. The expense of these alterations was defrayed by subscription headed by the Marquess of Ailesbury, who also gave the Portland stone steps for the turret staircase. John Ward gave a paten to the parish in 1831 and the screen dividing the chancel from the body of the church was restored by the vicar in 1832. In September 1837 repairs were carried out to the east window, at which time the coping was renewed and a stone cross placed at the apex, together with a similar cross at the apex of the north transept. The Marquess of Ailesbury met the total costs of some £15.10s. In April 1840, the end of the north transept was thoroughly repaired, with new copings and new heads to the buttresses carried out by John Lloyd for £7.14s.6d.

Revd William Collings Lukis, MA, who was born in Guernsey, succeeded John Ward in 1850. Educated at Trinity College, Cambridge, he was at East Grafton as perpetual curate between 1846 and 1850 and vicar of Great Bedwyn from 1850–55. He was rector of Collingbourne Ducis from 1855–62.

William Lukis lived at Bedwyn House in the High Street and was remembered as an archaeologist, who continued the excavations started by Revd John Ward at the site of the Roman villa in Bedwyn Brail, producing a very fine set of drawings of the mosaics found on the site.

A major restoration of St Mary's Church took place between 1853 and 1855, under the supervision of Thomas Henry Wyatt (1807–80), the well-known church architect, who designed St Katharine's in 1860. The work involved a rebuild of the nave and south aisle, replacement of the roof and repair of the old walls. A new east window and a new font and pulpit in Caen stone were supplied and the bells were rehung so that the heavy bells in the centre of the tower swung in the opposite direction in order to minimise the vibration. The restoration is said to have cost £2,000, which was raised by rate and subscription.

Revd John Dryden Hodgson, MA, succeeded William Lukis in 1855. He was the son of barrister John Hodgson, and brother of Henry Hodgson, Recorder of Ludlow. He was educated at Peterhouse, Cambridge, but was also a Fellow of Perne and Ramsey before being admitted to Lincoln's Inn in 1844. He was ordained in 1846 and served as curate of Sawbridgeworth in Hertfordshire between 1847 and 1849, of Great Baddow in Essex, 1849–51, and was perpetual curate of East Grafton from 1951–55. As well as serving as the vicar of Great Bedwyn from 1855–74, Dryden's other positions included: rural dean of Marlborough (1860–75), rector of Collingbourne Ducis (1875–1896), chaplain to the Marquess of Ailesbury and canon of Salisbury Cathedral (1878–96).

Dryden married Frances Ann, daughter of Revd John Thomas, vicar of Great Bursted, Essex. He died in 1896 aged 74. He is chiefly remembered for his remarkable visiting book, a record of parishioners and their children and their occupations for both Great Bedwyn and Collingbourne Ducis, which is now held in the Wiltshire County Archives in Trowbridge.

Chapter 7
RELIGION & EDUCATION

RELIGION
Early Days

Iron-Age people in Wiltshire would have worshipped universal deities found throughout the Celtic world as well as individual spirits associated with local cults. There is little archaeological evidence of these pagan religions but some images on pottery, coins and brasswork have been associated with Celtic gods and goddesses. The excavation of the disc barrow at Tor Mead (Forest Hill) produced some finds which were believed to be offerings to Gods to bring success to hunting and prosperity to crops.

The Romans usually made little attempt to suppress other religions in the territories they conquered; their gods tended to merge with the local ones, perhaps to increase their potency and acceptability. Mercury, who was regarded as the guardian of livestock and had special significance for woodland hunters, might well have supplanted the Celtic gods who had previously been worshipped in this area.

Christianity

The beginnings of Christianity in southern Britain date back to Roman times. A gold ring mounted with a cross from the third or fourth century AD was found at the Roman villa in Bedwyn Brail. This could be an early Christian artefact although the cross was never uniquely a Christian symbol. Nevertheless it is possible that the owner of the Roman villa was a Christian and, if so, it is likely that efforts would have been made to convert his British workforce. Historians believe that by the fourth century Christianity had become the major religion in Roman Britain; however, it is unlikely that it had totally supplanted all other pagan cults. Christianity among the Romano-British died out slowly after the Roman withdrawal at the beginning of the fifth century; this process was accelerated in areas dominated by the pagan Saxons. No Romano-British or early-Saxon graves have been found locally, probably because they are buried under buildings or well below plough-blade depth. The earliest indication we have of Saxons anywhere near our area is from pagan burials in a Saxon cemetery dating from AD450–500 at Collingbourne Ducis. There is also a report of a pagan temple at Harrow Farm (next to the A4) by AD625; the word harrow in Anglo-Saxon (hearg-wih or weoh) often refers to a temple or shrine. By the time of St Augustine's mission to Britain, which began in Kent in AD593, it seems that Christianity in this area had very likely lost whatever influence it might previously have enjoyed.

It then took some 40 years before Christianity began to reassert itself in Wiltshire with the conversion of the members of the West Saxon royal families. It would then have taken more time to filter through to the peasants and been fully accepted by them. It was not until AD905 that it was deemed necessary to build a church here: it is recorded that Alhund, the Bishop of Winchester, bought land in Great Bedwyn for the purpose. In support of this is an entry in a tenth-century manuscript copy of some Latin Gospels, which instructs that 'two parts of the tithes from Bedwyn and Lambourn should be used for the sustenance of God's servants at Bedwyn.' This implies the existence of a mother or minster church, which was staffed by several priests to serve its dependant chapels. The instructions came from a man called Æthelweard who, it is believed, was the Earl of the Wessex Provinces and died in AD998. These Latin Gospels are in the Berne Museum in Switzerland but a photograph of them is held by Devizes Museum.

Additionally the Domesday Book of 1086 states that a priest called Bristoardus held the church in Bedwyn and that his father held it before him in the time of Edward the Confessor (1042–66). There is no further evidence to suggest that this minster church was of monastic status, but it is not unreasonable to think that a significant church would have grown up as the focus of the large royal estate close beside King Alfred's (AD871–899) stronghold at Chisbury. At around this time Ramsbury had become the seat of a bishopric, so that is a more likely site for a monastery if one had ever developed locally.

Rectors

The lands of the Church were valued in the Domesday Book at 60s. and covered one-and-a-half hides (about 180 acres) which was par for the course for a minster church; this was but a small part of the overall Bedwyn estate of 80 hides and eight mills. Soon after, in 1092, King William II gave the tithes (revenue) from this Church property to Bishop Osmund at Old Sarum Cathedral. He in turn granted them to the rector of Bedwyn.

The rector of a parish was the person who recommended to the bishop who should be the vicar in charge of each church in his parish, as well as deciding how the tithe revenue was to be spent, other than on himself. We know the names of only six rectors (or prebendaries as they were sometimes called). One was Nicholas Wickham, who in 1405 visited the church of Little Bedwyn in the same year that Little Bedwyn's priest was first authorised to give the sacraments. Another, Thomas Beckington, was secretary and tutor to Henry VI and later became Bishop of Bath and Wells. Rectors had both moral and religious jurisdiction over their parishioners through the Church Courts. An interesting extract from the records of such a court on 10 May 1409 reads: 'Bedwynde... John Crop, defamed of having stolen Richard Colyngbourne's capons and hens, purged.'

The Dissolution of the Monasteries

Ordained priests controlled all matters connected with the Church. This situation lasted until the Dissolution of the Monasteries under Henry VIII. Then all the powers, which had been in the hands of the rector, were transferred to laymen and, in the case of Bedwyn, to the Duke of Somerset and his successors. In effect this transfer of religious authority and finances went to the wardens of Savernake Forest and stayed with them until 1847.

Medieval Times

In the early-medieval period the parish of Bedwyn covered some 14,000 acres. Contained within this area were five chapels of ease, some of which may at times have had a permanent chaplain, as well as at least one private manorial chapel at Crofton. Today only St Michael's at Little Bedwyn and St Martin's at Chisbury are anything more than ruins.

There are still signs of the chapel at Knowle although its history is lost. It was made of flint and sarsen stones in the shape of a simple parallelogram like St Martin's and the old East Grafton chapel of St Nicholas. Although there are no remains of the old East Grafton chapel, its history has been documented. It stood as early as 1302 in the field opposite the present church and its foundations and debris of stained

Right: *Latten pax found at East Grafton.*

Below: *Parish of Bedwyn in the fourteenth century.*

glass and pavement tiles were dug up in 1844 when the new church was being built. Later a farmer found a beautiful fifteenth-century gilt latten pax in a nearby hedgerow; this can be seen in Devizes Museum.

The chapel at Marten was standing in 1313 but was not served after 1486. The one at Wilton was known to exist in 1405 but passed out of recorded history 35 years later. The private manorial chapel at Crofton, first mentioned in 1317, had become dilapidated by 1405 and was last mentioned in 1414. The reasons for the abandonment of many chapels in this period could be attributed to depopulation following the Black Death and subsequent plagues.

The Vestry & Churchwardens

The Poor Law, which was introduced in 1601, made each parish responsible for the welfare of its inhabitants, and each year overseers of the poor were appointed from the landowners of the parish; they worked in close contact with the churchwardens, the overseers of the highways (or waywardens) and the constables (tythingmen), and had regular meetings of the Vestry, with the object of conducting parish and church business. Rates were raised for a church rate and a poor rate, based on property in the parish.

The duties of the churchwardens involved more responsibility than their present-day counterparts, and in addition to their regular church duties they were involved in pest control, checking that the public houses did not sell alcohol during the time of services, and helping official travellers financially. Vestries frequently purchased and ran fire-engines (Aldbourne has two good examples in the church). The churchwardens were, because of their greater responsibility, the senior members of the Vestry.

In many ways the overseers of the poor had a more difficult task, which involved weekly meetings in the church each Sunday to hear requests for clothes, shoes,

Knowle +

Chisbury +
St Martin's

+ Little Bedwyn
St Michael's

+ Great Bedwyn
St Mary's

Crofton +

Wilton +

+ Marten

+
East Grafton
St Nicholas's

medicine and medical attention. They were also expected to arrange employment for the able-bodied poor who could be put to work in road mending or knitting. Apprenticeships were arranged for children of the parish. In 1723 an Act of Parliament encouraged individual parishes to set up poorhouses as places of refuge, employment or punishment.

In the first half of the eighteenth century, the harvests were sufficiently good to feed the greater part of the population, resulting in fewer calls for the overseers of the poor to assist. However, this was not the case for later years, resulting in an increase in poor rates. Most families in rural areas were able to provide for themselves with vegetables that supplemented bought bread and pork, and home-brewed ale (small beer) was the main drink for most families. Home-brewing went into decline in 1780 after the introduction of Lord North's tax, which led to the formation of commercial breweries. Some poor people may have qualified to receive assistance from Friendly Societies from the latter part of the eighteenth century.

In 1834 an Act of Parliament, the Poor Law Amendment Act, moved the responsibility from the Vestry and overseers to the Unions of Parishes under poor law guardians; this move resulted in the workhouse in Wilton being constructed. As the nineteenth century progressed, the parish's responsibility for social conditions diminished progressively until the introduction of Parish Councils in 1894; these removed the Vestry's remaining social functions. The Vestry's sole responsibility with the Church was finally transferred when the Parochial Church Councils were introduced in 1922.

Churchwardens & Overseers of the Poor

1743 John Cumming and Christopher Abraham Shephard paid Land Tax at 4s. for Bedwyn church land.
Revd William Loggon was the Vicar and the Churchwardens were Thomas Cannon and Edward Tanner. For the year, Church Rate was £32.7s.11d. and the Church Rents were £9.18s.2d.

1745 The churchwardens were James Ralfe and William Pinckney. The overseers were Thomas Cannon, Edward Tanner and Daniel Bushell.

1746 The overseers were Thomas Scane, Robert Long, William Hawkins and John White.

1752 Revd W. Harrison was the curate and John White and Edward Tanner were the churchwardens.

1809–11 Thomas Hawkins and James Pike were churchwardens.

1812 Payment of £1 was made on 31 March to J. Wooldridge for washing the surplices and sacrament linen.

1829 The overseers of the poor were Mr Pike, Mr Tanner, Mr Hewitt, Mr Edwards.
Paid the Sexton's Bill for looking after the clock as usual: £1.5s.0d.
Paid Mrs Thatcher's bill (the Cross Keys) for sacramant Wine: £2.8s.0d.

1830 Paid John Hoare for maintaining the poor for 1 month in the workhouse: £7.14s.0d.

1833 Paid to James Ralph for maintaining the poor for 1 month in the workhouse: £5.8s.6d.

1839 Paid to William Jackman for maintaining the poor for 1 month in the workhouse: £7.1s.2d.

1841 24th March. J. Wooldridge one year's salary as Parish Clerk to Easter 1843: £8.0s.0d.

1842 18th April. James Pickett's Bill Paid for Repairing Church Windows: £3.3s.0d.

1852 Revd William Lukis was the Vicar and James Pike and Thomas Potter were the churchwardens.

1853 27th Jan. John Lloyd's Bill for Colouring the Church Walls and Ceilings: £8.8s.11d.
Mrs Thatcher's Bill for Sacramant Wine: £1.5s.0d.
Thomas Hercomb's Bill for repair to the bells and roof: £2.3s.9d.
Thomas P. Abery's Bill for parish chest: £1.18s.9d.
C.E. Wooldridge's Bill for attending to Church clock for half a year: £0.16s.3d.
Mr Pike's Bill for sacramaent bread: £0.4s.0d.
Four men putting tarpaulin on the church: £0.2s.6d.

1853 5th April. Mr Pickett the balance of this account in Part of his Bill for new leading part of the nave of the church: £15.4s.7d.

TOTAL EXPENSES FOR THE YEAR 1853: £44.18s.1d.

1856 14th April. Received of the Marquess of Ailesbury, One Year's rent of Church Land due Lady Day.: £18.0s.0d.

1872 Taxes Paid.
Ailesbury, Marquess: £586.16s.6d.
Edwards (Harding): £3.9s.4d.
Revd J.D. Hodgson: £7.10s.4d.
James Lidderdale: £2.14s.6d.
Thomas Norris: £7.11s.0d.
Charles Smallbones: £4.4s.0d.

Taken from a church document, 1836, held in Wiltshire Record Office.

St Mary's, Great Bedwyn

At the time of the Domesday Book, the population of the ex-Saxon royal estate of Bedwyn stood at around 1,000 people, not all of whom would have been concentrated in the main settlement at Bedwyn. The size of the Saxon church would probably have reflected the needs of the immediate population, but it has been suggested that the late-Norman one was more a statement of the power of the Church and in particular that of the Bishop of Sarum. Perhaps one should not dismiss this view when one finds that he commissioned the building of Devizes Castle, which was adjudged by the Crown as too sumptuous and consequently sequestered. In any event the present twelfth-century building lies above some impressive Saxon foundations so it is likely that the church here has been a landmark for some time.

The chancel was rebuilt in the mid- to late-thirteenth century in Chilmark stone, which is the same material as that used on Salisbury Cathedral. Underneath are blocks of sarsen stone, below which are graves from an earlier period indicating that the site has a very long religious connection. Flint is the main material used for the outer walls and it has been suggested that the source was the Roman villa in the Brail.

Above: *St Mary's Church seen from the north-west in 1830.*

Left: *The layout of St Mary's Church, Great Bedwyn.*

In the mid-nineteenth century the church was given an extensive Victorian-style makeover. Fortunately this did not completely alter all the original architectural features of the earlier church. The only work done by Lloyds the stonemasons was the new turret staircase, which leads to the belfry. The drawing *(left)* was completed before all these alterations took place, and if one accepts that the artist did not use too much licence, then it is possible to see the extent of some of the Victorian alterations. Notice the shortening of the window over a new north entrance and the very different pitch to the roof.

The earliest part of the present church is the nave. Its piers and arches are a combination of Norman and early-English features in a style which has sometimes been called Transitional (late-eleventh to twelfth centuries). The table below shows some of the features to look for when identifying the different architectural styles.

The narrow lancet windows of the chancel place its rebuilding in the mid- to late-thirteenth century.

Medieval Architectural Periods

Date	Style	Features to consider
1066–1200	*Norman*	*Chevron mouldings on rounded arches, volute/scalloped capitals to piers.*
1200–1300	*Early-English*	*Narrow pointed single light windows (lancet), rounded shafts to piers, stiff leaf mouldings on capitals.*
1300–1350	*Decorated*	*Lightly cut mouldings with ogee curves, slightly flatter arches.*
1350–1660	*Perpendicular*	*Wider windows, less pointed arches, some flat headed. Simple regularity of window tracery, embattlements added to towers and clerestories built above nave.*

All but the top entry are Gothic in overall style.

*Interior of St Mary's Church showing
chevron mouldings on the arches.*

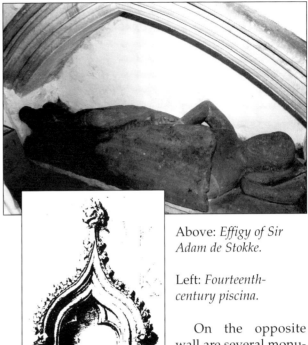

Above: *Effigy of Sir
Adam de Stokke.*

Left: *Fourteenth-
century piscina.*

The transepts were added before 1331 under the guidance of Sir Adam de Stokke and the crossing was rebuilt in the same period in the Decorated style. It probably replaced an earlier tower, which tended to be a feature of both Saxon and Norman churches. The final medieval alterations came around 1485 when the aisles were altered, the clerestory built above the nave and all the roof pitches flattened. The pierced embattlements were added to the tower at this time. The style is uniquely English and called Perpendicular.

Discoveries Made During Victorian Refurbishment

Between 1853 and 1855 during the Victorian refurbishments, which included rebuilding the dilapidated west wall, some segments of old stone coffins were found in the wall. The lid of one had a carved symbol indicating that it had been used for a Knight Templar. Also during this restorative work a number of ancient frescos were found on the walls of the transept, which have since been covered to preserve them. The north wall contained large figures of saints, bishops and knights. These knights wore armour which had two pieces of iron coming up from their shoulders; these eyelets were in fashion for only a short period at the beginning of the fourteenth century, and so this helps to date the transepts.

Interesting Features

Inside the church there are a couple of main features worth viewing. The first of these is the stone effigy of Sir Adam de Stokke in the south transept. He died in 1313. He has crossed legs, the sign of a crusader. Buried under the adjacent arch is his son Sir Roger de Stokke who followed him 20 years later.

Another main feature is in the sanctuary, on the south wall. It is a fourteenth-century Decorated piscina with a fine ogee head.

On the opposite wall are several monuments including an Elizabethan memorial to Sir John Seymour, father of Queen Jane, who was wife of Henry VIII and mother to Edward VI. Above the adjacent two brasses and placed in the lancet window are the remnants of stained glass brought to the church in 1901 from Wolfhall, Lady Jane's home.

The 1854 iron screen across the chancel is the work of a Collingbourne Ducis blacksmith called Jo Easeby. The Marquess of Ailesbury, whose family estate covered both villages, presented the screen but it is interesting to speculate as to why the Bedwyn blacksmith failed to be given the job.

A fine wooden screen dating from around 1350 would have stood in the crossing between the chancel and the nave. This screen was removed during the Victorian refurbishment and after a number of adventures it was returned in 1975 to its present position between the north transept and the crossing.

*The wooden
rood-screen
in its
original
position.*

One of the bells made by Henry Knight in 1671.

The preaching cross in St Mary's churchyard in 1800.

*Bell-ringers in 1901. Left to right, back row:
Billy Holloway (head porter), Jim Broadway (farmer),
Joey Read (vicar), ? Emerson (Smallbones shopkeeper), ?;
front row: Herbert Beckenham (gardener),
George Hart (blacksmith), Harry Ryman, ?, ?, ?;
sitting on floor: A. Ryman.*

The tower contains seven bells which represent one of the heaviest rings in Wiltshire weighing altogether 4¼ tons. The oldest bell was cast in 1633 and its inscription reads, 'In the Lord doo I trust IWD'. Three more date from 1671 and their inscriptions read 'Henry Knight of Reading made mee'. It is not known when bells first pealed out from St Mary's, but collections were made to fund some as early as 1405 and by 1553 there were five bells in the tower. The tower correspondent in 2003 is Stuart Sellwood.

The Churchyard

Outside the church between the war memorial and the north-west door is a preaching cross *(opposite)*, parts of which date from the 1300s. Although rather eroded, the painted figure is said to depict a bishop. In 1850 there were the remains of a sundial on the top, but this was replaced in 1889 by a crucifix. Part of the plinth is also a Victorian restoration. It is not certain that the cross was always in its present location in the village as

preaching crosses were sometimes to be found in market-places; perhaps the cross started its life in the High Street. However, there is a record from 25 November 1449 which relates to a London churchyard:

*... stode a crosse of the height of a man or more,
and that same
crosse was worshipped by the parisshens there
as crosses be
commonly worshipped in other churchyards.*

Also on the outside of the church and sadly not that easy to read, up on one of the buttresses of the southern transept, is a faded Greek inscription dated 1684. It is encouraging Christian warriors to persevere. This date is close to the end of the reign of King James II, the last Catholic king, and might have indicated that religious life in Bedwyn during and since the Civil War had not been uneventful. It has been suggested that the defaced wall statue behind the pulpit suffered from the attentions of Cromwell's soldiers.

St Michael's, Little Bedwyn

St Michael's Church in Little Bedwyn also dates from the late-twelfth or early-thirteenth century. Similar to St Mary's the earliest parts are in the Transitional style and it is built over an earlier Saxon church, although this may well have only extended under the present nave.

There were three distinct periods of construction; the circular arches over the north aisle and the rounded piers of both aisles are the earliest. The square-headed windows and flattened arches of the doorways indicate later Gothic work when the external flint walls were also renovated. The elegant 70-foot spire was a fifteenth-century addition.

Historically St Michael's interior is a little sparse apart from the fourteenth-century font but this has a Victorian cover. Of the four bells, two were originally cast in 1581 by James Wills of Aldbourne but were recast in the nineteenth century; the other two bells were cast in the seventeenth century.

Right: *St Michael's seen from the south-west.*

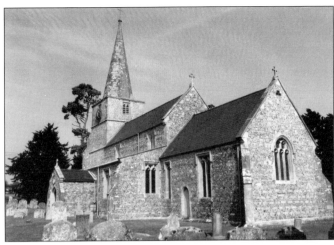

Above and below:
The arches over the aisles in St Michael's Church.

Carving on a capital of a column in St Michael's Church, Little Bedwyn.

WILTSHIRE GAZETTE AND HERALD THURSDAY JUNE 13, 1963.

LIGHTNING STRIKES CHURCH AT BEDWYN

THE top of Little Bedwyn Parish Church spire, including the cross, collapsed on Sunday night when it was struck by lightning in one of the worst thunderstorms the village has suffered in living memory.

The Vicar of Little Bedwyn, the Rev. P. E. Bird, with the damaged cross.

The lightning, which struck the spire, cracked it from top to bottom, sending debris through the roof of the church. It was 6 p.m. —but there was no Evensong for a service had been held in the morning by the newly-inducted incumbent, the Rev. Peter Bird.

"It was a terrific bang," commented a woman living in a cottage next to the church. "I knew something had gone, but it was pouring with rain and I couldn't get outside to see what. I can't remember a storm as bad as that one."

ROOF HOLED

As there is no immediate danger in the church, Mr. Bird has decided that it is safe to continue services there.

On the scene soon after the spire collapsed was people's warden, Mr. E. Harrison. He told a Wiltshire Gazette and Herald reporter: "There were three holes in the roof of the church caused by falling masonry but luckily the stones fell at an angle and most of them missed the church.

"A boy who saw it from his bedroom window, Robin Harris, said that the wrought iron cross just bent over and disappeared with the stones of the spire.

"The steeple is cracked from the top almost to the bottom corner. The top four courses are definitely unsafe and will have to come down. Most of the spire will have to be taken down and rebuilt I think but most of the stones are all right and can be re-used."

BUILT 800 YEARS

Mr. Harrison said that as far as he knew the steeple was the original built with the rest of the church about 800 years ago. "There are engravings on copper and lead, though, which show it has been attended to several times," he added.

An interesting feature of the church is the arches. One is pure Norman in style and the other Early English. And it appears they were both built by the same masons—the same who built Great Bedwyn Church.

"This shows that the church must have been built during the time of the transition of building styles," said Mr. Harrison.

There are also supposed to be two monuments in the chancel but these disappeared when the church was restored round about 1860.

The storm also blacked-out the village until this morning, as well as killing three lambs and a sheep on a farm. A house in Little Bedwyn was also struck by lightning.

The lightning damaged spire of Little Bedwyn Parish Church. Masonry was split and the iron cross hurled into the churchyard.

Little Bedwyn was definitely a separate parish of some 4,000 acres by the sixteenth century when its parish boundaries were independently delineated. However, there are grounds for thinking that 1405, by which time the vicar was authorised to give the sacraments, marks the independence of the two parishes, which continues up to the present day. The authority to give the sacraments (christening, marriage, burial) brought with it a voluntary donation to the vicar. There is no record of the creation of a prebendary at Little Bedwyn at that date.

In 1963 there was a lightning strike which extensively damaged the spire. It is ironic to recall that the advice given to the Parish Council less than a year before was that a lightning conductor was not necessary.

St Martin's, Chisbury

Within the parish of Little Bedwyn lies the thirteenth-century chapel of ease of St Martin's at Chisbury. St Martin reputedly dealt rather abruptly with heathens and perhaps a chapel in a pagan hill-fort dedicated to him seemed very appropriate. It is difficult to suggest a context for the present construction as other than a successor chapel, placed by or possibly over, the gateway to the Alfredian burghal-hidage fort. It is in the shape of a single parallelogram with no division between the sanctuary and the nave, which is very much in the Saxon style. The probable abandonment of the hill-fort in favour of the settlement below it in Bedwyn in the early-tenth century suggests that the original chapel is of ninth-century origin. The present building is made of flint with Bath stone for the worked parts. It was built when the early-English style was moving towards the Decorated and this can best be seen in the lancet form of the nave windows and the tracery of the sanctuary windows. There would have been a wooden screen across the sanctuary but all that remain are the marks for this on the walls.

John ApMan was St Martin's priest in 1534 on a stipend of £2.13s.4d. per annum, which was about a quarter that of the vicar at St Mary's. The chapel was out of use in 1547 at the time of the Reformation; the parishioners had then to make the journey down

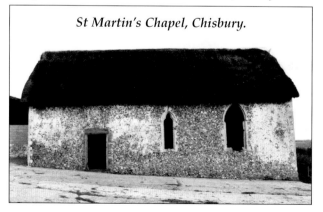

St Martin's Chapel, Chisbury.

to either Great or Little Bedwyn. The building was restored in 1942 and is now maintained by English Heritage. Currently one service a year is held there.

Church Records

The church records in Wiltshire have not survived intact and there are many gaps from before the Dissolution of the Monasteries. The nominal roll of vicars from 1548 can be found in St Mary's and from slightly later in St Michael's. The registers in St Mary's have also been well kept with entries on baptisms from 1553, marriages from 1539 and burials from 1538. In the case of Little Bedwyn the registers begin in 1722 and, apart from a few of the very early years, are complete. There follow certain details taken from medieval times:

In 1317 the chaplain of the private chapel at Crofton Braboef Manor was entitled to all the tithes from the demesne at Crofton and could hold a croft and the income from a barn. In turn he paid 13s.6d. to the rector of Bedwyn and 7d. to the lord of the manor. His duties seemed hardly arduous as he was prohibited from administering the sacraments and could only say Mass when the lord of the manor was present. Perhaps this was taken into account when one reads that in 1405 his Vicarage and chapel were in great disrepair.

In that year the vicar of Great Bedwyn was accused of frequenting taverns, an accusation he denied. In this he was ably assisted by his clerk who 'customarily sits with his ale when he ought to go with the vicar to visit the sick.' Who was leading whom astray? By 1412 the vicar was in more trouble as he had failed to appoint any chaplains, apparently as a result of the poverty of the Vicarage. It could have been worse; at a time of clerical celibacy, the priest of nearby Burbage was accused in the Church Courts by his parishioners of adultery with at least five wives by whom he had many children. By 1535 the value of the Great Bedwyn Vicarage showed little increase from the previous century – it was just £9. This contrasts with the fact that in the early-fifteenth century St Mary's was rich in plate, books and vestments and had a box covered in silk containing saintly relics.

In more modern times the Vicarage was still adjudged to be poor; it was valued at £20 in 1678 and £212 in 1830. Fortunately for the vicar his income around then was being supplemented by Parliament to the tune of £600 and by Marquess Ailesbury with £400. It was not until the twentieth century that a vicar could expect a regular income based on UK-wide parameters.

The Nineteenth Century & Beyond

The more modern religious buildings in this area date from the nineteenth century. When, in the 1850s,

Above: *The interior of St Katharine's Church.*

Left: *St Katharine's Church, Savernake Forest.*

the main hall in Tottenham House became too small for the congregation at daily prayers, St Katharine's in Savernake Forest was built. It was constructed of flint with ashlar stone dressings in early-fourteenth-century style under the direction of the architect T.H. Wyatt. It was funded through the Marchioness of Ailesbury and dedicated to her Russian mother Katharine Voronzoff, after whom a gate and toll-house along the A4 into Savernake Forest was also named. In the days soon after the Bishop of Salisbury consecrated St Katharine's, the congregation numbered around 160 of whom over a third were communicants. This gives an idea of the size of the staff at Tottenham House and the number of people employed on the land around it.

Unfortunately the accidental ammunition explosion nearby on 7 July 1945 caused extensive damage to the structure of the church as well as destroying nearly all the Victorian stained glass. Services were held for the next seven years in the schoolroom, mainly by the Revd E.G. Courtman, the vicar of Mildenhall. Largely through the efforts of Noel Tilley, the chairman of the Parish Council, and Admiral Portal, repairs were put in hand to recreate the church in its original style. This took six years and the church was reopened on Easter Day, 1952.

Methodism

The first reference that we have to the Nonconformists, as they were called, is to the Wesleyans who gained some support in Great Bedwyn in 1787. Establishing their own purpose-built chapel proved to be no easy matter and not until they had gained the approval of the landowner, the Marquess of Ailesbury, were any constructed. Prior to that, they had to make use of existing buildings, which then had to be certified for use. In Great Bedwyn this was in a cottage on the north-west side of Church Street and could well have been on the land currently occupied by the Vicarage. Records show that in 1825 Methodists were meeting at cottages in Crofton and at Bedwyn Common and that by 1828 a cottage in Chisbury was in use too. This could well be the one in the centre of the hamlet, which was used as a chapel for many years in the twentieth century.

By 1834 the Great Bedwyn Methodists had rented a room which served as a cooper's store and was part of the Old Malt House on Church Street. Around this time Mr John May provided a home for preachers in the farmhouse in Frog Lane, which burned down in 1938/39.

In Little Bedwyn there were a number of houses being used for worship prior to the building of the Methodist chapel in 1846. This was next to the Harrow Inn and its proximity limited the licence of the inn to six days a week. This did not change until late into the twentieth century.

There were reports of religious intolerance in those early days, but clearly this was no deterrent. By 1851 the congregation in Great Bedwyn numbered around 150 and perhaps this was influential in eventually gaining the Marquess of Ailesbury's permission for the purpose-built chapel in Brown's Lane. This opened in 1875 and a Sunday school was added later as a direct result of the efforts of the Evans family. Inside the chapel is a tablet with the words:

In memory of William and Elizabeth Evans, who for more than 40 years prayed, toiled and sacrificed for the Cause of God and the establishment of Methodism in the village...

William died in 1896 and his wife the following year. She was presented with a quilt in 1890 with motifs covering the history of the Bedwyn Society from

The Methodist chapel in Brown's Lane, Great Bedwyn.

Inside the Methodist chapel.

1797, the founding of the Temperance Society in 1840 and the Bazaar of 1890. The chapel became a private house some time after it closed in 1967.

Church Music

St Mary's Church Choir, Great Bedwyn, 1930. Left to right, back row: ? , ?, Arthur Middleton, Bert Davis, Ben Lloyd, Revd Phillips, Miss Bravery (organist), Mr Saunders, Mr Downton, Victor Bennett, ?, Kathleen Kempster; front row: ?, ?, ?, ?, Arthur Kempster, ?, ?, ?.

The harmonium in the south transept of St Katharine's Church.

The earliest form of church music came from enthusiastic parishioners in the church band. After the Middle Ages their instruments included fiddles, flutes, clarinets and sometimes drums and bassoons. Great Bedwyn even had an accordion player in the mid-nineteenth century.

Barrel organs began to displace the church band but their repertoire must have been limited to the number of barrels and the skill of the Parish Clerk, whose job it was to keep the machine working. In turn these were phased out in preference to the pipe-organs that are still used in 2003. The organ in St Michael's was electrified in 1972, prior to which it was hand pumped. The reward (on earth) for this labour was the equivalent of 50p in 1898 and this was not increased until 1948 when it jumped to 75p. St Katharine's now has a Willis organ; other examples of this excellent type of organ can be found in St Paul's and Salisbury Cathedrals. Before that the hymns were sung to the sounds of the harmonium.

Missing Treasures

Unfortunately all the treasures of the Bedwyn churches have not survived nor are they all here in the parish. We only know about some of them.

A list of the church plate in 1891 has a cryptic note to the effect that the commissioners of Edward VI took the considerable quantity of 42 ounces of church silver plate for the use of the King, leaving only 14 ounces to the parish. In other words, three-quarters of the churches' silver disappeared to shore up the state's finances after the death of Henry VIII or into the pockets of those running the country on behalf of his under-age son. The Lord Protector at the beginning of Edward's reign was his uncle, the Duke of Somerset, who was faced with some large costs for his proposed new mansion in Bedwyn Brail.

Apparently in medieval times, St Mary's had a small stained-glass window, which by 1724 had disappeared; its existence is recorded in documents at Holkham Hall in Norfolk. The window featured a crippled figure with a flagon by his side. The Anglo-French inscription, when translated, reads:

I am Peris, called vicar of this church
I am leaning on my crutch dressed as you behold
My cup is in my grasp and I'll drink without pretence
Behind me stands my can as cans are placed today
My can and cup I'll keep under my jurisdiction
That none who drinks therefrom escape my eye.

The rhyme and an image of the crippled drinker can be seen on a painted carving on the front wall of the Lloyds' stone-mason museum in Church Street.

Left: *Sketch of Peris, a figure once depicted in a stained-glass window in St Mary's.*

There are no records of a priest called Peris, but the window might refer to a crippled beggar who became a fixture at the front door of the church and thus earned the nickname 'vicar'. Perhaps he gained the affection and sympathy of the locals who arranged this memorial to him. The precise truth remains a mystery.

The late-Saxon copy of the tenth-century Latin Gospels (see Chapter 2) are in the library in Berne in Switzerland. In addition to the instruction concerning the use of tithes, the document also covers the manumission of two women slaves from Bedwyn. It is also the earliest reference to a guild in this Saxon royal burh. In the crossing are copies of the 40 or so patterns of the twelfth- or thirteenth-century locally produced pavement tiles, some of which were used to border the paving of the chancel. Most were made to be shown in pairs, and one set measuring 9 by 6½ inches depicts a clash between a mounted Knight Templar and a Saracen carrying a long lance. The original is in the British Museum and was last seen in the village in 1967 at the Church Exhibition in St Mary's.

Crusader and Saracen pavement tiles.

St Mary's was once home to an early-thirteenth-century parish chest made of oak and ornamented with later ironwork. It can now be found in the Victoria and Albert Museum and is an important piece of early-English furniture.

At one time the church boasted a copy of the earliest type of clock; one with only a single hand. George Hewitt, a Marlborough clockmaker, was asked in 1767 to make such an old-style clock for the church. The single hand worked its way round the four successive wooden dials until 1906 when a new one was bought through public subscription. Fortunately the old clock was rescued from James Shefford's carpenter's scrap heap for the sum of £2 and can be seen in 2003 with a new face on the church tower at Rustington in Sussex.

EDUCATION

Early Days

Before the government intervened, children's education throughout the country was a voluntary matter at the whim of the local church, charity or private individual. The earliest records show that there was a schoolmaster in Great Bedwyn in 1580

and 'that up to 1791 a Swiss held a school there'. By the eighteenth century education of the poor was seen as important for health and moral reasons. However, it was many years before the idea of a child's right to a general education became a reality.

In the meantime education was strongly tied to religious instruction as personified by the Society for Promoting Christian Knowledge, which funded the setting up and running of elementary schools. Eventually an overall National Society was formed in 1811 as a Church institution to arouse interest in the elementary education of the children of the poor and to encourage the building of schools for this purpose.

Nineteenth-Century Schools

Perhaps in response to these efforts there were, in 1818, three or four day schools in Great Bedwyn parish attended by 70 children. No doubt some of these children came from the independent parish of Little Bedwyn where there was no record of any schools at that time. Some 15 years later, however, Little Bedwyn had two schools with 20 pupils while the number of children at school in Great Bedwyn had doubled and spread across some 13 schools.

In Great Bedwyn, William Cox set up a charity on 18 December 1799 for ten boys, aged between five and ten, to be taught (for free) to read the English language, and to repeat by heart the catechism of the Church of England as well as an old version of the fifteenth psalm. This confirms the strong link in those days between education and religion. He died in 1812 but it was 1824 before the accumulated rents and interest on the land in Frog Lane was sufficient to fund the appointment of a master. This was Josiah Wooldridge who, in addition to being the Parish Clerk, was five times portreeve of Bedwyn (the senior elected official of the borough market and whose staff of office can be seen in Devizes Museum). If the boys' parents wanted them to learn to write or to be capable of arithmetic, which incidentally was Josiah's subject, then they had to pay, but at half the rate of those children not on charity. Fees at a typical dame school, as they were termed, would have been around 1d. a week. When Josiah died in 1837 his son took over the teaching of these children.

Great Bedwyn National School

The Education Act of 1831 gave formal responsibility to parishes for the education of the poor. As very limited government funds were available and as these were tied to the size of local contributions, it is not surprising that establishing a National School in each parish was a slow process. In Great Bedwyn's case it was the generosity of the Marquess of Ailesbury who contributed four-fifths of the £380 needed for the building and the land. The village school was built by John Lloyd, and was completed by 1835. The master's

Pupils and staff of Great Bedwyn School between the two world wars.

salary was 15s. a week. It is interesting to compare this with the income of 1d. a week per pupil at a typical dame school. The initial 30 pupils rose to around 130 by 1856. These would have included, from 1846, the ten boys and girls being educated by the Cox's Charity.

Little Bedwyn National School

Some of these children came from Little Bedwyn until 1840, when a school was opened in a room to the left of what is now Denby Cottage opposite the footbridge over the canal and railway. Prior to that there had been a school in Church Street. It was not until 1854 that the school was moved to its permanent home next to the Vicarage. We have to assume that the mason responsible for carving the '4' of 1854 had not benefitted too much from his education, as the figure is backwards!

St Katharine's National School

In Tottenham House Park the wooden building which was being used as a school was converted into a summer-house in 1858. A new school was opened in 1865 next to the church and is still in use as a primary school in 2003.

In the nineteenth century St Katharine's National School only took girls; the boys either went elsewhere or just did not attend. It was not until the 1870 Education Act that local authorities were given the power to compel children between five and ten years to go to school. It is of interest to note that in 1871 nearly a quarter of those getting married in this area had to sign the church register with an 'X'.

Little Bedwyn School is now a private residence.

St Katharine's School, Savernake Forest, in 1999.

*Mrs Turner, head teacher of St Katharine's School,
with some of her pupils in 1920.*

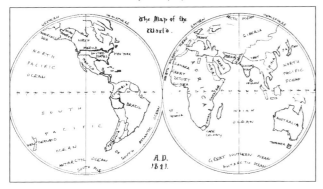

*World map, 1841. In 2003 it is displayed in the surgery
in Church Street, Great Bedwyn. It is a listed object.*

Teaching Styles

The style of teaching at national schools was largely based on the monitorial system. Most often the school had just one teacher who was responsible for keeping order in the one room of the school; teenage monitors each tried to make their group memorise items of information through mechanical repetition. With books, writing materials and paper in short supply, holding the pupils' attention must have been a daunting task.

The Decline of Dame Schools

As more resources were given to national schools so the number of dame schools decreased. The best example we have today of the probable structure of a dame school is in the terraced houses next to the bakery on Church Street. One of the rooms in No. 5 still has bands of wood at desk height to protect the walls, and the windows inside Nos. 5 and 6 still bear scratch marks made by idle hands. Before being repaired by Lloyds' labourers many years ago, the 9-inch brick squares on the floor were in perfect condition under the area of the 18-inch wide desks around the walls. Further out there was a 2-inch deep gutter where feet had scuffed and worn the bricks away. The door inside one of the rooms in

No. 5 is still in two halves with a solid iron bar, which can be slotted across to close off the bottom half. With the top half open, Miss Wooldridge, the teacher in the 1820s, could keep an eye on her pupils as well as cook. We do not know when her school in Church Street closed but a Miss Wooldridge is recorded as the schoolmistress at the National School in 1842. The record of Miss Franklin's dame school in Crofton ceases after 1866. This was held in an old thatched cottage, which was on the site of one of the current brick-and-slate houses. Some have suggested that it was also on the site of the medieval St John Hospice, which had lands in Crofton.

Teaching Standards

With the limited government support through grants based on attendance and exams came the Inspectors. Their reports give an insight into conditions in the schools. In 1859 Great Bedwyn had 70 pupils in a room with boarded floors and parallel desks. Instruction and discipline were fair but of an elementary kind, perhaps because the master was uncertificated. By 1878, with 153 pupils, space per child was around 10 square feet, the desks were tiered and new desks had been affixed to the infants' gallery. Given that the classrooms must have been very crowded, it is not surprising that desks were tiered so that those at the back were still easy to supervise from the front of the class. However, by 1894 matters had got worse, perhaps in part due to a falling off of the essential local contributions needed to run the place.

Fortunately a new headmaster arrived: the well-respected and experienced Edward R. Pole who had been master at Little Bedwyn some time before. The dark and dismal main rooms that were badly in need of better ventilation were rapidly transformed over an extended harvest break of some seven weeks, by putting in windows at both ends of the building as well as replacing the curtains between classes by fully boarded partitions. The inspection report for the following year described the school in glowing terms.

Edward Robert Pole, Headmaster

Edward Pole was a graduate of St Mark's College, Chelsea, the earliest Church of England teacher-training college. He spent two years there and straight

*Edward R. Pole,
headmaster of both
Great and Little Bedwyn
National Schools.*

after graduating in 1864 he became master at Little Bedwyn. He remained there until 1885 when he moved to Ramsbury before his final move to Great Bedwyn. The annual inspection reports covering his last decade in charge at Little Bedwyn are all highly complimentary. For example, the one for 1879 reads: 'This is a good rural school. The children are diligent and interested in their work. They might, however, be tidier in their writing.' Perhaps some things never change. Mr Pole's own school records from his time at Little Bedwyn contain some interesting entries too:

29 March 1878: A very severe snow storm on Friday prevented every child from attending school...
4 February 1888: Small attendance as no path has yet been cut through the snow to Froxfield...

The weather was not the only factor to affect attendance in this farming community, for example: 'attendance poor this week, many children potato picking and attendance not so good at end of the week, several away hay making.'

Overcrowding & Epidemics

As the size of the school has not materially changed, it is clear that accommodating the 200 children of E.R. Pole's time must have caused problems. One of the effects of this overcrowding was in the number of times the school had to close as a result of epidemics; these were not just from influenza but also from diphtheria and typhoid, cases of which were sadly sometimes fatal. Attempts were made to disinfect all surfaces and even dispose of all pens, pencils and crayons before reopening. Some primitive hand-washing facilities were provided for the boys in 1909, but the girls and infants were left to take their chances as before. The insanitary earth closets remained until around 1920 when buckets were provided.

The Twentieth Century

Eventually all elementary education came under the control of Local Education Authorities. Many new secondary schools were started at which there was a proportion of 'free places' selected by an examination of 10–11-year-olds. The school-leaving age was gradually raised until in 1918 it became 14. At the same time a distinction was made between junior and senior education and senior schools started to be established.

In the 1930s pupils in Great Bedwyn were divided into seven standards and all except the oldest sat six to eight abreast along oak forms with worktops on heavy cast-iron bases. The oldest sat in dual desks, as did the infants who were in smaller versions. There were two classrooms which could be entered through the front door, with the larger one to the left being further subdivided by a curtain. A visit to the

The cookery class of 1916 in Great Bedwyn.
Left to right, back row: *?, ?, Winnie Hawkins, Pat Webster, ?, ?;* middle row: *Kitty Scorse, Violet Scorse, ?, ?, ?, ?;* front row: *Maggie Elkins, ?.*

doctor's surgery gives an indication of the space available as the interior wall running at right angles to the front door is still in the same place. Where the receptionists now work was a further classroom with the segregated cloakrooms at either end. Classes were not segregated, but gates that stood around 6 feet high divided the playground, so that the boys and girls never met at play. Each side had their own bike sheds and toilet block. The caretaker had the thankless task of carrying the buckets to the trenches dug by the boys in the school gardens (the current allotments). Central heating, such as it was, comprised a coal stove in each of the three class-rooms. In the 1940s and '50s some use was made of the Methodist chapel in Brown's Lane as overflow accommodation for some classes.

Great Bedwyn became a primary school in 1963 (before this pupils had received their full education there). A total of 46 pupils attended in 1965 and in 1972, when Little Bedwyn School closed, another ten children joined the school. The children's home, based in the Old Vicarage and run in the 1960s and early 1970s by Tom and Dorothy Tribe, had sustained Little Bedwyn's existence. However, when this closed the village school became unviable.

The school on Church Street closed in 1994 and in 2003 its thriving successor can be found at the end of Farm Lane.

The new primary school in Farm Lane, Great Bedwyn.

Little Bedwyn School group, 1903.

Little Bedwyn School group, 1929. Left to right, fourth row: *Jim Elkins, Jim White, Ben Pazzard, Tommy Meadham, Frank James, Frank Newman, Doug Womersley, Ray Mundy;* third row: *Joan French, Mary Pounds, Kath Allen, Peggy Womersley, Vera Mason, Gladys Lawrence, Fay Picken, Florrie Lawrence, Daisy Claridge;* second row: *Roly Elkins, George Lovelock, Poppy Pazzard, Phyllis Mason, Alice Bint, Mary Womersley, Gwen Fisher, Ted Bird, Billy Fisher;* front row: *John Claridge, 'Bonny' Claridge, Tony Mason, Alf Claridge, Joe Womersley, 'Soner' Bint.*

Class of Great Bedwyn School, early 1950s. Left to right, back row: *Mr Cunningham (headmaster), Les Brooks, Robin ?, ? Paddington, Don Hawkins, Clifford Beckingham, Winifred Lovelock, Sylvia Burridge, ?;* third row: *David Claridge, Gordon Legg, ?, Jean Edwards, Mary Alderman, Margaret Alderman, Dennis Lovelock, Felicity Hill, Michael Hill;* second row: *David Regan, Ronald Crame, Harold Hawkins, Brian Hart, Brian Butler, Cyril Dines, ? Mildenhall;* front row: *Reg Mills, Daphne Hoare, Linda Blundy, Gwen Hedges, George Leonard, Brian Poole, Peter Kimber, Gerry Baldry, Stan Edwards.*

The bell is rung for afternoon lessons in September 1999.

Chapter 8

A WALK AROUND THE VILLAGES

Left: *Great Bedwyn Jubilee Lamp.*

Below: *The centre of Great Bedwyn, with Wayside Cottage and Bedwyn House.*

GREAT BEDWYN

If we start at the Chains in the centre of the village, note the Victorian lamp standard erected in 1887 as Queen Victoria's Jubilee Memorial, sited on the traffic island. The medieval Town Hall once stood on this spot, and it is from here that we can get a very good view of the centre of the village.

Walking along the left-hand side of Church Street, and away from the Chains, we pass Tudor Cottage, previously called Wayside Cottage, and at one time the property of Dr Elias Fraser, formerly of Bedwyn House. The next house, at one time a butcher's shop, immediately opposite the Corner House, was run by Cyril Bryant, who used to kill his animals in a field to the rear of the premises. Later owners included Mr Kitkat and Jo Davis who kept the business from the 1930s until the 1980s. It is probable that part of this house predates the fire of 1716.

Crossing the approach road to Coster View, we come to the bakery, which was originally started by the Bartholomew family, who later moved to Bournemouth. The Bartholomews had previously worked in the old bakery that was owned by the Evans family who had been owners of the village shop. Two sons, Fred and Billy Bartholomew, ran the

Church Street, looking north.

Left: *New housing development and Manor farmhouse* (centre).

Below left: *Moonraker's Cottage.*

Below: *St Mary's Church.*

Right: **The preaching cross in the churchyard of St Mary's.**

Main picture: *Lower End, Church Street.*

bakery for many years, before selling to Kelland of Swindon, who in turn sold the business to a Mr Collier in 1925–26. By 1932, the Haines family owned the bakery; the Merritts took over from them in 1984.

Proceeding along Church Street, we pass a continuous row of eighteenth-century cottages, which were rebuilt after the 1716 fire in Great Bedwyn. It is worth noting the plinth of the first four houses, which projects out. Nos 5 and 6 formed part of a nineteenth-century dame school (see Chapter 7); No. 6 was the home and workplace of Mr Little, the village glazier, known affectionately as Putty Little. He was a member of the Home Guard in the Second World War and his face can be seen among the photos in Chapter 10. The house was subsequently bought by Dr Fenn, where he ran his surgery.

No. 7, Wessex House, consists of three original dwellings. It was sold by the Marquess of Ailesbury to Mr Charles Smallbones in 1915. Various owners followed, including the Woods who ran a shop which faced Church Street, later to be run by the Broads. In 1953 the Midland Bank had a small branch within the main building (it had previously been located in No. 8 Church Street, at one time the home of Mr Robbins, a retired stationmaster). A draper's shop and a hair-dresser were incorporated into the cottage to the rear, and beyond the cottage the area was used as a coal yard owned by the Broad family. Bob Broad used large vehicles, and to enable access he removed a bedroom over the entrance, leaving just the ceiling.

Continue along Church Street, passing various cottages with well-proportioned dormer windows. No. 12 Church Street was an earlier Post Office. We soon come to nineteenth-century Manor Farm House, set back from the road. It is a red-brick house with a slate roof; the house together with outhouses are part of the farm run by the Kerr family who took over from Nevins Thomas Potter, who ran the farm in 1881. Earlier tenant farmers included James Pike in 1816. A private development now covers the original pig farm, farmyard and granary, which stood on staddle stones.

St Mary's Church, an imposing building which dates from 1092, when a prebend of Bedwyn was founded, was largely rebuilt in 1853–55, although it retains some original details. These include a four-teenth-century wooden rood-screen in place in 2003 between the crossing and the north transept. The screen was rescued from Warren Farm, where it had been stored from 1853 until 1919, when it was taken to the Victoria and Albert Museum, where it joined the early-thirteenth-century oak chest. It was finally reinstated in 1975. (For more details on the church see Chapter 7.)

There are five buildings of note further up Church Street to the west. The large field on the left is called Great Mead. At the end of Great Mead we come to a clap-boarded and thatched barn, previously used by the Abery family as a carpenter's shop.

Immediately beyond the turn to Wilton, we can see Mill House, a stone-built double-fronted house facing the railway and canal, built in the first half of the nineteenth century close to the site of Upper Mill, by Benjamin Lloyd for his own use. Previously the grounds included watercress beds (formerly the mill leat) run by the Philips family who sent watercress by rail to Paddington. Crossing the road and returning to the centre of the village we find Moonraker's Cottage, which in the 1940s was up for sale for £40! It was bought by George Smart of Brail Farm and later was purchased by the Haine family, together with Brail Farm. In 1949, it was bought by George Frederick Bance for £600 before being sold to a Mr Goldsmith, who in turn sold it to the Earl of Wilton. Dorothy Jobling, the Wilton family nanny, lived there in her retirement.

Some late-Victorian houses are followed by a row of council-houses, built as 'Homes for Heroes' immediately after the First World War. Most of these are now privately owned.

Around the site of the modern Vicarage are two older priests' homes. Pear Tree House was the Vicarage until 1878; Glebe House was the original Vicarage designed by George Gilbert Scott, who shared his name with his father. It was completed in 1878 and is the largest house in the village. To create the entrance to the present Vicarage an attractive thatched cottage occupied by the Standing family, whose well was sited halfway up the present drive, was demolished. Evidently brass and antiques were thrown into the well as ballast! There are then three pairs of late-nineteenth century cottages, all well designed with contrasting brickwork and slate roofs. To the rear of Pear Tree House lies Garden Cottage,

Right: *The cottage at the bottom of the Vicarage garden, with the Standing family outside, c.1930.*

The Old Rectory (Glebe House).

Left: *Garden Cottage.*

Right: *Lt-Cmdr and Mrs Dunn at Garden Cottage.*

Left: *Pair of cottages opposite St Mary's Church.*

Right: *Dr Elias Fraser's wife planting a tree to commemorate the silver jubilee of George V, 1935.*

Left: *The Croft, 94 Church Street, formerly a farmhouse.*

Right: *Corner House, Church Street.*

Below: *The Wharf.*   Right: *Frogmore Farm.*

so named by Cmdr D. Dunn, who added to an existing stable in 1950, and who was one of the founders of the Friends of Great Bedwyn Church Trust.

Beyond the Cutting Room (previously the reading-room) is the present Post Office, which was at one time the fire station. This forms part of the mason's yard, in which we can still see the village pump, now separated from the pavement by a brick wall. The Lloyds' stonemason museum contains an extraordinary range of examples of a mason's craft. Behind the Post Office on a site now occupied by a row of holiday cottages, was a Second World War rope factory run by the Betteridge family (Arthur Betteridge was a fine craftsman and built horse-drawn wagons) and demolished in the 1990s. Note the large cut stones forming part of the boundary wall; stone was reused from an earlier building.

Great Bedwyn National School, largely funded in 1835 by the Marquess of Ailesbury and built using dressed limestone, now serves the village as a doctor's surgery. Continuing past the only thatched cottage set at right angles to Church Street, we see two well-constructed red-brick and plain-tile roofed houses, separated by a yard. To the left is an old farmhouse and to the right is the Old White Hart, which ceased to be an inn during 1875. It later became Powell's shop, which sold sweets and tobacco. More recently it was owned by the late Tom and Mary Davison. The Corner House, whose garden joins the start of the High Street, was part of the Ailesbury estate, until being bought by Thomas Place of Northallerton, Yorkshire, in 1932. It was bought in 1933 by Sir Felix Pole, general manager of the Great Western Railway and chairman of Associated Electrical Industries, although he never lived in the house. Later owners included Sir Patrick Scrivener, a diplomat and one-time ambassador to Syria, as well as Dr Kingston, who had his surgery in what is now an artist's studio.

Retracing our steps to follow the alternative walk across Great Mead, cross the railway line passing Church Lock. Note the skewed brickwork construction of the canal bridge, and the stonework carried out by Benjamin Lloyd, who was superintendent of masonry in the early-nineteenth century. Above and to the front is Coster Hill, and beyond Bedwyn Brail, the site of a Roman Villa. Turn left along the tow path to the wharf, now an unsurfaced car park, but previously the site of Wally Lovelock's large work-shop, used for his trade as a wheelwright and carpenter. The wharf was also used by the village fire brigade who practiced their fire drill there. The hose was so old that water spurted from many holes!

Walk along Frog Lane with The Wharf on your left (a long thatched building with stabling at the far end, which at one time had a small shop). Opposite is a modern dwelling on the site of Frogmore Farm, converted from two separate dwellings. One of these was owned by Dame Mary Railton, Director of

Dame Mary Railton and Miss Lola Holt at the opening of the Village Hall.

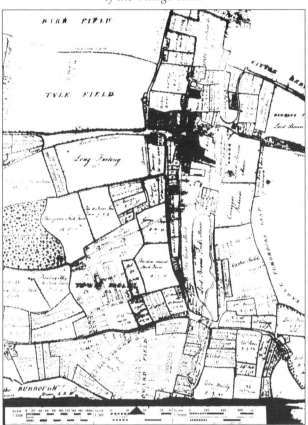

1753 map of Bedwyn and Stokke.

Looking west along Brook Street.

101

Left: *Sweetbriars on Brook Street, home of Nurse Webster.*

Below: *Brook Street, looking towards the centre of the village. The Railway Cottages are in the foreground.*

Above: *The corner of Brook Street and Farm Lane.*

Right: *Farm Lane.*

Below: *The Maltings.*

Castle Cottage, birthplace of Dr Thomas Willis.

WRAC, 1954–57, and her memorial is in Great Bedwyn's church. She died in 1992. Miss L. Holt, a member of the family who owned the White Star Shipping Line, lived in the other dwelling and gave generously towards the cost of the new Village Hall. Frogmore Farm, where the Blundy family lived, was burnt down in 1925. Continuing along the lane passing the new Village Hall we come to the canal and a lock. This is near the site of Burnt Mill or Little Mill, which is shown on a map of 1753, attached to a Deed, and is referred to as Streat's Mill. Returning to the main road, turn to the left, away from the centre of the village. This will take us to Sweetbriars, at one time a farmhouse with a dairy to the rear, formerly owned by Nurse Webster, a much-loved local figure.

We then come to a small brick and flint building with bottle glass inserts in the wall. This was briefly a village lock-up. Further along we see an attractive group of thatched and tiled cottages on either side of the road, before we reach a brick-and-tile-roofed house set back from the road to the left. This was originally the George Inn, later to be called the Horse and Jockey; it is now divided into three dwellings, and the right-hand house incorporates the beer cellar. Behind, the Hawkins family farmed Jockey Green Farm, also known as Merle Down Farm, where the family made bricks. The remains of the brick kiln are still to be seen to the right of the lane leading to Burridge Heath. We now retrace our steps and cross both bridges to see to the right, Railway Terrace, a row of Victorian cottages which are contemporary with the arrival of the broad-gauge Berkshire and Hampshire Railway Extension, and dated 1862.

Continuing up Brook Street, towards the Cross Keys public house, we pass a group of cottages to the right; the middle house was formerly a shop run by Mrs Gigg, whose husband William was the general builder in the village. This stretch of road was formerly known as the High Street. The houses were sold at auction by the Ailesbury estate in the late 1920s.

Turn right into Farm Lane, once known as Jubilee Street with the most complete group of eighteenth-century cottages in the village. At the far end we reach The Maltings, which won a European Architectural Heritage Award in 1975, in the category 'new uses for old buildings'. A date stone on the Kiln House shows '1868+ CS' (Charles Smallbones), but the roof construction indicates that the floors were most likely of an earlier date. Charles Smallbones owned The Maltings until 1920. During the Second World War the building was used to house prisoners of war. The Cranstone family, formerly at The Wharf, came in 1945 to run a coal business there. However, from July 1951 the name Ryan occurs in the deeds; later they ran the village shop from the front of the building and opened a petrol station. Francis Smith (Smiths of Axford) ran The Maltings as a transport depot between 1955 and 1970.

The next building on the right is a thatched cottage with an oversized chimney. The name, Castle Cottage, was first recorded as such in 1955 – before it was referred to as the Old Castle. It was thought to have been so named because of its one-time ruinous state. The house is chiefly noted as the birthplace of the celebrated physician, Thomas Willis, MD, on 27 January 1621. Thomas Willis was named after his father, also Thomas, steward to Sir Walter Smyth, a Bedwyn MP. He became a leading authority on blood circulation within the brain, and a founder member of the Royal Society. Castle Cottage is noted for its limestone and flint chimney-stack with circular chimney and mouldings, stone fireplace with flat arch and high-level cornice above, two-pointed arch wooden doorways with mouldings and a number of heavily cambered tie beams, together with other reused timbers.

Later owners include Josiah Wooldridge, who, according to John Ward, vicar of Great Bedwyn, 'was a most worthy man, an excellent mathematician'. He kept a school at Bedwyn and was first master in 1824 of Cox's Foundation. He was many times portreeve of the borough and was particularly active during the riots of 1830. On the evening of 21 November, it was reported that three mobs were lying in the vicinity of Bedwyn. Early on Monday morning Mr Wooldridge swore in the special constables, 45 of whom were mounted, and all of them supplied with an ashen cudgel, and a few with pistols. 'Not one rioter ventured into the town...'. More recent owners included the Smallbones and Cranstones.

Returning to the centre of the village, after passing an attractive brick and thatched cottage opposite Castle Cottage, we cross the well-thought-out design for the Castle Road council-houses, where at this point, pairs of houses follow the contours of the bank. Here is the Harts' old blacksmith's property, which has been converted into a dwelling.

At the end of Farm Lane, we return to the Cross Keys. The bottom step by the entrance is said to be at the same height as the top of the spire on Salisbury Cathedral. The adjacent Georgian building features a replica of an old Sun Insurance mark. This is No. 15 High Street, built c.1750, possibly by Thomas Bird, who at the time of the 1743 Court Leet was one of the town's two ale-tasters and bread-weighers. By 1851 it was inhabited by Thomas Hill, grocer, who most likely owned the shop next door. During the early 1900s it was lived in by shopkeepers and after the First World War Captain Scott lived there, followed by the Wilkins family, who also ran the adjacent store. After the Second World War Arnold Kerr and his family lived in the house briefly, before moving to Manor Farm. In 1961 the house was bought by Dorothy Stopford, the daughter of a bishop, who had the distinction of being delivered by Dr W.G. Grace, the famous cricketer, in his capacity as a GP. Architecturally one of the most interesting buildings in the village, note the attractive mixture of local bricks – both red-brown and blue-grey. In addition, the doorcase is a an example of fine brick dentilled eaves. To the rear is the garden and an adjacent paddock (part of Hillbarn House garden in 2003).

The next building was a shop, originally known as Thomas' Shop, and successively owned by the Scotts as a chemist dispensary, and the Wilkins who ran a general store. The last owner to use the house as a shop was Phil Sykes who lived in Bedwyn House opposite, and ran the shop as a general store on his retirement.

By a large tree at the side of the road is Stocktree Cottage, which forms part of the Hillbarn property. Stocktree was purchased by Lord Bruntisfield in 1963/64, from Lord Wilton, together with the adjoining field. This allowed him to develop a lower-level garden. At this time the house was modernised, and became a guest-house for weekend visitors.

Hillbarn House, named after Hillbarn Farm near the Wilton windmill, was once three cottages, running at right angles to the street; access was gained by a farm gate. A Mr George Smith, a London antiquarian bookseller, converted the three cottages to form one house, and is remembered for being the possessor of an original set of

Hillbarn House.

Shakespeare plays. Mr Smith sold the property to the Earl of Wilton in 1959, who had briefly owned Ramsbury Manor and who, in turn, sold Hillbarn in 1963 to Sir Victor Warrender (later Lord Bruntisfield) who was the last surviving godchild of Queen Victoria. He was instrumental in employing the well-known garden designer, Lanning Roper, to plan the garden. The house and estate, consisting of adjacent cottages and fields on Coster Hill, were bought by Alastair Buchanan in 1971, as part of the Hillbarn estate.

Continuing up the High Street, we pass a row of Ailesbury estate cottages, with interesting brickwork and ornate chimneys. Opposite the turn into Brown's Lane and straight ahead, is the Three Tuns Inn, a painted brick building with sash windows and a tiled roof. Outwardly it is an eighteenth century building with an earlier interior. The first house in Brown's Lane was Nash's Farm. Mr Nash ran a steam traction business. A bicycle shop also existed there.

Continuing along Brown's Lane, the Methodist chapel was erected in 1875, together with its adjoining school, which in the Second World War became St Joachim's Roman Catholic School. We then pass two eighteenth-century cottages on the north side of the road and descend through a cutting until we reach the end of Castle Road. On the right-hand side, we come to a long and low thatched building, covered with old advertisements, where Miss Napier lived. She was

something of an eccentric and was, amongst other things, involved in the Newbury Dog Rescue organisation and instigated the Bedwyn dog-racing day. Beyond are the modern developments of Wandsdyke and the new primary school, and near to the railway line are Spaines (1966) and The Knapp (1971). On the 1753 map of Great Bedwyn and Stokke, a Revd Thomas Shepherd is listed as the owner of Spaines, and the Revd Streat as the owner of Farm Mead in Farm Lane, a property that ran down to the river.

Returning to the High Street, we come to Foxbury Place, a new development, which retains some of the old pig-farm buildings which form the nucleus for a group of mostly single-storey retirement dwellings, incorporating two courtyards. Head towards the centre of the village, passing the Royal British Legion hall (rebuilt in 1982) and Bedwyn Motors, built on the site of two cottages, a continuation of the eighteenth-century row in Back Lane. Crossing over the road we come to a row of three reconstructed brick and tile cottages on the site of Portreeve Close. The middle cottage is named Shefford after Peter Shefford and his family, who bought it from the Ailesbury estate in 1929. The Sheffords are one of the earliest recorded Bedwyn families. The village stores were owned by the Evans family from before 1830 until 1986 (and leased to Stanley Lee, 1944–55). Mr Haines took over the shop when he married Joan Evans. It was purchased by Mrs Cooper in 1986. It was known as the Top Shop, and Haynes Edwards' shop was the Bottom Shop.

Bedwyn House was, for many years, the Vicarage and in the 1851 census we find the name of Revd William Collings Lukis of Bedwyn House. He was a keen amateur archaeologist, who together with his predecessor Revd John Ward carried out excavations on the site of the Roman Villa at Bedwyn Brail. Later on, after the new Vicarage was built, Dr Elias Fraser and his wife lived at Bedwyn House. Dr Hancock and his family not only lived in the house but also had a surgery there; their daughter was Betty Gauntlett. Phil and Kay Sykes came to live in Bedwyn once Phil had retired from Standard Chartered Bank in the Far East, taking over the ownership of the house from a close relative in 1947. The Barn, now a separate house, was once part of Bedwyn House. It is now known as the Butler's Pantry because it was originally the servant's quarters. At one time it was also used by a playgroup.

An additional walk, passing the Three Tuns Inn, continues up Forest Hill and passes several modern houses, until an Edwardian house to the left is

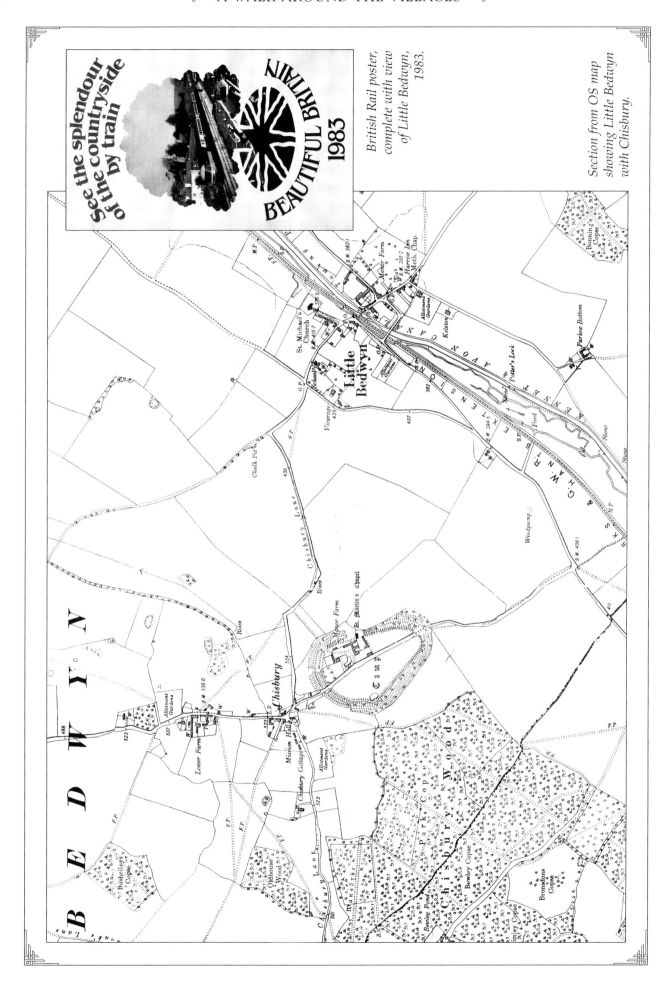

See the splendour of the countryside by train

BRITAIN BEAUTIFUL 1983

British Rail poster, complete with view of Little Bedwyn, 1983.

Section from OS map showing Little Bedwyn with Chisbury.

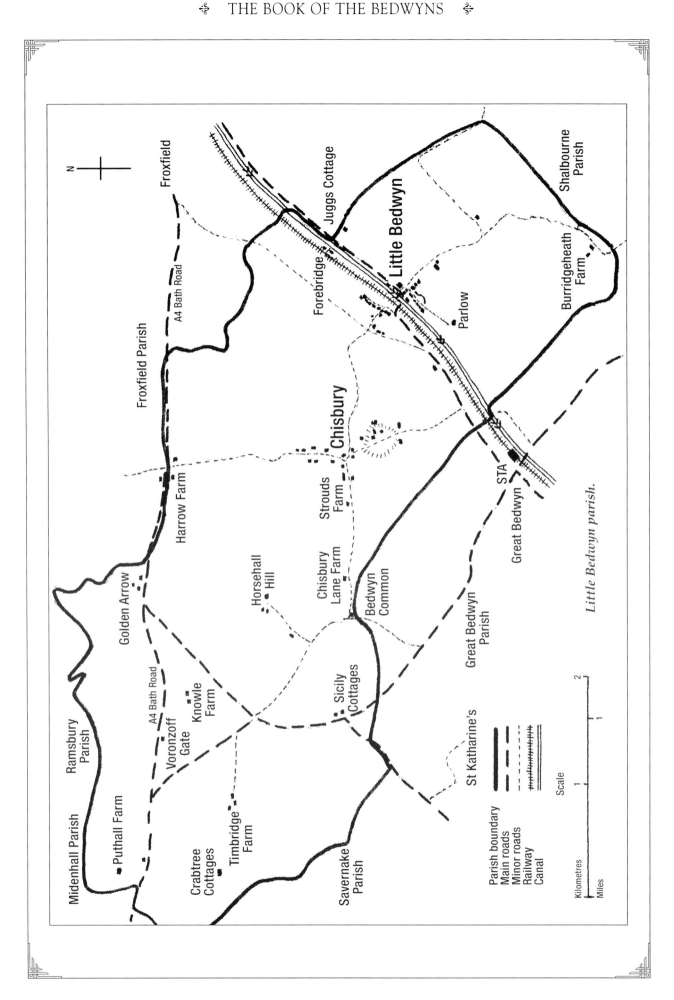

reached. Tor Mead was built for a Miss Bryant, and was later bought by a Mrs Watney who lived there with her sister (members of the brewing family). Dr Fenn lived in one of the Victorian houses opposite.

Little Bedwyn

Over the years the parish of Little Bedwyn, which includes Chisbury village, has varied from one-half to one-quarter the size of Great Bedwyn with the population peaking at nearly 600 in the 1840s and then falling to just under 300 in 2003. Little Bedwyn, as is the case with Great Bedwyn, was normally spelt with an 'i' until late in the nineteenth century. It was also frequently referred to in documents and plans as 'East' or 'Est' Bedwin and occasionally as 'Bedwin Parva'. The village, a mile to the north-east of its larger neighbour, was established on either side of the River Dun with a ford and possibly a wooden footbridge, taking the High Street across the small river. The division of the village is fairly equal with the older north-west side having the church, the nineteenth-century Vicarage, the old schoolhouse, the sites of earlier schools and the previous sub-Post Office. The southeast, now larger, side has the manor-house and the site of the earlier Manor Farm, the old forge, the Harrow Inn, the old general shop and the previous Vicarage.

This division became more dramatic in 1799 with the coming of the Kennet & Avon Canal, built in the valley of the River Dun. The canal was crossed by a swing bridge situated at the High Street and it seems that by this time the river had also been bridged. Some 60 years later, in 1862, the Berks and Hants Extension Railway, from Hungerford to Devizes, arrived as a single track, following the route of the canal and with a level crossing on the line of the High Street and the canal swing bridge. In 1895 the length of the line, by then owned by Great Western Railway, was converted to double track and at this time the road between the two halves of the village was diverted to the southwest where a new large brick and steel bridge was built to span the river, canal and railway. The earlier crossing then became solely a pedestrian route with a fixed bridge across the canal and a high-level footbridge across the railway and river, as it is today.

The view from the 1895 road bridge has become a favourite of photographers from far and wide, particularly when a steam train is scheduled. The juxtaposition of Little Bedwyn Lock, the railway, attractive village houses, the village green and the 800-year-old church in the background, has been the subject of many photographs and paintings and in the early 1980s featured on a British Rail poster.

There are seven listed buildings in the conservation area that is in the centre of Little Bedwyn village and 30 other houses in the area are considered 'significant unlisted buildings'. Also of particular note is the number of impressive, mature trees in the village centre, sheltering the roads.

Aerial view of the north-west side of Little Bedwyn village.

Our walk starts on the north-west side of the village, at Church Meadow. This village green of one-and-a-half acres, bordered by the River Dun, Church Street and St Michael's churchyard, is owned by the Little Bedwyn Playing Field Trust. In the eighteenth and first half of the nineteenth century it was a farmyard with two substantial barns, which were demolished between 1841 and 1884, possibly when the railway was built, and the area then reverted to pasture. The Trust was established in 1987 to purchase the meadow and ensure that this sensitive site in the centre of the village was protected from any unacceptable development. Funding for this was generously provided by Richard Tucker, present owner of Little Bedwyn Manor, the SW Farmer Trust, set up by a previous owner of the Manor and estate and by the District and County Councils. Church Meadow is used, together with Church Street, as the site of the annual Little Bedwyn Street Market, a village fête designed to raise funds for St Michael's Church. It is also used for an annual volleyball tournament, for village barbecues, the annual Bonfire Night celebrations and other village occasions. A boule pitch has also been created at one end.

Walk across Church Meadow with the waters of the gentle River Dun (where the Trust owns half of the fishing rights) lapping the banks on the south-east side, and go through a gate to Sandy's Wood. The Trust was able to purchase this site (a further one-and-a-half acres) next to the meadow and around the church boundary in 1992, where a woodland has been created. A total of 400 trees were planted (mainly indigenous varieties, particularly beech, but also with about 40 sponsored specimen trees including mulberry, copper beech, Scots pine and oak). There is a grassy dell with a picnic table and a wide avenue leading up to a seat at the highest point of the woodland. The wood was named after Sandy Kilpatrick who selected the trees and organised the planting, doing the major part of the work himself.

Returning to Church Meadow and looking to the north-west, one glimpses an attractive vista of Church

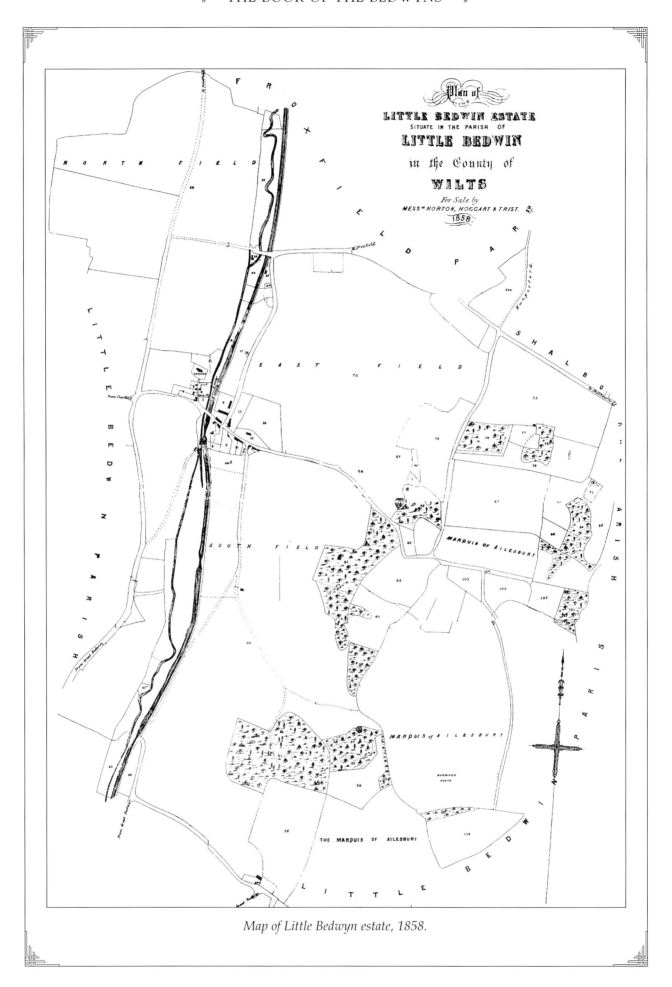

Map of Little Bedwyn estate, 1858.

A map of Sandy's Wood, behind the church.

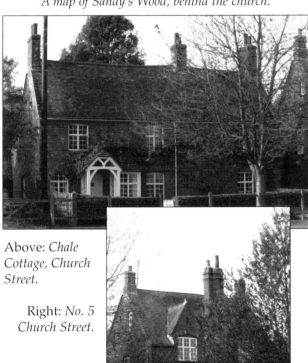

Above: *Chale Cottage, Church Street.*

Right: *No. 5 Church Street.*

Street. These five houses, all of different styles, were built in the eighteenth and nineteenth centuries but almost certainly on the sites of earlier houses. The house on the left, No. 1, was two dwellings until the 1980s. Next door, Chale Cottage was christened by William and Eve Gauntlett who spent their honeymoon at Chale on the Isle of Wight in the 1930s. This is almost certainly the oldest house on Church Street and is thought to have been the miller's house in the eighteenth century. It also housed a school during the first part of the nineteenth century and, later in the century, the village Post Office.

The middle house, the only one listed, has its date, 1860, shown in a circular stone plaque on the façade. This house has an unusually tall central chimney stack and was also originally two dwellings. It was constructed very much in the Ailesbury-estate decorated-brick style of that period. One side of this house was the home of the village blacksmith, Arthur Pavey, and his wife Dolly, until the mid-1970s. Next door, June Cottage is of a different character but happily nestles into its setting between its larger neighbours. Closest to the church is Jubilee Cottage, which was previously two thatched cottages joined together and now substantially extended since the early 1980s.

St Michael's Church, at the end of Church Street, dates from the twelfth century and is described in more detail in Chapter 7.

At the other end of Church Street and across the road is Old Manor Cottage, also listed. This thatched, three-bay, timber-framed house is probably the oldest in the village, dating from the seventeenth century. It is believed that, as Court Farm, it was one of the three farmsteads in the centre of the village in the early-eighteenth century, the others being Manor Farm across the Dun and a farmstead adjacent to the church. Sam Farmer, owner of the estate, bought this cottage early in the twentieth century on the condition that the lady living there at the time could stay for the rest of her life. This did not prove to be one of Sam Farmer's best deals (see Chapter 6) as she lived to the ripe old age of 99!

Towards the footbridge is a pretty terrace of three listed seventeenth- or eighteenth-century timber-framed thatched cottages. Attached at the western end as a matching projecting wing, is the nineteenth-century brick-and-slate-roofed Old Post Office. The last postmistress of this sub-Post Office, who retired in 1990, having served for 60 years, was Mrs Kit Mills, then the longest-serving postmistress in Wiltshire. Mrs Mills' stepfather, Mr Panter, had been the village shoemaker and shoe repairer in the early years of the last century and plied his trade from the house.

The other two houses in this terrace are Denby Cottage, which now includes the other smaller wedge-shaped Old Cottage and which, for a period in the early-nineteenth century, housed a small dame school and, at the eastern end, Violette's Cottage.

St Michael's Church.

Above: *Church Street,
Little Bedwyn, in the
late-nineteenth century.*

Right: *Church Street,
as seen from the footbridge
in 1912. Winnie Andrews
(from the Harrow Inn) is
in the foreground.*

*A double wedding
group in Church Street, 1901.
Sisters Sarah and Ellen Hawkins
married James Marshall and
John Shuttleworth.*

Schoolchildren with the Bishop of Salisbury, early 1950s. Old Manor Cottage is in the background. Included in the picture are: Roy Lance, George Freeman, Duncan Loft, Alan Roberts, Tim Gauntlett, Janet Huntley, Alan Lance, Chris Gauntlett, ? Rosier, Polly Freeman, Jenny Tuttle, Trevor Bolland, Colin Brooks, Robin Harris, the Bishop, Brian Burgess, David Huntley, Rosemary Martin, Mr Harrison, Mrs Harrison, the vicar.

Left: *Horse-drawn water cart, for supplying the traction engines, at the pump near the footbridge in the early-twentieth century.*

Left: *The old Post Office and listed Denby and Violette Cottages.*

Right: *Crossing Cottage, Little Bedwyn, 1970s. The building was demolished when the Thames Water pump house was built on the site.*

Above: *Little Bedwyn School.*

Left: *Maypole dancing at Little Bedwyn School, 1920s.*

Above: *The wedding of Muriel Smith (the vicar's daughter) to Henry Rivington, June 1904.*

Left: *Little Bedwyn Lock, Church Meadow and the church in the 1940s.*

Next to this group is a mid-nineteenth-century house, the eastern part of which is Avon House and the western part, Avon Cottage. Opposite these houses and close to the footbridge, Railway Cottage was built in the 1860s from where the level crossing was controlled. This later housed the Post Office and was demolished in the early 1970s when the Thames Water pump house was built on the site. Edwin Gauntlett, a previous owner of the estate, reminisced in a newspaper interview in 1950 about crossing the railway line with a donkey, around the turn of the century, when the animal stopped in the middle of the line and refused to budge. A train was coming so 'the donkey had to be carried out of harm's way.'

Going back past Old Manor Cottage and up School Hill, one arrives at the Victorian school building on the left. This was one of the national schools built throughout the country in the mid-nineteenth century, principally with local funding, in this case largely from the Ailesbury family. The school and schoolmaster's house, in the western wing, was built in 1854 – the date is clearly set in patterned bricks right across the gable of the east wing but the '4' is the wrong way around. The school closed in 1971 and its modernisation and conversion to two houses was completed in 1981, the year of the royal wedding of Charles and Diana. A special brick commemorating this event was placed in the eastern wall. Sir Felix Pole, general manager of GWR in the 1920s, was born here, where his father was headmaster from 1864–85.

Going on up the hill and left at the crossroads brings one to the Old Vicarage, which has parts of an earlier eighteenth-century house at its core. It was built in the early 1860s, supposedly because the vicar complained that while writing his sermons he was disturbed by the trains on the newly-built railway line immediately adjacent to the earlier Vicarage. In the middle of the twentieth century this Victorian Vicarage became a children's home, run by Mr and Mrs Tribe. This finally closed in 1970, precipitating the closure of Little Bedwyn School. In the grounds to the west of the Vicarage, the old stables and an outbuilding have been converted to make Southdown, a cottage with beautiful and extensive views to the south-west. At the entrance to the Old Vicarage is a group of ten impressive lime trees; these, together with a mature copper beech at the south-facing front of the house, and other Scots pines and ash trees, are features of the view to the north-west from the village below.

Going back down to Church Meadow and climbing the footbridge, there are lovely views either way from the top – to the east over the canal, Church Meadow and Church Street to St Michael's, and, to the west, over Little Bedwyn Lock and the canal. If you are lucky there might be a 125 express from Plymouth to Paddington thundering immediately below your feet or, just possibly, a restored classic steam engine.

Above: *The White House (an early Vicarage).*

Right: *Mrs Mary Jane Cooke of the White House.*

Below: *Little Bedwyn Manor and the Game Larder.*

Little Bedwyn Manor.

The Great Barn and Manor farmyard, as seen from the footbridge.

Over the bridges on the left was the village canal wharf, bordering the Manor farmyard. Throughout the nineteenth and well into the twentieth century, many tons of grain were loaded onto canal barges at this wharf. On the right is a Georgian building: the White House. This was once a Vicarage, built soon after 1800 when the previous one was demolished to make way for the canal. It is now converted to form three houses; the White House, Old Orchard and the stables and coach-house conversion, White House Cottage. In 1873, not long after the vicar had moved to the Vicarage up the hill, the White House was sold by the Marquess of Ailesbury to Mr George Cooke for £500. Mrs Cooke lived at the White House until her death at the age of 102 in 1939. At the age of 101 she was still on the school management board and a member of the Parochial Church Council.

Continuing up High Street alongside the high brick wall of the Manor stables and farmyard one arrives at the junction with the Hungerford–Great Bedwyn road. Here, at the corner of the farmyard wall, is a lovely eighteenth-century, octagonal, brick game larder with a conical tiled roof, topped by an elaborate black and gilt weather-vane showing a boar's head. This was built originally as a village lock-up and has been known in recent times as the Roundhouse or the Game Larder, reflecting its present use.

Centre: *Line drawing of the weather-vane on the Game Larder.*

The Georgian manor-house is opposite and is made up of a north-west range, built about 1750, and a more elegant south-west block of about 1800. It seems likely that the north-west part was built on the site, or was a remodelling, of an existing farmhouse. If it was an entirely new building it seems unlikely that it would have been sited so close to the roads on two sides. The south-west range is of a grander style with a Tuscan porch and pediment. It is not entirely symmetrical as there are two windows on one side of the front door and three on the other. The apparent corner windows on the upper floor are expertly painted on the brick to match the others and do not appear to be windows blocked up to avoid the window tax.

The manor-house was probably built by the Streat family and their descendants, the Kents, who owned Little Bedwyn estate for most of the eighteenth century. The road opposite the front of the manor-house, leading to Great Bedwyn, was constructed when the new bridge across the canal and railway was erected in 1898. This road created a grander approach to the manor-house and Sam Farmer, who then occupied the house, planted trees lining the road and erected small white posts and chains along this section of the road to set off the approach. The trees, a selection of Scots pine, beech, ash and holly are now very impressive and a real feature of the village but the posts have long since disappeared. At the corner of this road to the bridge is The Poplars, situated alongside the canal, with a marvellous aspect to the south-west.

Threshing on Little Bedwyn estate, 1930s.

The road from the bridge approaching the manor-house, constructed around 1898.

Sam Farmer reading in the garden at Little Bedwyn Manor, 1920s.

A garden party at Little Bedwyn Manor in the 1960s. Left to right: Pat Cadet, Jack Mills, William Gauntlett.

High Street with the village shop (the nearest house).

This sizeable house was built in the late 1970s, one of only ten new houses built in the village since the end of the Second World War.

Opposite the listed manor-house is an attractive group of stables and farm buildings. A large barn, timber-framed, weatherboarded and originally thatched (it is now tiled), was erected in the first half of the nineteenth century. There is also a smaller granary barn on staddle stones to the north-east; along the Hungerford road and beyond are new farm buildings erected in the twentieth century.

Continuing up the High Street there is a view on the left, over the high brick wall, of an impressive eighteenth-century brick gazebo in the gardens of the manor-house. Opposite and further up the road there is a terrace of four cottages, also listed. The façade of this row is nineteenth-century brick but other parts, including the chimney-stacks, denote seventeenth- and possibly even sixteenth-century origins. The end cottage, nearest the Harrow Inn, was the village general shop until late in the twentieth century. William Gauntlett recalls Mr Wise with a long black beard, who ran the shop shortly after the First World War. He always seemed to be wearing a black hat. William's mother, Winifred Gauntlett, helped Mr Wise with the complications of ration books at this time and when he gave up the business he gave her the pewter measures he used in the shop as a present. The shop ceased to operate in the early 1970s when the last tenant, Walter Huntley, who had previously been chauffeur to Sam Farmer, and his wife Nellie, retired. The only shop left in the village was then the sub-Post Office, which sold sweets, soft drinks and postcards, in addition to conducting Post Office business.

Turning right into Kelston Road at the Harrow Inn, nineteenth-century Stockwell Cottage is set back from the road on the right. In Kelston Road there is a terrace of four estate cottages on the right. These were built around 1860 when the estate was owned by Robert Lee Cooper Bevan, who lived at Fosbury Manor, south of Little Bedwyn, near Oxenwood. Set into the brickwork of the façade of this terrace is an impressive stone carving of the Bevan family crest – an attractive touch on what were essentially farm-workers' cottages. Next to these are two modern houses, Wansdyke and Savernake House, which were built in the late 1980s on previous allotment gardens. Then comes the 1960s mansard-roofed Greenacres, originally built for the farm manager of the estate. After this is the only twenty-first-century addition to the village, Kensington House, built in the old orchard of Kelston House.

On the opposite side of Kelston Road is an impressive crescent of four pairs of linked houses – the Farmer Cottages. These were built, three in 1936 and one in 1961, by the S.W. Farmer Trust, which was established through the will of Sam Farmer. People who had worked on the estate could live in these

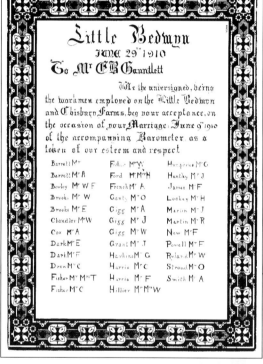

Above: *Parlow – originally Parlow
Bottom Cottages, the gamekeeper's
and woodman's houses.*

Top left: *Windmill Cottages and Chisbury Hill,
with St Martin's Chapel.*

Left: *Scroll with wedding gift from farm employees
to Edwin Gauntlett, 1910.*

Below: *Sam Farmer's traction engines working
at Chisbury, early-twentieth century.*

houses at a small rental and with utilities provided. However, towards the end of the twentieth century, with the mechanisation of agriculture, there were insufficient people who qualified and in 1996 the Trust sold the houses to a housing association. In 2003, two of the houses are occupied by people who had worked on the estate. These are two generations of the Martin family, Arthur, now 93, and son Michael and his wife, Brenda. Both Arthur and Michael were gamekeepers on the estate, as was Arthur's father, Oliver, who was killed in the First World War.

Kelston House, on the right, was built in 1910 when Edwin Gauntlett married Winifred Tanner. She came from Bath and Edwin is said to have proposed to her at Kelston, on the River Avon between Bath and Bristol, hence the name of the house and the road. Edwin Gauntlett was a nephew of Sam Farmer (his father was Sam Farmer's half-brother) who worked with him in running the estate and purchased it after Sam's death in 1926. As with most houses in Little Bedwyn, Kelston House, has been extended and altered significantly over the years but its basic Edwardian character has been preserved.

Going on down the hill, Kelston Road appears to be solely a farm road with extensive views south-west along the canal to Great Bedwyn and west to Chisbury hill-fort. However, at the bottom, a quarter of a mile from Kelston House, is Parlow. Until the mid-1970s this was Nos 1 and 2 Parlow Bottom Cottages, built in the 1870s for the gamekeeper and woodsman on the estate. Latterly and until the 1960s, pigs were kept in the two barns, 80 yards to the south-east. It is a reflection of the relatively prosperous nature of farming in the 1870s, compared with the agricultural depression years of the 1880s and '90s, that architectural features such as gothic-style windows and decorated brickwork were put into such a modest pair of houses. The two houses were joined together in the 1970s and extended to the west in the 1980s. The public road ends at the gate to Parlow but the 'green road', now a bridleway, was originally one of the routes between the two villages.

Harrow Inn, 1920s.

'Along the Green Roads of Britain'
by J.H.B. Peel (1976)

Now I began to look for an old friend, Little Bedwyn, whose gardens at the appropriate season illustrate the hamlet's name, a dialect word, bedwind, meaning 'clematis'. Presently I sighted the church tower among trees on the far side of the water. Bisected by the railway and the canal, Little Bedwyn is beautiful, unpretentious, sequestered. It's southern and higher half contains two handsome houses, several cottages and the Harrow Inn, a name well suiting thirsty men who, having ploughed the fields, scatter the seed and then return to harvest it...
Little Bedwyn is indeed an old friend of mine.
I am always glad to reach it, and always sorry to leave it.

Little Bedwyn High Street looking south towards the Harrow Inn.

Across the canal and railway, along the road to Great Bedwyn and amongst the very few houses visible from here, are the two Victorian Windmill Cottages, which until the mid-twentieth century had a wind-operated water pump in the adjacent field.

Going back up Kelston Road, at the junction with High Street, is the Harrow Inn, now a successful restaurant of a high standard, which attracts a clientele from far and wide. Turning to the right, next to the Harrow is the nineteenth-century Myrtle Cottage, named after Myrtle Mead, née Lance, whose family ran the inn. Myrtle married Tom Mead from Chisbury and they lived in this cottage for many years. The small space between the Harrow and Myrtle Cottage was once the site of a Methodist chapel and for this reason the Harrow was not able to obtain a seven-day licence until the early 1980s.

Beyond Myrtle Cottage, there were previously four cottages, occupied by the Claridge, Womersley, Bird and Bint families (they were demolished in 1936). The one furthest south was a particularly ramshackle cottage, known as the 'mud hut', which was inhabited latterly by an old man known as 'Ferret Bint'. On the site of these cottages is twentieth-century Blandings. As might be imagined, the original owner was a fan of P.G. Wodehouse. The house has a stone plaque, set into the brickwork by the front door, detailing the names of the people principally involved in the construction of the house in the early 1990s.

Approximately 100 yards further along the lane is the Old Dairy. In recent years this has been altered for use as stables with a large grain dryer adjacent. Another 100 yards beyond here brings you to the New Dairy, extended in 2000, but since moth-balled, due to the difficult environment for dairy farming. A new house, Bonnings Cottage, was built here for the dairyman in the 1990s.

Back down High Street towards the manor-house and turning right onto the Hungerford road one comes to the new farm buildings, and then The Old Forge. The last blacksmith, Arthur Pavey, retired in the 1960s and it is now a private house. A quarter of a mile towards Hungerford is Hollytree Cottage, dating from the eighteenth century. In the 1960s, this was a police house where the local policeman, Alec Yates, lived with Kathy. Restoration in the late 1980s uncovered a curved inglenook fireplace and a bread oven, which contained a child's hobnailed leather boot and an old ink pot. Just beyond here is the little hamlet of Fore Bridge. Bridge Cottage, formerly Nos 1 and 2 Wayside Cottages, on the south bank of the canal, with the towpath running past its windows, dates back to the early-eighteenth century and was a pair of thatched cottages until the late 1970s. Closer to the bridge is the site of Little Bedwyn's other inn, the Windsor Castle. This was apparently built in the middle of the nineteenth century and was sold by Mr Thomas Wise in 1868 to Mr Robert Bevan, who then owned Little Bedwyn estate, for £150.

The Windsor Castle later became a private house where Mr Mason, the local wheelwright and coffin maker, lived. Finally, in 1951 an order was approved by Marlborough and District Council for its demolition 'within 28 days', because it was unfit for habitation. There was a workhouse at Forebridge in 1792, which was occupied as three tenements in 1841 and demolished by 1884. This may have been done to facilitate the construction of the railway or maybe it was demolished and the Windsor

Bridge Cottage and Fore Bridge.

Castle, which was described as 'modern' in the 1868 sale particulars, was built on the site.

Across Fore Bridge itself, one of John Rennie's attractive canal bridges, there are three houses. On the left is Riverside, a pair of nineteenth-century cottages converted to a single house in the mid-twentieth century by Mick and Sylvia Kington whose families have lived in Little Bedwyn, Chisbury and Froxfield for many years. Earlier in the twentieth century two generations of the Barrett family lived here. Winnie Barrett, born in 1914, later married Charlie Mabbutt who looked after the cart-horses while Winnie was 'in service' at Little Bedwyn Manor. Next to Riverside is the little Riverside Cottage, converted from an outbuilding and opposite is Crossing Cottage, built with the advent of the railway in the early 1860s to control the crossing. In 2003 the crossing is only a pedestrian path across the railway, which leads across the field to the upper road to Froxfield. However, in earlier times it was clearly a more important route for wheeled traffic continuing up the track directly across the present Hungerford road, past Juggs Wood and North Standen to Hungerford. About 100 yards up this track, south of the Hungerford road, is Juggs Cottage, built in the twentieth century but extensively altered and extended in the late 1900s.

It is a short walk westwards along the canal back to Little Bedwyn village with lovely views across the canal to the Church Street houses, St Michael's Church and Sandy's Wood. The view is enhanced, on many evenings, by the soft floodlighting of the church, one of the village's millennium projects.

A more extensive walk would have included the two houses over a mile south of the village at Burridgeheath, which has been part of Little Bedwyn estate at various times during the last two centuries. These are Burridgeheath Farm and Foxwood Farm, which was converted and significantly enlarged from barns and stables in the 1980s. Closer to the village is the twentieth-century Four Oaks, which has beautiful and extensive views down to Little Bedwyn village.

CHISBURY

Situated on the northern flank of the hill-fort, Chisbury village has a cruciform plan. Starting at the crossroads, a sunken lane, known locally as The Shoot, goes south through the earth banks to the hill-fort itself. This is now a Grade I listed monument but over the years there has fortunately been only limited development in this fairly clearly defined central area of the hill-fort. On the east side is

Bridge Cottage, as seen from across the canal.

Chisbury Manor.

Woodland House, Chisbury.

Left: *Lower Farm, Chisbury.*

Above: *No. 9 Chisbury,
previously three farm cottages.*

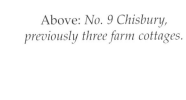

Left: *Chisbury Cottage.*

Chisbury's most impressive house, Chisbury Manor, a well-proportioned Georgian house built in the late-eighteenth century. It is on the site of a Jacobean house and an earlier fourteenth-century manor-house, which is said to have incorporated:

... a hall, with a high chamber at the west end and roofed with stone slates, a tower, containing a chapel and a chamber and roofed with lead, and a latrine roofed with tiles; it had a gatehouse and probably a moat.

Chisbury Manor has had a more settled ownership than most large estates. For 300 years, from the late-thirteenth century, it was owned by the Cobham family whose long connection with the estate ended when, in the early-seventeenth century, Lord Cobham was accused of high treason for involvement in a plot to replace James I on the throne by Arbella Stuart (see Chapter 4). The manor was then acquired by Edward Seymour, Earl of Hertford and descended with the Savernake estate lands of the Seymours and subsequently the Ailesburys.

Chisbury Manor was occupied, in the 1950s, by General Sir Brian Horrocks, a corps commander in Montgomery's forces in the North African and European campaigns of the Second World War. At the time he held the position of Black Rod in Parliament. A new house was also built in the 1980s in the grounds of the manor, in keeping

Joan Sherman, G.I. Bride.

with the manor-house and incorporating an octagonal tower. Next to the manor are the farm buildings of Chisbury Manor Farm, now operated as a stud. Close by on the eastern edge of the hill-fort is the thirteenth-century St Martin's Chapel, which is described in Chapter 7.

At the southern bank of the hill-fort there are two houses, one on either side of the road. To the east is Chisbury Manor Farmhouse, built in 1941 and to the west Woodland House, also built in the twentieth century and then hugely altered and extended in the 1980s. Both of these houses are in commanding positions, looking down over Little Bedwyn to the east and Great Bedwyn to the south-west and with extensive southerly views over

three counties: Wiltshire, Berkshire and Hampshire.

Returning through the evocative environment of the hill-fort to the crossroads, the road north passes Stroud's Farm, run in the second half of the twentieth century by Brad Stiles, and Park House, the latter having doubled in size with major extensions at the start of the twenty-first century. Further along is the late-Georgian farmhouse of Lower Farm with its farm buildings and a duck pond across the road. Before the road drops steeply down to the Bath Road the eighteenth-century house, prosaically known as No. 9 Chisbury, is located. Originally three cottages, it has beautiful and extensive views to the north and west. At the junction with the Bath Road are two houses close to the busy road. To the east of the road to Chisbury is Harrow Farm Cottage, an attractive thatched cottage, built around 1765, and to the west is Harrow Farm, an earlier inn. Across the Bath Road there used to be an area of the stream called the Washpool. Sheep were once washed here on their way to market.

Back again to the crossroads, one of the cottages on the southern side was certified in 1828 for meetings of Wesleyan Methodists and continued to be used until 1864. There is an attractive group of eighteenth- and nineteenth-century cottages around the triangle at the crossroads. To the west down Chisbury Lane is a large brick Mission Hall built by the Marquess of Ailesbury in the mid-nineteenth century as a carpenter's shop but later used for Nonconformist services. Further along are some of the few new houses in Chisbury: a late-twentieth-century house on the right and then six council-houses, The Robbins, built in 1921, followed by two older Robbins Cottages. On the other side of Chisbury Lane is a large early-twentieth-century house called The Laurels. This was built by Mr Chinnery who ran a wholesale fruit and vegetable business there in the 1930s. He had five delivery lorries which took locally caught rabbits up to the markets in London and brought back fruit and vegetables.

Continuing along the lane, which becomes sunken and is prone to serious flooding, the last house on the right behind high hedges

Left: *Mrs Gigg and Mrs Mills at a tea party at Chisbury at the end of the Second World War.*

Right: *At Stroud's Farm, Chisbury.* Left to right: *Ray Mundy, Don Hillier (bending), Harry Waters, ?, Terry Wright, ? Johnson, Rhoda Hillier.*

Below: *Chisbury Jazz Band outside the Bell at Ramsbury, c.1934.* Left to right: *Nell Newman, Frank Newman, Walt Newman, Roy Kington, Billy Webb, Len Pearce, Billy Norris, Billy Butcher.*

is eighteenth-century Chisbury Cottage. This is close to the site of a Tudor farmstead called Thorn Place and has been occupied by the Bishop family for many years. Chickens and turkeys were raised here in the years following the Second World War.

Owl's Castle, Savernake Forest.

Finally, on the eastern road from the crossroads there are only two houses. First and immediately on the corner of the road is Hollyhocks House, an eighteenth-century cottage, which was occupied for some time by an elderly reclusive thatcher. It was restored to a family house in the 1990s. Next, up a long driveway is nineteenth-century Fort Cottage, built on the ramparts of the hill-fort. This was converted in the 1990s from a cottage used as an office for many years by Chisbury Manor Farm and later by a trust providing holidays for disadvantaged children. The road, known locally as Colley Copse Hill, winds down to Little Bedwyn village, with beautiful views towards the church and over the surrounding countryside – a satisfying way to complete the ramble around Chisbury.

A more extensive walk would have included a number of other distinctive houses and farms north-west, towards Marlborough. Chisbury Lane Farm along the western road from the village has been one of the Chisbury farmsteads for centuries. Further along this road and close to the turning to Bedwyn Common is Buckwood, with the parish boundary running along the edge of its garden. Up on the hill north of Chisbury Lane Farm is the eighteenth-century Upper Horsehall Hill Farm, which has a long and well-documented history. At the bottom of the hill is the seventeenth-century, timber-framed andthatched Lower Horsehall Hill Cottage, so full of character and original beams that in the Little

Bedwyn Millennium Parish Map it was painted as if in a tree!

Over the crossroads and on the Great Bedwyn–Marlborough road is Timbridge Farm, another old farmstead and an interesting eighteenth-century farmhouse with Georgian and Victorian additions, including a pair of Venetian windows. Through its farmyard, across the field and on the fringe of the forest is Owl's Castle, converted and extended from two forestry- and farm-workers' cottages. Further to the west and reached from the Bath Road, deep in the forest are the two Crabtree Cottages, which look like something Hansel and Gretel might have stumbled across. The small area of Little Bedwyn parish north of the Bath Road is close by and includes Puthall Farm and its cottages. Adjacent is the site of the medieval hamlet of Henset, abandoned in the Middle Ages.

East of Puthall on the Bath Road is first the Victorian Voronzoff Gate, built in 1856 and named after the Russian family of a nineteenth-century Marchioness of Ailesbury, and then Knowle Farm and its cottages. Just beyond the turning south to Great Bedwyn is one of the relatively few modern developments in Little Bedwyn parish. This is the Golden Arrow petrol station, a neighbouring bungalow and the Klondike Restaurant, a former transport café renovated and altered during the 1990s and now a Canadian-themed restaurant.

South of the Bath Road and towards Great Bedwyn there are beautiful bluebell woods and opposite is the drive down to Knowle House, an impressive early-Georgian mansion, which has the ruins of a small fourteenth-century chapel in its grounds. This was the site of some of the oldest archaeological finds in Wiltshire, including axes and artefacts dating back to the late-Palaeolithic period. Towards Great Bedwyn and close to the junction of the road to Tottenham House and St Katharine's are Sicily House and Thistle Cottage in a small area known as Thistleland.

Upper Horsehall Hill Farm, Chisbury.

Above: *Crabtree Cottages, Savernake Forest.*

Left: *Knowle House.*

Below: *Voronzoff Gate, Bath Road.*

Above: *Great Bedwyn Bowls group – 1930s.*

Left: *Arthur Betteridge, owner of the rope factory, with Jack Lloyd and George Bance. They won a bowls club trophy in the 1930s.*

Bowls club in 1949. Left to right: George Batchelor, ? Rebbick, ? Robbins, Jo Davis (bowling), Sir Brian Horrocks, Mrs Winifred Gauntlett, Jack Lloyd, Ralph Hitchman, Arthur Wells.

Chapter 9

RECREATION & SOCIETY

The history of Great and Little Bedwyn does not fit neatly the divisions into which, for the sake of convenience, we parcel our history. The nineteenth century passed into the twentieth without any discernible change in the patterns of life and work in our villages. Queen Victoria's golden jubilee was commemorated with the erection of a stately iron lamppost and Farm Lane was re-christened Jubilee Street, but life went on much as it had done since the canal was built. During the following century, in spite of two world wars, the advent of the motor car and the landing of the first man on the moon, in social and economic terms the villages remained backwaters until the influx of newcomers in the 1980s and after. A significant number of the village families recorded on the map of 1750 were still resident in Great Bedwyn in the 1950s, and many remain in 2003. Whereas Little Bedwyn has suffered the loss of almost all its traditional local families, Great Bedwyn itself has retained a good number. Their continuing presence and influence helps to give Great Bedwyn a sense of community and of connection with the past which many other villages have lost.

Nevertheless, village society did change and evolve during the course of the twentieth century. One major factor was the decline of the power and influence of the Ailesbury family. Ever since Norman times, the hereditary warden of Savernake Forest had been a dominant, if remote, influence on village life. Unlike many local villages, including Little Bedwyn, Great Bedwyn was technically never a part of Savernake Forest. Nevertheless, with its two MPs it had, throughout history, functioned as the forest's market town. Until the late 1920s, when they were auctioned off, many village houses were owned by the Ailesburys. The Ailesbury weddings and their funerals took place at St Mary's Church in Great Bedwyn. The weddings were public occasions of great importance and photographs still exist showing the borough's streets decked with flowers and imported greenery as well as festive crowds. Although too grand to regard themselves as such, the Ailesburys acted as village squires. Tottenham House, which employed no fewer than 60 gardeners in the early-twentieth century, offered work to many villagers. In many ways the local economy depended on Savernake Forest and the forest was

owned by the Ailesburys. Dray horses, kept in the old stable yard of the Cross Keys, were used to haul timber. The life of Tottenham House and of the great family who resided there, was of consuming interest and importance to residents of the Bedwyns in the years before the Second World War.

Until the mid-twentieth century the Bedwyns, like all other Wiltshire villages, remained socially stratified. The great majority of residents were cottagers who worked on the land as ploughmen, hedgers, ditchers and shepherds. Others, 'roadmen', were employed to keep the highways in good repair; many others worked on the Great Western Railway. Many of the village's men were employed at Dodsdown brickworks. Village girls needed to find work as soon as they left school at the age of 14; many went into service or worked at the big house as maids or cooks, while others became shop assistants. Bedwyn society remained almost as impoverished as it had been when Cobbett visited in the early-nineteenth century.

Even after the Second World War some village men re-cycled their gas masks as dinner bags! Most working men went off to tend their allotments in the spring and summer after work. In addition to the allotments in Back Lane, there were also two allotments in Brook Street – one on the right as one leaves the village, adjacent to the wharf, and one on the left between the Blundy pig farm and the Horse and Jockey public house. Keeping allotments was an economic necessity rather than a preferred method of recreation.

Those who can remember the days before the Second World War affectionately describe a village community where everyone knew everyone else. It was a society strong on good neighbourliness, where people helped each other out in times of trouble. Families were divided into 'church' and 'chapel'; the 'church' families tended to buy their groceries at the village shop (now No. 13 High Street) whereas the 'chapel' folk shopped with Evans on the opposite side of the road (now the Stores). Attending either church or chapel was the norm and villagers would dress in their Sunday best and attend two services each Sunday. If anyone failed to attend questions would be asked. After church, it was customary to go for a good walk, weather permitting. The church choir was large and well regarded. Much social, as well as religious, activity centred on the church.

The local gentry took a keen, if paternalistic, interest in village affairs, and in the well-being of local families. Between the wars, Miss Bryant of No. 15 High Street (she later had Tor Mead built in Forest Hill), Mrs Egerton, Mrs Hancock, the doctor's wife, (from the Old Vicarage, now Bedwyn House, in High Street) and Mrs Arthur Kerr (the farmer's wife from Manor Farm) got together to provide social events for the village people. There were sandwiches, cakes, games, fun and laughter. A 'Doctor's Social' was held in the evening of Boxing Day and the ladies got together to provide food and musical entertainment for the village. Lord Finlay, the distinguished judge (of Fairway, Forest Hill) took a keen interest in the school, of which he was a governor, and talked to the schoolchildren at Christmas parties. (Lord Finlay used to dress less formally than his chauffeur, Mr Killick, so local people used to jokingly refer to them as Lord Killick and Mr Finlay!) Local clubs were established and some (such as that for bowls) were even patronised by the vicar, while Dr Hancock took an interest in the Royal British Legion. After the Second World War Sir Brian Horrocks, the distinguished soldier who lived for a time at Chisbury Manor, also supported both of these organisations. Apparently when attending a Legion function, Sir Brian chose to stand with the men, rather than the officers. On one occasion, one old soldier, not recognising the great man, said in a loud stage whisper, 'And who's the old b****r in the silly hat?'

Able villagers rose to positions of responsibility. Kathleen, the daughter of the village cobbler (who lived and worked at Cobbler's Cottage in Farm Lane) was a bright girl who became a student teacher at Great Bedwyn School. She won a place at Marlborough Grammar School, so had to walk through the forest every morning to Savernake Station to catch the train to Marlborough. Later, she attended Salisbury Training College to take a teacher-training course and returned to the village to teach at her old school. With some coaching from Lady Finlay of Fairway in Forest Hill, she later became a notable headmistress of Great Bedwyn School. She introduced a school uniform, succeeded in getting a number of local children into Marlborough Grammar School and produced a number of plays, including *What Happened to George*, which was a great success. Kathleen married Mr Bennett, who became station-master at Great Bedwyn. They later lived in one of the new council-houses in Church Street.

Little Bedwyn, which had a manor-house in the centre of the village where many villagers were employed, looked more towards the occupants of the manor and the owners of the estate rather than to Tottenham House and the Ailesburys. From 1874 to 1926 Sam Farmer lived at the manor-house and from 1910 his half-brother's family, the Gauntletts, lived at Kelston House and later at the manor-house. Sam Farmer, who had no children, was a more remote 'village squire' but the Gauntletts are remembered for many acts of generosity to the village community.

By the late 1930s, sports were flourishing at Great Bedwyn School. The boys had both football and cricket teams, whilst the girls played hockey and netball. There were matches against other local schools, especially Little Bedwyn, Burbage, Shalbourne and Marlborough Grammar School, the great enemy.

In the earlier part of the twentieth century, most cottagers had little leisure or money for recreation. Women were kept busy with chores such as washing and ironing, but at harvest time they would also help out on the farms. They were also sometimes sent into the fields to gather stones for road building.

The remoteness of the village community provided an incentive for entertainment to be brought to the village, since it was difficult for people to travel to and from the town. After the First World War a travelling cinema came to the village to show films in the Challoner Ellis Hall (the old Village Hall in Frog Lane) every month or so. The first mobile library took the form of a woman on a bicycle with a large wicker basket full of books. The local branch of the Women's Institute was started in the early 1920s by Mrs Gauntlett from Little Bedwyn and Mrs Hancock. There were outings, classes, plays and pantomimes. Membership grew rapidly and at one time there were about 100 members.

Davis the butcher ran a little unofficial betting shop from his premises in Church Street (now No. 111). Women were his main clients. Every day the evening papers were carried from the station and thrown down on the front steps of the Cross Keys. The women would gather round and the lucky ones would rush down to Davis' to claim their winnings.

It is not known when football was first played in the villages. The minute book for Great Bedwyn Football Club for the season 1908–09 has, however, survived. It reveals an efficient and well-run club, presided over by the Great Bedwyn GP, Dr Frazer. C. Waddup was elected captain for the season and many well-known local names played in the team, including W. 'Wally' Mills, H. and J. Lloyd, E. Smallbones and Fred Hart. In the season, 26 games were played, of which 16 were won, one was drawn and nine lost. Money raised from social events, subscriptions, the sale of jerseys and gate money from the matches played was spent on items such as a new football bladder (1s.9d.), J. Bartholomew for cutting the grass (4s.) and 15s. for the hire of a brake to take the team to Thatcham. Of the 15 players who scored goals in 1908/1909, it seems that only one, Edward Lovelock, was killed in the First World War.

Unfortunately, most of the score books and minute books of the football club have been lost, so it is not possible to give a comprehensive account of what was the village's most popular sport (at least

Great Bedwyn Football Club, winners of the Marlborough League, 1908–09.
Left to right, back row: H. Bennett, R. Wyld, F. Parsloe; centre: H. Lovelock; J. Lloyd, C. Waddup,
H. Evans; front: W. Mills, E. Atkins, G. Smart, W. Hart.

Great Bedwyn
Football Club,
1921–22. Left
to right, back
row: J. Symes,
F.G. Hart,
R. Gooding;
third row:
F. Heaver,
C. Vivash,
E. Wilde,
J. Taylor,
E. Hollister
(trainer);
second row:
C. Jerram,
F. Rosier,
R. Callaway;
front row:
W.J. Tilley,
B. Bird.

Bedwyn Football Club,
c.1930. **Left to right, back row:** *A. Lewer, C. Callaway, W. Baker, H. Richardson, H. Martin,*
P. Hoare, B. Lovelock, T. Hollister (trainer); **front:** *J. Hillier, J. Brooks, S. Bolland, N. Tilley, J. Grace.*

Winners of the Swindon Advertiser Cup. Left to right, back row: *A. Hart, B. Butler, A. Cox,*
J. Mills, R. Eastmond, C. Beckingham; front row: *D. Hutchins, C. Clements, B. Cox, P. Cox, T. Perry.*

until after the Second World War). Several local players remember how the Great Bedwyn team worked its way up the Swindon and District League. It was in the fourth division in 1953 and a photograph of the team (including goalkeeper George Chapman, left back Reg Coward, plus Frank Offer, Les Perry, Terry Perry and Brian Hart) has survived. By 1962 it won the Advertiser Cup, having reached the final the year before. Great Bedwyn did well to win the prestigious Newbury Graystone Challenge Cup on two occasions (3-2 against Bucklebury in 1957/8, and 6-2 against Kintbury Rangers in 1961/2). John Mills managed the Great Bedwyn team after he gave up playing in 1969 and in that year the team did well; it came top of the Second Division.

The village was not without its stars. Brian Hart, described in an article in the *Newbury Weekly News* as 'The Cannonball Kid', had a terrific kick, and was also able to head the ball well. He was one of the best players to come out of the village. He had a trial for Arsenal, but did not want to leave the area. He played for Newbury Town and Basingstoke, until a broken ankle ended his football career. Two local men played for Wiltshire in 1960: John Mills (goalkeeper) and Alan Hart (left back). The former also played for the Wiltshire Association of Boys' Clubs in the early 1950s.

Cricket had been less popular than football in the village even though it is believed to have been played here at least since the 1850s, at one time on the water meadow at Lower End, south of the canal. The *Marlborough Times* for September 1859 reported:

The concluding match of the season was played on Monday, the 12th inst., at Hungerford Park, between the Great Bedwyn and Hungerford Park clubs, which ended in favour of the latter with 58 runs to spare. After the game the party adjourned to the Bear Hotel, and partook of a most excellent dinner... A most agreeable and pleasant evening was spent.

Cricket grew in popularity after the Second World War; a meeting was held in Great Bedwyn School in January 1946 to revive both cricket and football. This was well attended, despite 28 January being a 'wild and tempestuous night' and resulted in the foundation of Great Bedwyn Sports Club, which had the football and cricket clubs as subsidiary committees. Village men were returning to civilian life after serving their country and their involvement in local sport was seen as an important factor in helping them return to normality. George Cranstone, then a coal merchant, was elected chairman and Ted Haines, village grocer, served on the committee. George Cranstone later became the captain of the Great Bedwyn cricket team. Club members included Ralph Block, Ernie Brown, Percy Hoare, Alf Claridge, Arthur Kempster, Andrew Blundy, Ted Mills and Cyril Burgess. John Mills joined in 1947, Frank Offer in 1949, Bert Appleford, Ernie Crook and Wally

Late-Victorian Bedwyn cricketers, with Shawgrove in the background.

Great Bedwyn Cricket Club, at Bewley Farm, 1950. Left to right, back row: A. Regan (scorer),
F. Offer, K. Bailey, R. Wells, J. Scarlett, A. Claridge, E. Mills (umpire);
front row: G. Cranstone, L. Hart, A. Blundy, E. Brown, M. Berry, J. Mills.

Great Bedwyn Cricket Club versus ITV (World of Sport), 1972. Left to right, back row: D. Upton,
P. Coppock, R. Davies, N. Durden-Smith, J. Bromley junr, J. Bromley senr, A. Franklin, R. Gardham,
J. Baker, M. Archer, W. Whipps, M. Beer; front row: D. Crook, J. Roff, J. Mills, F. Offer, D. Bonner,
T. May, B. Hart, B. Nutley, P. Tilley, R. Kempton, S. Edwards.

Whipps in 1953, Gordon Stone in 1954, Brian Hart and John Roff in 1955, Mick Hand in 1957 and Noel Tilley in 1958. Before 1946 cricket was played on the football field in Brown's Lane, but in 1946 it moved to Bewley Farm, where it stayed until 1962, when it moved to its modern home in Frog Lane.

Cricket has long been associated with the Stone family. Bob Stone did not play the game himself, but his son Gordon did, and has been an energetic club chairman for over 25 years.

The history of the cricket club is well documented from 1946–2000. Ivor Rowell has written an official club history, which includes records, averages, facts, figures and statistics, although scorebooks for seven years in the 1960s are lost. In all matches since 1946, the club has played about 1,700 games. Bedwyn batsmen have scored a grand total of 188,000 runs at an average of 15.14 each. Our bowlers have taken almost 12,000 wickets in 54,000 overs at an average of 15.04 each. Peter Tilley has the distinction of appearing in most matches; he has played 975 times since 1946. A. Martin has achieved the best ever bowling figures for the club; in 1948 he took ten wickets for 11 runs in six overs against Marlborough College Die Hards. In 1955 Great Bedwyn bowled

Gordon Stone presents Reg Eastmond with a trophy to commemorate 50 years' service to Great Bedwyn Cricket Club.

Great Bedwyn's team were the first winners of the Savernake League in the silver jubilee year, 1977.
Left to right, back row: *T. Mills (umpire), P. Tilley, J. Joel, P. Barrett, M. Hand, T. Wright, K. Stokes, B. Nutley, J. Mills (umpire), Mrs B. Crook (scorer);* front row: *P. Gilbert, B. Hart, D. Crook (captain), D. Bowden, D. Collis.*

Oxenwood out for ten runs, but in 1957, it bowled Burbage out for a grand total of just four runs! J. Joel became the first ever player to score a century for Bedwyn when he scored 110 not out against Ramsbury on 28 July 1968.

Little Bedwyn had its own football and cricket teams from time to time but with a much smaller community this was not on the same organised basis as Great Bedwyn. Matches were played on the field between the school and the old Post Office.

Harry Mills of Upper Horsehall Hill, Chisbury

Harry Mills achieved national fame in 1955 when, at a church fête in the grounds of Little Bedwyn's manor-house, his own pet crocodile, Croc, bit and nearly severed his thumb. This required emergency treatment by unbelieving staff at Savernake Hospital. The story hit the UK headlines and as far away as Australia, particularly when the press learnt that this was just one of Harry's many exotic pets.

Harry lived all his life in a cottage at Upper Horsehall Hill Farm, near Chisbury, where both his father and grandfather had also lived. He started building his menagerie in 1952 when he bought an unidentified snake in Reading, soon to be followed by a grass snake and some European Green Lizards. In the same year, Harry saw an alligator advertised for sale in a Sunday newspaper. This arrived by train from Croydon, wrapped in cotton wool and sealed in a cardboard box. It was only 11 inches long at this time but was eventually to grow to 4½ feet. At first it lived in the house with Harry but eventually had to be rehoused in a garden shed which he arranged to have heated to tropical temperatures. After fielding frequent questions about the difference between alligators and crocodiles, Harry decided to buy a crocodile. London Zoo obliged but advised him that, unlike alligators, crocodiles are untameable. Croc proved this point.

Over the following years Harry acquired monkeys, bushbabies, a python, a boa constrictor, a brace of rat snakes, marine toads, chipmunks, terrapins, tortoises, lizards, pigeons, mynah birds and parrots. His cottage was visited by school coach parties and TV camera crews and in 1956 he appeared on TV in the 'Dave Allen Show'.

When, eventually, the crocodiles, alligators and pythons had gone, Harry shared his cottage with a golden mantilla from Madagascar, one of the world's rarest frogs at just 1½ inches long, a 20-year-old Mexican red-kneed tarantula, a cage full of African Giant Snails and four bird-eating spiders from Chile.

It is worth mentioning that despite the demands of his collection of exotic wildlife, Harry for many years made time to serve as a Little Bedwyn Parish Councillor and as an active member of the Royal Observer Corps and the postwar civil defence organisation.

People of the Parishes

Bedwyn outing to Salisbury, c.1920. Left to right: *Arthur Skippence, Mr and Mrs Saunders, Jennie Webster, Nurse Webster, Pat Webster, Len Lovelock and wife Annie, with Amy Lovelock in front, ?, ?, ?.*

Beaters for the shoot at Stokke between the wars.

*James Shefford and his wife,
grandparents of Peter Shefford
who ran the newspaper
business in Great Bedwyn.
James was a carpenter on
the Ailesbury estate in the
early-twentieth century.*

*Little Bedwyn Youth Club outing to the seaside, 1950s.
Left to right: Norman Burridge, Brian Burgess, Roy Brooks, Rodney Miller,
Pat Jeanes, Colin Brooks, Alec Roberts, David Huntley, Terry Brooks.*

Sam Farmer (left) and his nephew Edwin Gauntlett (right). Three generations of the Farmer and Gauntlett families farmed Little Bedwyn estate for almost 100 years from 1874.

Local Land Girls during the Second World War, 1939–45.

Muriel Mundy of Little Bedwyn.

Below: *Arthur Skippence.*

Above : *Chisbury forestry workers, c.1950s. Harry Waters is on the far left.*

Below: *Wedding in Little Bedwyn of Muriel Smith and Henry Rivington, 1904.*

Fred Lance and his sister Myrtle, Little Bedwyn, 1950s.

Chapter 10

BEDWYN AT WAR

Great Bedwyn Church Parade, 7 July 1926.

THE FIRST WORLD WAR

As the war memorials record, all three parishes played a full part in both world wars. The memorials commemorate only those who did not come home, so it is the rolls of honour, such as those in St Katharine's Church, and photographs of events including the Church Parade in the High Street in 1926 that are a more accurate reflection of the commitment of all the villagers as a whole.

As typical examples of the country's response in August 1914, it is poignant to note that of the three Bedwyn men who enlisted in Devizes into the 6th Battalion, Wiltshire Regiment, on the same day (their Army numbers are consecutive) two died on 25 September the following year and the third six weeks later. Frank Edwards, Leonard Hart and George Stagg are all commemorated on the Loos Memorial in France.

One of the most notable memorials is at Arras and was designed by Sir Edwin Lutyens. The names of John Gigg and Charles Harris, serving in the 1st Royal Berkshire Regiment, can be found there. They were killed within five days of each other in the spring of 1917. The spring offensive that took place the following year took the life of Oliver Martin of Little Bedwyn, whose name is amongst the 14,644 missing men recorded on the Pozieres Memorial to the north of Albert. Fred Cope, whose family came from Folly Farm, has his name on that most famous memorial, the Menin Gate at Ypres. Every evening at 8p.m. the traffic along the busy thoroughfare is stopped and the Last Post is played by Belgian buglers under the memorial.

ROLL OF HONOUR *Men & Women from the Parish of ST KATHARINE'S, Savernake Forest, who served in the King's Forces in the Second World War 1939–1945 on Foreign Service.*

Roland Barratt
Donald Bartholomew
Leslie Bartholomew
Maurice Brazier
The Lady Rosemary
Brudenell-Bruce
John Cantillon
Henry Cantillon
Rt Hon. the Earl of Cardigan
George Norman Chapman
Victor Charlwood

William Cope †
Willam Douglas Crosby
Charles Donaldson
Quentin Foote
William John Jobe
Frank King
Stanley King
Owen Legg
Alfred George Martin
James Martin
John Martin

Albert Henry Mills
Leonard Mills
Peter John Roberts
Stanley Rushent
Arthur Stroud
Henry Vincent
Alfred James Waters
Henry Charles Waters
Frank White
Lesley Lionel Wootton

On Home Service

Ivy Barratt
Joy Bartholomew
Marie Avis Bell
Norah Brazier
Frederick Cope
Edward Harold Ellison

Dorothy Trixie Hillier
Frederick Sydney Lewington
Harold George Lewington
Rose Lewington
John Mansfield
Edith Mansfield
Frank Edward Pike

Lillian Price
Arthur George Stone
Desmond Crosbie Trench †
George William Tandy
Havis Joan Tandy
Mary Watchman

† The two men who were killed in the war.

Great Bedwyn Church Parade in the late 1940s.

Belgian Refugees

The war had another very obvious impact on the three parishes, with the arrival of about 40 Belgian refugees, who stayed until their homes had been liberated in 1918. In No. 43 High Street there were nine members of the Van Gaals family but it is not known if they alone occupied the house, which was normally inhabited by one of Betteridge's employees. Most other refugee families were much smaller and in the case of the d'Haeves were put up in Nos 71 and 75 Railway Terrace by the Taylor family.

THE ROYAL BRITISH LEGION

In 1922 the Marquess of Ailesbury donated the land on which the Legion building stands. An old Army hut was brought over from Upavon and this was the clubhouse until 1980. In the beginning the hut was called the Ailesbury Comrades Club but it soon became known as the Bedwyn branch of the Royal British Legion.

In 1982 the new building, still in use in 2003, was put up under a lot more than the guidance of Jim Wild, the chairman of the branch. Fund-raising was begun in 1963, but by 1979 when planning permission had been given, only two-thirds of the costs had been raised. Builder Jim Wild, who agreed to do much of the work free of charge, saved the day. The president of the branch and chief fund-raiser was Col Peter Garrett, who sadly died a month before the new building was opened.

The Royal British Legion building.

CHALLONER ELLIS HALL

The Challoner Ellis Hall was built on the site of the present Village Hall in 1926. It was used as the headquarters for a summer camp for North London schoolchildren. In the winter months the Social and Entertainment Committee organised many events there. This committee was an offshoot of Great Bedwyn's sewing circle, formed during the First World War to provide gifts from home for the troops.

During the Second World War there was still the same desire to do something for the lads and dances were run in the hall to raise money for a gift for each returning serviceman. The Americans, based in the forest and in Tottenham House, were appreciative and generous attendees. For the British soldiers who were based locally, a canteen was run in the old reading-room (now the Cutting Room Hair Salon). In the event each serviceman received a leather wallet containing a £5 note.

In 1944, a War Memorial Committee evolved, and in 1949 the Challoner Ellis Hall was bought for the village. A year later it was being used by the WI, the Mothers' Union, for infant welfare and for a weekly children's dance class. In addition it was used by a commercial cinema circuit showing 16mm films once a week, as well as by the Food Office for exchanging ration books, by the Young Farmers' Club, and for boxing matches, wedding receptions, dances and whist drives. A lot of very similar activities take place in 2003 in its successor hall that was opened in 1982.

THE SECOND WORLD WAR

Perhaps the bombing of civilian targets and the great likelihood of invasion made villagers feel much more in the front line in the Second World War. Or maybe it was the lectures given by an Army Major from Chisbury in the chapel schoolroom. He ran them for air-raid wardens, demolition workers and the Home Guard. At the end of the lectures an exam had to be passed; an Army sergeant from Marlborough supervised this. The exam involved being able to test for the presence of gas, identify five gases and then demonstrate getting into a gas mask when incarcerated in the gas van, which was parked in the yard behind the Cross Keys. The head warden was Mr Smith who lived in the centre of the village. Once the wardens were qualified they had to help other villagers learn how to don a gas mask, but it is unlikely that everyone had to enter the gas van to prove they could do it. The wardens' main duty was to patrol the area to ensure the blackout was being observed; offenders could find themselves up before the magistrates in Marlborough.

The village had its own fire brigade that manned a handcart on which was a rather old hose. Fire practice on the wharf drew onlookers who enjoyed the spectacle of water spurting from the perished hose and the efforts of the men pumping the 'engine' by hand. The team leader was Mr Saunders who lived in Cobbler's Cottage on Farm Lane and his encouraging cries of 'pump up, pump up' must have drawn forth a few choice Wiltshire phrases.

Evacuees, mainly from the East End of London, were billeted in homes for a short while early in the war. Their relatives were able to visit by train, mostly on Sunday mornings. Those that were Catholics were allowed to hold Mass in the school on Church Street. When the evacuees had settled down, two Girl Guide groups were set up for the girls, one of which was run by Muriel Mann.

Pillbox just off the Crofton Road.

Anti-tank defences across Beech Grove Bridge.

Land Girls contributing to the domestic economy during the Second World War.

Great Bedwyn Home Guard, 1941. Left to right, back row: *Alf Parker, Charlie Broad, George Tandy, Reg Bowley, Jack Lovelock, Stan Rosier, Les Davis, Arthur Kempster, Vic West, Haines Edwards, Sid Dowton;* third row: *Vic Heaver, Ben Lloyd, George Hawkins, Les Wilmot, ?, ?, Bill Killick, John Wilkins, Putty Little, Dan Kerr;* second row: *Bill Dines, Norman Tosh, Ned Wild, Jo Davis, Padgett Cook, ? Hylton, Vic Bennett, ?, George Cranstone;* front row: *Ernie Brown, Ted Mills, ? Davis, Reg Cope.*

THE BOOK OF THE BEDWYNS

Little Bedwyn Home Guard in 1941. Left to right, back row: *Bill Mundy, Frank Keen, Bert Sainsbury, Ernie Luker, Stan Bolland, Joe Waters, ?, George Myall;* middle row: *George Pike, Len Pearce, Billy Webb, Ray Mundy, George Batchelor, Ron Head, Arthur Martin, Arthur Mills, Peter King;* front row: *Maurice Martin, Bill Mead, John Wildash, William Gauntlett, Arthur Pavey, Bill Harris, Arthur Tarry.*

The Kennet & Avon Canal was fortified as the major defensive line after the Channel coast. German tanks would have found it impossible to climb up out of the near-vertical banks of the canal even if they had been able to wade or swim across. There are still many pillboxes to be seen to the north of the canal today, which would have formed the framework of the defence.

Fortunately the defences were never put to the test, which was probably a great relief to the men manning the anti-tank gun post near the old Savernake Forest Hotel. The site can be seen in the hedgerow to the north-east of the bridge over the old railway line.

Both Bedwyns had their own Home Guard platoons. The men would have been very familiar with the weapons they were given, as most would have used them during the First World War. Vic West remembers laying an unofficial telephone cable from the Home Guard hut on Costers to the home of the detachment commander Padgett Cook at Brail Farm. The cable needed to be strung above ground and fixed to insulators. His helpers were Ben Lloyd, Les Davis and Arthur Kempster.

A local policeman, Sgt Stokes, started a Royal Observer Corps detachment in January 1938. It enlisted special constables; John Lloyd was in charge

with George Kempster as his deputy. Their post consisted of two chairs and a canvas windbreak beside a telephone pole on the sports field. Whilst there were wires to the pole, there was no connecting box in May 1938. The aiming post for orientating their instrument was the windmill at 43 degrees. When not in use the kit was stored in the bowls club's hut. However, when war was declared the post was upgraded with a plotting table and the telephone connecting box arrived. A 1941 photograph shows the detachment with its self-help hut; a timber and corrugated-iron structure with an open plotting area and a cubby hole for brewing tea. The job of the two-man team on duty was to spot, log, and report all aircraft to the Operation Room in Bristol. On one occasion they reported a low-flying Junkers 88 bomber following the canal. It was intercepted over Reading and chased out to sea. Perhaps it was looking for the ammunition depots, which were scattered all over this part of Wiltshire, particularly in Savernake Forest. The nearest one to Great Bedwyn was in Horse Copse on Forest Hill. During the war, 20 men, nearly all of whom were from the two Bedwyns, manned the post. For a time Lt-Col Gerald Lauderdale, who came from Marlborough, was one of the team.

The Rope Factory

The rope factory, which started production in 1940, was another example of the villages' contribution to the war effort. Sisal and hemp were used to make ropes for hammocks, rifle pull throughs, camouflage nets and slings for artillery field guns. Scramble nets were made for use in the Dieppe Raid of 1942. Arthur Betteridge ran the factory from a couple of 30-foot long sheds behind the Post Office, which were normally used as workshops; he built coaches and was a wheelwright and coffin maker.

The guy ropes for tents were tied up in bunches of 12 and piled up in a stack at one end of the shed ready to load onto the lorry and be taken to the station. He used to run a sweepstake on the number of packs in the stack and rewarded the winner with a bar of chocolate from his own sweet ration. The 30 or so workers were paid £2 per week for an eight-hour day shift and Daisy Betteridge is reported as earning £3 per week in 1948 making nets for vegetable markets. The factory finally closed in 1948.

Royal Observer Corps Detachment in Great Bedwyn, 1941. Left to right, back row: Noel Tilley, George Kempster, George Alexander, George Bushnell, Frank Sturgiss, Stan Bolland, Percy Hoare, Harold Pinching; front row: Jim Bowyer, Wally Lovelock, Jack Lloyd, Tom Cummings, Charlie Gauller; crouching at front: Arthur Shefford, Albert Standing.

Did Churchill Visit Bedwyn?

During the war the Minister of Information, Brendan Bracken, lived in Folly Farm Cottage. There are reports that despatches were delivered to him by light aircraft. A local farmhand, possibly Mr Holmes, was sometimes told to run a harrow over the fields to the west, presumably to flatten any wheel ruts and keep the field safe for landings.

There is a rumour that Churchill visited his close friend and together they worked on some of his speeches. Rumour even has it that he may have broadcast them from there. The supporting evidence of the hole in the window frame for the cable to the mobile transmitter is no longer visible as Folly Farm was extensively renovated after the war.

Billeting

The use of so many woods as ammunition depots, which needed constant guarding, meant that many soldiers were billeted locally. Perhaps the most obvious were the Americans who moved into Tottenham House in large numbers in 1942.

The Postwar Years

On 2 January 1946 there was yet another major accidental ammunition explosion in Savernake Forest. Such are the quirks of blast waves that the cottage at No. 56 Church Street was structurally damaged whilst other buildings including the houses at St Katharine's, much closer to Savernake Forest, were undamaged. No local people were among the small casualty toll but the incident is remembered for the heroism of those who were first on the scene, and whose efforts to move unexploded ammunition trucks prevented a far worse disaster. Major Kenneth Biggs and Staff Sgt Sydney Rogerson were both awarded the George Medal, the peacetime equivalent of the Victoria Cross.

After the war a fund was set up to buy the land owned by the Cross Keys and convert it into a recreation ground. Nine chestnut trees were planted overlooking the playing field to commemorate the nine Great Bedwyn men who died as a result of the Second World War. From the same fund the villagers were able to buy the old Challoner Ellis Memorial Hall and rename it simply the Memorial Hall.

THE COLD WAR

In September 1959 the Royal Observer Corps' Observation Post was geared for nuclear war. It was moved to a shelter 20 feet below the ground in a hardened concrete shelter some 16 feet by 7 feet wide. The roof of the shelter can still be seen in the same compound as the water-pumping station on the road between the Bedwyns. Its new role included reporting on radioactive fallout and nuclear strikes. There was room in the shelter for three beds and rations for two weeks. Some 34 people served in the Royal Observer Corps post after the war, with A.C. Emslie as the chief observer until 1972 and Harry Mills of Chisbury thereafter. The post remained operational until the ROC stood down in 1991.

Crofton Farmers.
Left to right: *Eddie Ellison, Robert Vines, Bill Powell.*

Returning to the farm.

Making hay bales.

Chapter 11

A New Millennium

Since the Second World War the character of nearly all villages throughout the UK has changed. Whilst the number of agriculture-related jobs have decreased dramatically, the number of people who now live in the country has grown. This drift from town to countryside has been the result of a number of factors – behind them all lies the typically English dream of owning a place in the countryside. The modern high levels of car ownership and the expansion and improvement to the trunk-road network has enabled many people to continue to work in towns and cities without being tied to the somewhat unsatisfactory public transport system. This influx of urban peoples has in some cases totally changed the character of the villages and hamlets into which they moved. The most obvious example is the week-enders who have no need of many local services. Consequently primary schools and small village shops close. Governmental financial stringency compounds the problem through the centralisation of education and medical facilities, the reduction in the number of police stations and their levels of manning and the closure of 'uneconomic' public transport routes to name but a few. With most people owning both a car and a freezer, it has become more convenient and quite often cheaper to shop in a supermarket rather than the local village store.

The Bedwyns have perhaps been more fortunate than many other communities in absorbing these changes and yet retaining some of the great attractions of country living. Having places within the parishes designated as conservation areas and being in an area of Outstanding Natural Beauty has helped to avoid some of the excesses, which have hit other Wiltshire settlements. Those who do not come from a rural background have often tried to impose urban or suburban values on their new community, such as insisting on no bonfires, no farms producing cow manure and mud in village centres and starting up cultural societies. While these ideas may have admirable motives at their core, some 'progress' may not be that beneficial, particularly if it breaks down

First meeting of the Great Bedwyn Cubs in September 1999 with Jon Jordan and Richard Holmes.

Left: *Great Bedwyn Parish Council meeting in September 1999.* Councillors, left to right: *George Gilbert, Nigel Henderson, Roger Durie, chairman Gordon Stone, Jack Minterne, Mark Thomas, Sally Rhodes, Rosemary Cummins, John Thomson, Bill Burrows.*

Right: *WI ladies selling harvest produce.* Left to right: *Vera Coleman, Pam Bailey, Hilda Brown, Betty Spong.*

Below: *WI meeting in the Village Hall, September 1999.*

Retired Mens' Lunch Club in the Cross Keys, September 1999. Left to right: *John Maslin, Tim Fuller, Keith Irwin, Peter Swaine, Brian Bailey, Raymond Duveen, Douglas Stewart, Carlton Younger, Tom Gilmartin.*

the social basis of village life. The rapid inflation of house prices and the shortage of affordable homes for rent or purchase is a very present threat in 2003.

The changes that have taken place over the last 50 years or so have been highlighted in the collage of photographs on the surrounding pages. The recent trend has been for an agriculture-based community working locally to become a dormitory for commuters and a haven for a retiring population. Great Bedwyn is clearly well down this route but there are still very obvious signs that Chisbury and Crofton have not lost their farming focus. Little Bedwyn is perhaps somewhere in the middle with only two of its residents in 2003 also residing in the village in 1950.

To celebrate the millennium Great Bedwyn produced an exhibition entitled 'We Are History' which sought to reflect the villages at the dawn of the new millennium from the perspectives of the inhabitants of all generations. This included a substantial photographic record, some of which has been reproduced in this volume. Little Bedwyn celebrated the millennium by commissioning a local artist to produce

a map of the village reflecting all aspects of the locale *(see page 150)*. The original hangs in St Michael's Church. Great Bedwyn also produced a Village Design Statement in keeping with Wiltshire's scheme to involve village residents in shaping the future planning of their villages. The statement was published in the spring of 2003.

Hand-bell ringers in St Mary's Church, September 1999. Left to right: *Myrtle Swaine, Hilda Brown, Shirley Nicholas, Wilma Hessey, Yvonne Maslin, Janet Gregory.*

Two cooks (Les Davis and Arthur Kempster) at the Regency Fair, 1966.

Regency Fair horse and cart.

Left: *The Regency Fair in 1966. Percy Lewer is on the stand beneath the lamp and Revd Neale is to the right. To the right beneath the flag is Lord Bruntisfield, owner of Hillbarn House.*

Below: *Pig roast held to celebrate the royal wedding of Prince Charles and Lady Diana in 1981. Ted Mills and Les Davis are on the right of the picture.*

Below: *The lease for the reading-room came to an end in September 1980. Left to right: back row: Robert (Buster) Fenn, Arnold Kerr, Gordon Stone, Dick Vines, Philip Sykes; front row: Frank Dean, Peter Haine, Kenneth Cummins, Mary Davison, Kathleen Sykes, Brenda Rome, Anne Buchanan.*

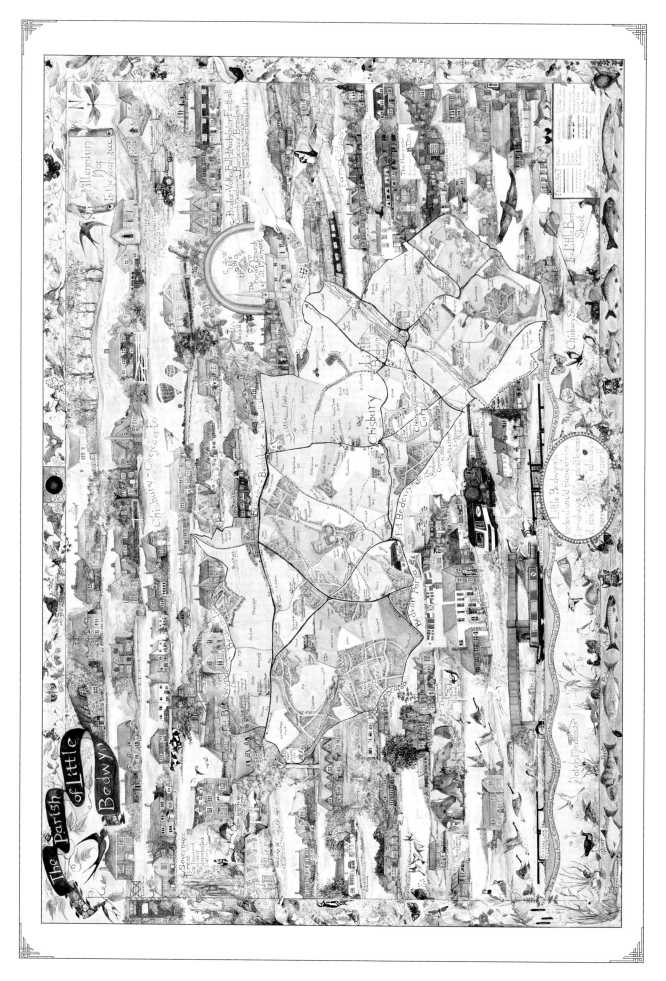

Chronology

BC

    Stone-Age earthworks constructed at Crofton.
    Stone-Age implements used at Knowle Farm.
    Stone/Bronze-Age bowl barrows constructed near Stokke Manor.
    Bronze-Age mace head used at Tor Mead, Great Bedwyn.
    Iron-Age hill-fort built at Chisbury.

AD

200–500: Roman road through Crofton linking Winchester with Mildenhall (Cunetio).
    Villa built in Bedwyn Brail: coins and pottery of this period have since been found.
    Villa near Tottenham House with tessellated pavement.
    Bedwyn Dyke built or enlarged.

672/688 Cissa rules Berkshire/Wiltshire from Chisbury.
675 Battle of Bedanheaford (Crofton) between Wessex and Mercia.

778 Earliest known surviving charter covers Little Bedwyn and Chisbury.

880s King Alfred makes Chisbury one of his strongholds in fight with the Danes.

905 Bishop of Winchester buys land for a church at Great Bedwyn.
    Bedwyn is the centre of a large royal estate.
975? Bedwyn Bible indicates primitive guild in Great Bedwyn.

1050–68 Mint in Great Bedwyn.
1086 Domesday Book – the settlement at Bedwyn was assessed for a tax of one night's provisions for the King and his royal retinue.
1092 Bedwyn becomes part of the Bishopric of Salisbury.
    Saxon churches in Great and Little Bedwyn start to be refurbished.

1100s Hospice for the Order of St John founded, probably at Crofton.

1200 3 December – King John visits the estate at Bedwyn.
1295 Right to elect two MPs created with the Model Parliament.

1442/3 Two visits by Henry VI.

1530s Courtship of Jane Seymour of Wolfhall by Henry VIII – marriage in 1536.
1540s Church plate seized by Commissioners of Edward VI.
1548 Construction of grand mansion in Bedwyn Brail begins for Edward Seymour, Duke of Somerset, Earl of Hertford and Protector of the Realm, but stops in 1552 upon his execution.
1582 Tottenham House becomes principal Wiltshire home of the Seymours.

Opposite: *Little Bedwyn's Millennium Map was devised and painted in 2000 by Angela Rawson. The original (46 x 28 in.) hangs in St Michael's Church. It depicts the parish, showing every house, together with flora, fauna and village activities.*

1621	Dr Thomas Willis (founder of the science of neurology) born in Castle Cottage, Farm Lane. His father (also Thomas) was steward to Sir Walter Smyth, one of the two MPs to the borough.
1641	Royalist troops quartered in the village.
1661	Silver Borough Seal given by Daniel Finch
1716	April – fire at Bedwyn destroyed 28 homes. Damage valued at £1,662 and goods worth £787.
1799	Construction of Kennet & Avon Canal reaches Great Bedwyn.
	Water diverted from the water-mills, which puts corn grinding into decline.
	Lloyd family arrive and work on canal bridges and tunnel.
1812	First beam engine at Crofton constructed by Boulton & Watt.
1817–20	Brick kiln of Robert Hawkins provides bricks for buildings in Church Street.
1821	6 November – William Cobbett rides through 'a group of shabby houses, upon a hill... the whole not intrinsically worth a thousand pounds.' Population of 850.
1821	Great Bedwyn Friendly Society formed.
Early 1800s	Knight's Mill burns down and is subsequently known as Burnt Mill.
1832	The Reform Act abolishes rotten boroughs. Great Bedwyn loses its right to elect two MPs.
1834	Great Bedwyn National School opens.
1854	Little Bedwyn National School opens.
1861	St Katharine's Church built.
1862	Construction of railway from Hungerford to Devizes through Bedwyn. Railway station built.
1864	Branch line to Marlborough built.
1864	St Katharine's School opens for girls only.
1870	Demolition of the old Town Hall in Great Bedwyn.
1875	Methodist chapel built in Brown's Lane.
1898	Midland and South Western Junction Railway (later GWR & BR) constructs branch lines from Marlborough to Andover through Savernake Junction.
1914	Belgian refugees billetted in the area.
1920–22	Council-houses built at the west end of Church Street. Garage built in High Street.
1926	Challoner Ellis Memorial Hall built in Frog Lane.
1929/32	Estate tenants buy tied houses from the Ailesbury estate.
1938/39	Forestry Commission receives long lease over Savernake Forest.
1945	Ammunition explosion in Savernake Forest damages St Katharine's.
1946	Hawtrey's Boys' Preparatory School established at Tottenham House (closes 1985).
1963	Lightning severely damages spire of St Michael's Church, Little Bedwyn.
1972	Little Bedwyn school closes.
1975	Restoration of The Maltings in Farm Lane wins European Architectural Heritage Award.
1982	Royal British Legion hall replaces ex-Army hut erected in 1926.
1982	New Bedwyn Memorial Hall opened.
1990	Queen Elizabeth II opens restored Kennet & Avon Canal.
1993	New primary school built and old Victorian school converted into doctor's surgery.

Glossary

Assart:	Woodland cleared for agricultural purposes.
Borough:	Town with customs and privileges; own court.
Burgess:	Inhabitant of borough with special privileges.
Burh:	Fort.
Close:	Enclosed field.
Copyhold:	Land held by title deed; on manorial court roll.
Cordwainer:	Shoemaker (not a boot maker). Originally using Cordovan Spanish leather. In practice, cordwainers also made many other objects from leather, such as bottles.
Cottager:	An unfree peasant holding a small piece of land.
Demesne:	Lord's manor; all proceeds from the land go the to lord, not to those working on it.
Danegelt:	Bribe paid to Danes to stop them raiding English territory.
Dissenters:	Non Roman Catholic or Church of England Christians.
Emphysema:	Thickening and hardening of the lung walls reducing oxygen intake and causing difficulty with breathing.
Herepath:	Army road.
Hide:	Land unit of taxation, generally taken to be approximately 120 acres but depending on fertility of soil. Originally it signified the amount of land which could be ploughed annually by a team of eight oxen. Has also been assessed as amount of land needed to support one family.
Hundred:	Local administrative areas usually covering 100 hides.
Husbandman:	Farmer who worked with animals. By the 1700s this had become a general term for a farmer.
Latten Pax:	Image used in communion service.
Myasthenia Gravis:	A breakdown in the nerve pathways, causing extreme muscle weakness.
Pcruke maker:	Wig maker.
Prebendary:	See rector.
Rector:	Priest who recommended person for position of vicar. In charge of each church in his parish and controlled how tithe money was spent.
Reeve:	Senior administrative official in a town/estate.
Serf:	Lowest ranking unfree peasant with few privileges.
Sheriff:	King's representative; principal administrator in a shire.
Tithe:	Tax.
Villein:	Highest ranking dependant peasant owing his lord duties and services in return for land.
Yeoman:	A landowner who farmed his own fields (usually only a small amount of land). He was part of a system that formed a bridge between the break-up of feudalism and the agricultural revolution of the eighteenth and nineteenth centuries.

Place Names

Local Place Names and their Origins

Modern Name	Era of origin	Early Name
*****bury	Saxon	Burh, byrg, fort, eg Cissa's fort.
*****ley		Leah, clearing.
*****ton	Saxon	Tun, enclosure.
Bedwyn	Celtic	Possibly Bedd (grave); gwyn (white) believed ploughed out, at SU 280654.
		Or, a valley where wild clematis grows.
	Roman	Or, Bedum; part of mill stream which turns the wheel.
Brail	Norman	Enclosed area of forest.
Collingbourne	Saxon	Place of Cola's people who live by the stream.
Crofton	Saxon	Crostone in 1086 – farm with or by a croft.
Frogmore Farm	Medieval	1249 home of William de Froggemere.
Grafton	Saxon	1086 farm by the grove.
Ham	Saxon	Settlement.
Hamm	Saxon	Meadow, enclosed pasture.
Harding	Saxon	Hardene, boundary valley in charter of AD778.
Harrow	Celtic	Hearg wih or weoh, temple or shrine.
Hatchett		Forest gate.
Hillbarn	Medieval	1281 home of Thomas atte Hylle.
Kennet	Celtic	Cynetan, Cunetio? Recorded in AD939.
Kinwardstone	Saxon	First written in 1086, Chenenuare stan.
Knowle	Medieval	Cnoll, hillock.
Marten	Saxon	Place with a pond.
Puthall Farm	Saxon	Putta's augh or corner of land, AD778.
Rudge		Ridge.
Savernake	Celtic	Safernoc – first written record, AD934.
Timbridge	Medieval	1229 Tymerigg ridge which provided timber.
Wolfhall	Saxon	Piece of land frequented by wolves.
Wex...	Saxon	Wax.
Wil...	Saxon	Wool.

Information based, in part, on *Place Names of Wiltshire*, English Place Name Society (ed.), *Vol. XVI* (1939).

Bibliography

PUBLISHED SECONDARY SOURCES

Adams, W.M., *The Two Bedwyns* (Marlborough, 1906).

Adams, W.M., *Battle of Bedwyn AD675* (Marlborough: Maurice & Co., 1903).

Campbell, J., *The Anglo Saxons* (London: Penguin, 1991).

Chandler, J., *Stagecoach Operation through Wiltshire* (Salisbury: South Wiltshire Industrial Archaeology Society, 1980).

Chandler, J., *Vale of Pewsey* (Bradford-on-Avon: Ex Libris, 1991).

Chandler, J., *The Day Returns* (Bradford-on-Avon: Ex Libris 1998).

Chandler, J., *Marlborough and Eastern Wiltshire* (Salisbury: Hobnob Press, 2001).

Clew, K.R., *The Kennet & Avon Canal* (Bradford-on Avon: Moonraker Press, 1985).

Cochrane, C., *The Lost Roads of Wessex* (Newton Abbot: David & Charles, 1969).

Cunliffe, B., *Wessex to AD1000* (London: Longman, 1993).

The Earl of Cardigan, *The Wardens of Savernake Forest* (Marlborough: 1949).

Ellis, P., *Roman Wiltshire and After* (Devizes: Wiltshire Archaeological and Natural History Society, 2001).

Griffiths, N.G., *Battles of Saxon Wiltshire* (Norfolk: Anglo-Saxon Books, 1996).

Hackwood, F.W., *Inns, Ales and Drinking Customs of Old England* (London: Bracken Books, 1985).

Haslam, J., *Anglo-Saxon Towns in Southern England* (Chichester: Phillimore, 1984).

Hill, D., *An Atlas of Anglo-Saxon England* (Oxford: Blackwell, 1984).

Hoare, Sir R.C., *Ancient History of Wiltshire* (Watchfield: EP publisher for Wiltshire County Library, 1975).

Maggs, C.G., *Midland and South West Junction Railway* (Newton Abbott: David & Charles, 1980).

Major, A.F., *Early Wars of Wessex* (Poole: Blandford Press, 1978).

Maurice, D., *The Book of the Marlborough Doctors* (Stroud: Sutton, 1994).

Mitchell, V., *Western Main Lines – Newbury to Westbury* (Midhurst: Middleton Press, 1978).

Roberts, C., *And So to Bath* (London: Hodder & Stoughton, 1940).

Stedman, A.R., *Marlborough & the Upper Kennet Valley* (Marlborough, 1960).

Stenton, J., *Anglo-Saxon England* (Oxford: OUP, 1989).

Welch, M., *English Heritage Book of Anglo-Saxon England* (London: Batsford with English Heritage, 1992).

Young, G.M., *Origins of West Saxon Kingdoms* (London: Oxford University Press, 1934).

PAPERS HELD IN THE WILTSHIRE COUNTY RECORDS OFFICE, TROWBRIDGE, WILTS.

Eighteenth Century Coroners Bills, County Record Office.

1753 Map of Great Bedwyn.

Census Returns.

Church Warden's Accounts.

The Ailesbury Estate Papers, Vols 1–9.

Kennet & Avon Canal Act (1794).

Wiltshire Archaeological and Natural History Society Library Sources.

Wiltshire and Swindon Record Office, Trowbridge, Wilts.

PERIODICALS

Archaeological Journal Vols LXXV & LXXVI.

Bedwyn History Society, *The Bedwyn Chronicles* (1995– 2003).

Bedwyn and Shalbourne & District Nursing Association Minute Book.

Family Tree Magazine

Medieval Archaeology, Vols 24 & 25

Savernake Hospital Contributory Scheme Collecting Book, 1941.

Victoria County History: Wiltshire (2001)

Wiltshire Archaeological Magazine, Vols 14, 28, 33, 41, 46, 47, 52, 55, 61, 77 & 88.

Index of Family Names

SUBSCRIBERS

Margaret V. Alderman, Great Bedwyn, Wiltshire
Brian and Annette Alford, Great Bedwyn, Wiltshire
Pamela Allen, Savernake Forest
Gordon Anderson, Hungerford, Berkshire
Eileen Andrew (née Barrett)
Peter and Helen Angus, Great Bedwyn
Mr and Mrs R.S. Ash, Gt Bedwyn
Tony and Meg Atkins, Inkpen
Kenneth and Joy Aust (née Edwards), Gt Bedwyn, Wiltshire
Dawn Bacon, Great Bedwyn, Wiltshire
Jasper Bacon, Tisbury, Wiltshire
Dawn Bacon, The Castle, Bedwyn
Brian and Pamela Bailey, Great Bedwyn, Wiltshire
Mr George Bailey, formerly of Great Bedwyn, Wiltshire
Janet Bailey, Spaines, Great Bedwyn
Susan Ballthy (née Cranstone)
William Bance, Gt Bedwyn
Susan Bance, Gt Bedwyn
The Barlows, Great Bedwyn, Wiltshire
Harry Bartholomew and the late Mary Bartholomew, Great Bedwyn
John Bartholomew, Ashley Heath, Hampshire (formerly London)
Graham M. Bathe, Woodgreen
Dr Walter Chisholm Batten, Apple Tree Cottage, Bedwyn Common
Albert Roy Beckingham, Great Bedwyn, son of Albert Charles and Treanious Emily Beckingham
Anne Bendall, Great Bedwyn, Wiltshire
Phil and Val Bichard, Great Bedwyn
Dianne Billing, Great Bedwyn
Mr Edward C. Bird, Great Bedwyn, Wiltshire
Shirley Bishop
Thomas Blagrave, 1522–1590 Great Bedwyn
Ruth Ullathorne Blok, Great Bedwyn
Daphne and Barry Blundy, Brook Street, Great Bedwyn
T. Blundy, Great Bedwyn, Wiltshire
Philip, Assunta, William, Patrick and Martin Blunt, Brook Street, Great Bedwyn
Ann and Colin Boothroyd, Great Bedwyn, Wiltshire
D.R. Bowden
Mr and Mrs J.J.R. Bracey-Gibbon, Bedwyn House
Wendy and Noel Bradbrooke, Bournel, France
Irene Brady, Gt Bedwyn
Emma L. Brady, Great Bedwyn, Wiltshire
Charlie Brainch, Great Bedwyn
Kay E. Brind (née Painting), Newbury, Berkshire
Terry Brooks, Hungerford, Berkshire
Mr and Mrs L. Brooks, Castle Road, Great Bedwyn
Roy Brooks, Great Bedwyn
Stan and Ruby Brooks, Great Bedwyn, Wiltshire
Hilda K.E. Brown, Great Bedwyn
Bryony Brown and Steve McKenzie, Tilehurst (Reading)
Dave and Gill Bruty, Brook Street, Great Bedwyn
Jane and Graham Bryant, Great Bedwyn
Mr and Mrs Tony Burch, Crofton, Wiltshire
C. Burgess, Great Bedwyn, Wiltshire
The Burt Family, Little Bedwyn, Wiltshire
Stuart Calkin, Hatherden, Hampshire
Kenneth A., Alastair J., and Elizabeth J. Callaway, Great Bedwyn, Wiltshire
Ronald and June Cannings, Great Bedwyn
Christopher and Birdie Cannon
The Earl of Cardigan, Savernake Estate, Marlborough
The Carlisle Family, Great Bedwyn, Wiltshire
Kevin and Sue Challen, Great Bedwyn
Joan Chapman, The Knapp, Gt Bedwyn
Phillip and Michaela Cheese, Great Bedwyn, Wiltshire
Kerry and Don Childs, Great Bedwyn
Sandra Chivers, Newbury
Jenny Clack, Great Bedwyn, Wiltshire
H.J. Claridge, Lifelong resident of Little Bedwyn and Great Bedwyn
Mrs L. Clarke, Great Bedwyn, Wiltshire
Mr Peter R. and Mrs Alexandra F. Coleman, Great Bedwyn, Wiltshire
Anne Court, granddaughter of Edwin B. Gauntlett, Little Bedwyn, Wiltshire
Ruth Cousins, daughter of Edwin B. Gauntlett, Little Bedwyn, Wiltshire
Mark (Jake), Sarah and Emily Cramsie-Smith, Great Bedwyn, Wiltshire
C. and E. Cranstone
Lorna Cronje, granddaughter of Edwin B. Gauntlett, Little Bedwyn, Wiltshire
Kenneth and Rosemary Cummins, Great Bedwyn
Pat Davies, Hungerford, Berkshire
N.P. Davies, Marlborough, Wiltshire
Beryl Davis, Brightwell-Cum-Sotwell, Oxon
Mrs Beryl K. Davis (née Hart), Wallingford, Oxon
A. Dawson, Great Bedwyn, Wiltshire
Betty Dines, Great Bedwyn, Wiltshire
Martin and Anna Ditchburn, Back Lane
Penny I. Dixon, Great Bedwyn
Rachel Katrina Dixon, Great Bedwyn
Janet and Roger Durie and Family
Raymond and Pamela Duveen, Gt Bedwyn
Stan and Janice Edwards, Great Bedwyn, Wiltshire
Brian Edwards, Devizes, Wiltshire
Susan N. Ennion, Shalbourne, Wiltshire
The Evans, East Grafton, Wiltshire
Simon and Fionna Filipiak, Great Bedwyn
David Hugh FitzWilliam-Lay, Bloxham, Great Bedwyn
Christopher FitzWilliam-Lay, Bloxham, Great Bedwyn
Hugh FitzWilliam-Lay, Bloxham, Great Bedwyn
Val Murrie/Stephen Fox-Andrews, New Zealand/Australia
Margaret Fox-Andrews (née Gauntlett), Nottingham
Karin and Alice French
R. and M. Fry, Bournemouth, Dorset
Peter Fryer, Great Bedwyn, Wiltshire
Mr and Mrs Leslie Fryer, Ramsbury, Wiltshire
P.R. and Mrs M.E. Fuller
Dr and Mrs Simon Furey, Froxfield
The Gardner Family, Great Bedwyn, Wiltshire
Colonel and Mrs Roger Garnett, Great Bedwyn/France
William T. Gauntlett, Akaroa, New Zealand
W. Bruce Gauntlett, Brimslade, Wiltshire
Betty Gauntlett (née Hancock), Ramsbury, Wiltshire
David Gauntlett DFC, Ramsbury, Wiltshire
Diana Geater, Hungerford
Fiona Gibb, Great Bedwyn
Alison Gibb, Great Bedwyn
Commodore and Mrs Ian Gibb, Great Bedwyn
Ken Gigg, Chandlers Ford, Hampshire
Mr Thomas J. Gilmartin, Great Bedwyn
Tom Gilmour, Great Bedwyn
Pat and Brian Glazebrook, Great Bedwyn
Anthony H. Gotley, Great Bedwyn, Wiltshire
Denise Emily Wells and Roger Grant, The Stores, Great Bedwyn
Elizabeth and Thomas Griffiths, Great Bedwyn
Pip and Roz Haines, N. Ireland
Phillip Hand, Auckland, New Zealand
Rodney and Jennifer Harrison, Great Bedwyn
Brian Hart, Great Bedwyn, Wiltshire
Mr A.J. Hart, Pewsey Vale, Wiltshire
Alan Hart, Wootton Rivers, Wiltshire
Angela Hawkins, Gt Bedwyn
Kenneth W. Hawkins, Rubery, Birmingham
Graham Anthony Hawkins, Great Bedwyn, Wiltshire
Bernard Charles Hawkins, Glewstone, Herefordshire
Grenville Desmond Hawkins, Thatcham, Berkshire
Peter Mark Hawkins, formerly Great Bedwyn
Jean and Robert Heard, Wilton, Wiltshire
Marilyn Heilmann, Farm Lane, Great Bedwyn
The Henderson Family, Brook Street, Great Bedwyn
Wilma Hessey, Great Bedwyn
The Hewitt Family, Great Bedwyn
Judith Hiller, St Katharines
John and Barbara Hillier
J.M. and L.A. Hitchman, Great Bedwyn, Wiltshire
Mrs R.J. Hitchman, East Kennett, Wiltshire
David Hoare, Great Bedwyn, Wiltshire
Kevin J. Hoare, Great Bedwyn, Wiltshire
William C. Hoare, Ambleside, Cumbria
The Hobson Family, Great Bedwyn
Mr and Mrs R.J.S. Holmes, Great Bedwyn, Wiltshire
Wendy Holmes, Great Bedwyn
David and Jane Homer, Chisbury
Pam Hope, formerly of Great Bedwyn, Wiltshire
Drs Hoshang and Chitra Bharucha
Susan E. Hotham, Chadlington, Oxfordshire
Mildren and Raoul Houghton, Great Bedwyn
Martin and Jan Hudson, Great Bedwyn, Wiltshire
David Huntley, formerly of Little Bedwyn
Andrew and Jacky Hutchison
A.R. and M.F. Jones, Great Bedwyn
Roger and Sue Jones, Little Bedwyn
Louize Juniper, New Zealand
Arthur Kempster, Winterslow
Ralph J. Kennington, Great Bedwyn

Janette Kersey (Claridge)
Sandy and Ann Kilpatrick, Little Bedwyn
Mary Kilpatrick, Edinburgh
John King, London
Michael E. King, Great Bedwyn, Wiltshire
Robert and Alison Kirtland, Kirtland, Abingdon
Anthony R.T. Klalber, Great Bedwyn, Wiltshire
Kamini Knill, Great Bedwyn
Janet Lambourne (née Huntley), formerly of Little Bedwyn
Alan and Nan Lance, Truant House, Froxfield
Fred and Juma Lance, Ramsbury, Wiltshire
Mary Rose Lewington (née Aldred), Great Bedwyn, Wiltshire
Mrs James Liddiard, Savernake
Benjamin Lloyd, Back Lane, Gt Bedwyn
Marjorie A. Loft, Great Bedwyn, Wiltshire
Barrington L. Long, Great Bedwyn, Wiltshire
Maurice and Julia Lovelock, Great Bedwyn, Wiltshire
Dennis Lovelock, Great Bedwyn, Wiltshire
Gloria and Bob Lucas, Little Bedwyn
Jean Luker, Chisbury
Ian and Sheila Mackintosh, Little Bedwyn
John Mann, Avebury
Jacqueline Mann, Arizona
R.C.W. Mann, Great Bedwyn
Jeffrey Mann, Pewsey
Muriel P. Mann (née Gigg)
Bill and Di Marchant Smith, Great Bedwyn
Pat Martin and Brenda Martin (née Evans), East Grafton
Louisa Villiers Maskell, Horsehall Hill
Brenda Mason, Great Bedwyn, Wiltshire
Bruce R. Mason, The Cross Keys Inn, Great Bedwyn, Wiltshire
Richard and Mary May
Mrs Thora McDonald, Great Bedwyn, Wiltshire
Mary McLachcall, granddaughter of Edwin B. Gauntlett, Little Bedwyn,
Rita McVittie, East Grafton, Wiltshire
Jessamy and Nigel Milliner
John Mills, Great Bedwyn, Wiltshire
Harry and Megan Mitchell, Great Bedwyn
John and Monique Moore, Savernake, Wiltshire
Helen Beazley and Mark Mordey, Great Bedwyn (from 17 September 2003)
Muriel Mundy, Great Bedwyn, Wiltshire
Mrs Francis Naumann, Great Bedwyn, Wiltshire
Travers Nettleton, Stokke Common
Leslie and Shirley Nicholas
John and Shar Nokes, Little Bedwyn
Tony and Brenda Nolson, Great Bedwyn, Wiltshire
Kate Norris (née Cranstone)
Mrs Joan Offer, Great Bedwyn
William and John Offer, Great Bedwyn, Wiltshire
Suzanne Offer, Great Bedwyn, Wiltshire
Frank Charles Henry Offer, Hungerford, Berkshire (lived Great Bedwyn)
The Old School Surgery, Great Bedwyn
Dr A. Paddon, Little Bedwyn, Wiltshire
Louise and John Painting, Great Bedwyn
Adrian P. Parker
Chris and Val Patrick, Aughton, Wiltshire
Nic and Sadie Payne, The Kennet and Avon

Elizabeth Jane Pearce, Great Bedwyn, Wiltshire
Stephen and Shirley Pearce, Great Bedwyn, Wiltshire
Nicholas J. Pearce, Great Bedwyn, Wiltshire
The Pearsall Family, Great Bedwyn, Wiltshire
Bob and Sue Peel, Great Bedwyn, Wiltshire
Clive Pellett, Great Bedwyn
Catriona Perazzo, London
Major General Ken Perkins, Bedwyn Common
Leslie L. Perren, Great Bedwyn, Wiltshire
A. Perren, Great Bedwyn
Pam and Terry Perry, Great Bedwyn
Julia Perry, Great Bedwyn, Wiltshire
Steve and Sue Pocock, Brook Street, Great Bedwyn
Mark and Fiona Pollard, Royal Tunbridge Wells
Mr B.R. Pounds and Mrs A. Pounds (née Hart), The Old Forge, Great Bedwyn
Clare Powell, Great Bedwyn
Philip S. Powell, Great Bedwyn, Wiltshire
Mary Powell, Burbage, Wiltshire
Gracie Randall, Great Bedwyn, Wiltshire
Angela F. Rawson, Pewsey, Wiltshire
Don Reeve
A.J. and P. Regan, Church Street, Great Bedwyn
Miss A.E. Regan, Brook Street, Great Bedwyn
Michael Regan, Rabley Wood View, Marlborough
John Regan, North View, Hungerford
David Regan, Tanyrhendy, Talog, Carmarthen
Mr P.A. Regan, Woodlands, Overton
Miss K.D. Regan, Sweet Hill Lane, Portland
Amy Rhodes, Castle Road, Great Bedwyn
Ben Rhodes, Castle Road, Great Bedwyn
Martin J. Rhodes, Great Bedwyn
Jane P. Riall, Great Bedwyn, Wiltshire
Jeanne Roach, Great Bedwyn, Wiltshire
John E. Roff, Great Bedwyn, Wiltshire
Simon Roff, Great Bedwyn, Wiltshire
Jeremy E. Roff, Great Bedwyn, Wiltshire
Angela and Frank Rose, Little Bedwyn
Philip C. Rowlands, Great Bedwyn, Wiltshire
Margaret and Peter Ruck, Tuebingen, Germany
John Russell, Gt Bedwyn, Wiltshire
Daphne Ryan (née Hoare), Redlynch, Wiltshire
Mrs John Sampson, Newbury, Berkshire
David, Jan, Emma and Ben Savage, Great Bedwyn, Wiltshire
Helen Sciba, Great Bedwyn, Wiltshire
Mrs Jenny Scott, Great Bedwyn/Edinburgh
Martin Scott, Melbourne, Australia
Stuart Sellwood, Great Bedwyn
Monica Seymour, Great Bedwyn
Kate Shears, Hungerford, Berkshire
P. Shefford, Hungerford
Peter and Karen Shellswell, Great Bedwyn, Wiltshire
Joyce Shergold, Great Bedwyn, Wiltshire
Yvonne Slade, Church Street, Great Bedwyn, Wiltshire
Norman Smart, Collingbourne Ducis, Wiltshire
Kenneth and Georgia Smith, Great Bedwyn, Wiltshire

Steve Smith, Granary Road
Harriet Smith, Great Bedwyn, Wiltshire
The Snelling Family (Chris, Elizabeth & Jessica, Alicia and Luke), Kensington House, Little Bedwyn
Audrey and Ivy Spalding, Bromsgrove.
Holt Family, Great Bedwyn
Mr D. Staning, Burbage, Wiltshire
Justine and Christian Stephens, Froxfield
Alan Stevenson, Brighton
Alex Stevenson, Great Bedwyn
Maria Anna and Audrey E. Stone, Froxfield
Carol Ann Stone
George B. Stone
Gordon R. Stone, Bewley Farm, Great Bedwyn
Andrew R. Stone
Andrew and Karen Stratford, Great Bedwyn, Wiltshire
Tim and Bar Summers, Chisbury, Wiltshire
Major and Mrs Peter Swaine
Felicity A.M. Swift, Bude, Cornwall
Professor Lindsay Symon, CBE, TD, FRCS
John and Belinda Talbot, Wilton
David Terry, Hungerford
Michael Terry, Burbage
Linda, Leigh, Elizabeth and Anna Thomas, Great Bedwyn
Rita Thompson
John and Sally Thompson, Great Bedwyn, Wiltshire
Hazel J. Tilley, Stokke Common, Great Bedwyn, Wiltshire
Ernest Tomlin, Great Bedwyn, Wiltshire
Jean Tsushima, Great Bedwyn
Robin Tubb, Hungerford Bellman with Bedwyn connections
Mrs Susan E. Tuckey, Great Bedwyn
Ruby Twyning, Hungerford, Berkshire
Bobbi M.W. Urquhart, Nairn, Scotland
Brenda and Keith Urwin, Great Bedwyn, Wiltshire
Martin, Jo, Hannah and Sam Vine, Great Bedwyn, Wiltshire
Mrs Norma Vines, Crofton, Wiltshire
Squadron Leader Paul Vivash, Great Bedwyn
Rosemary Wakeford
Michael Walker, Shalbourne, Wiltshire
John Walley, Little Bedwyn, Wiltshire
John F.W. Walling, Newton Abbot, Devon
Evelyn R.E. Walter, Shalbourne, Wiltshire
Malcolm Ward, Sydney, Australia
Mr and Mrs Waugh
Barbara Weatherburn-Lee, Gt Bedwyn
Joy Y. Webb, Great Bedwyn, Wiltshire
Liz and William White, Great Bedwyn
Admiral and Mrs Wilkinson, Manor Farmhouse, Great Bedwyn
Kevin Williams, Great Bedwyn
Paul, Karen and Tegan Williams, Gt Bedwyn, Wiltshire
Debbie Williams, Great Bedwyn, Wiltshire
Peggy Williams (née Shefford)
Miss H.L. Wilmott, Great Bedwyn
Mr and Mrs R.H. Wilmott, Bedwyn Common
Mark James Wootton, East Grafton, Wiltshire
Michael and Alison Wreford
Elizabeth Wright, Shalbourne
Mrs C.A.M. Yeates (née Bolland), Devizes, Wiltshire
Calton and Dee Younger, Gt Bedwyn

Community Histories

The Book of Addiscombe • Canning & Clyde Road Residents
Association & Friends
The Book of Addiscombe, Vol. II • Canning & Clyde Road
Residents Association & Friends
The Book of Axminster with Kilmington • Les Berry
and Gerald Gosling
The Book of Bampton • Caroline Seward
The Book of Barnstaple • Avril Stone
The Book of Barnstaple, Vol. II • Avril Stone
The Book of The Bedwyns • The Bedwyn History Society
The Book of Bickington • Stuart Hands
Blandford Forum: A Millennium Portrait • Blandford Town Council
The Book of Bramford • Bramford Local History Group
The Book of Breage & Germoe • Stephen Polglase
The Book of Bridestowe • R. Cann
The Book of Bridport • Rodney Legg
The Book of Brixham • Frank Pearce
The Book of Buckfastleigh • Sandra Coleman
The Book of Buckland Monachorum & Yelverton • Hemery
The Book of Carharrack • Carharrack Old Cornwall Society
The Book of Carshalton • Stella Wilks and Gordon Rookledge
The Parish Book of Cerne Abbas • Vale and Vale
The Book of Chagford • Ian Rice
The Book of Chapel-en-le-Frith • Mike Smith
*The Book of Chittlehamholt with
Warkleigh & Satterleigh* • Richard Lethbridge
The Book of Chittlehampton • Various
The Book of Colney Heath • Bryan Lilley
The Book of Constantine • Moore and Trethowan
The Book of Cornwood & Lutton • Compiled by the People of
the Parish
The Book of Creech St Michael • June Small
The Book of Cullompton • Compiled by the People of the Parish
The Book of Dawlish • Frank Pearce
*The Book of Dulverton, Brushford,
Bury & Exebridge* • Dulverton & District Civic Society
The Book of Dunster • Hilary Binding
The Book of Edale • Gordon Miller
The Ellacombe Book • Sydney R. Langmead
The Book of Exmouth • W.H. Pascoe
The Book of Grampound with Creed • Bane and Oliver
The Book of Hayling Island & Langstone • Rogers
The Book of Helston • Jenkin with Carter
The Book of Hemyock • Clist and Dracott
The Book of Herne Hill • Patricia Jenkyns
The Book of Hethersett • Hethersett Society Research Group
The Book of High Bickington • Avril Stone
The Book of Ilsington • Dick Wills
The Book of Kingskerswell • Carsewella Local History Group
The Book of Lamerton • Ann Cole & Friends
Lanner, A Cornish Mining Parish • Sharron
Schwartz and Roger Parker
The Book of Leigh & Bransford • Malcolm Scott
The Book of Litcham with Lexham & Mileham • Litcham Historical
& Amenity Society
The Book of Loddiswell • Reg and Betty Sampson
The New Book of Lostwithiel • Barbara Fraser
The Book of Lulworth • Rodney Legg
The Book of Lustleigh • Joe Crowdy
The Book of Lyme Regis • Rodney Legg
The Book of Manaton • Compiled by the People of the Parish
The Book of Markyate • Markyate Local History Society

The Book of Mawnan • Mawnan Local History Group
The Book of Meavy • Pauline Hemery
The Book of Minehead with Alcombe • Binding and Stevens
The Book of Morchard Bishop • Jeff Kingaby
The Book of Newdigate • John Callcut
The Book of Nidderdale • Nidderdale Musuem Society
The Book of Northlew with Ashbury • Northlew History Group
The Book of North Newton • Robins and Robins
The Book of North Tawton • Baker, Hoare and Shields
The Book of Nynehead • Nynehead & District History Society
The Book of Okehampton • Radford and Radford
The Book of Paignton • Frank Pearce
The Book of Penge, Anerley & Crystal Palace • Peter Abbott
The Book of Peter Tavy with Cudlipptown • Peter Tavy
Heritage Group
The Book of Pimperne • Jean Coull
The Book of Plymtree • Tony Eames
The Book of Porlock • Denis Corner
Postbridge – The Heart of Dartmoor • Reg Bellamy
The Book of Priddy • Albert Thompson
The Book of Princetown • Dr Gardner-Thorpe
The Book of Rattery • By the People of the Parish
The Book of St Day • Joseph Mills and Paul Annear
*The Book of Sampford Courtenay
with Honeychurch* • Stephanie Pouya
The Book of Sculthorpe • Gary Windeler
The Book of Seaton • Ted Gosling
The Book of Sidmouth • Ted Gosling and Sheila Luxton
The Book of Silverton • Silverton Local History Society
The Book of South Molton • Jonathan Edmunds
The Book of South Stoke with Midford • Edited by Robert Parfitt
South Tawton & South Zeal with Sticklepath • Radfords
The Book of Sparkwell with Hemerdon & Lee Mill • Pam James
The Book of Staverton • Pete Lavis
The Book of Stithians • Stithians Parish History Group
*The Book of Stogumber, Monksilver, Nettlecombe
& Elworthy* • Maurice and Joyce Chidgey
The Book of Studland • Rodney Legg
The Book of Swanage • Rodney Legg
The Book of Tavistock • Gerry Woodcock
The Book of Thorley • Sylvia McDonald and Bill Hardy
The Book of Torbay • Frank Pearce
*Uncle Tom Cobley & All:
Widecombe-in-the-Moor* • Stephen Woods
The Book of Watchet • Compiled by David Banks
The Book of West Huntspill • By the People of the Parish
Widecombe-in-the-Moor • Stephen Woods
The Book of Williton • Michael Williams
The Book of Witheridge • Peter and Freda Tout and John Usmar
The Book of Withycombe • Chris Boyles
Woodbury: The Twentieth Century Revisited • Roger Stokes
The Book of Woolmer Green • Compiled by the People of the Parish

For details of any of the above titles or if you are
interested in writing your own history, please contact:
Commissioning Editor Community Histories, Halsgrove
House, Lower Moor Way, Tiverton Business Park,
Tiverton, Devon EX16 6SS, England; tel: 01884 259636;
email: katyc@halsgrove.com